Managing Finance, Resources and Stakeholders in Education

withdrawn from stock.

1 4 JUN 2023

MBA in Educational Management by Distance Learning

This book, *Managing Finance, Resources and Stakeholders in Education*, is a core unit for one of the modules of the MBA in Educational Management offered by the EMDU, University of Leicester.

The other modules in this course are:

Human Resource Management in Schools and Colleges
Managing Finance and External Relations in Education
Managing the Curriculum
Research Methods in Educational Management

For further information about the MBA in Educational Management, please contact the EMDU at emdu@le.ac.uk. For further information about the books associated with the course, contact Paul Chapman Publishing at http://www.paulchapmanpublishing.co.uk

Educational Management Research and Practice series

Managing People in Education (1997)
  edited by Tony Bush and David Middlewood
Strategic Management in Schools and Colleges (1998)
  edited by David Middlewood and Jacky Lumby
Managing External Relations in Schools and Colleges (1999)
  edited by Jacky Lumby and Nick Foskett
Practitioner Research in Education (1999)
  edited by Marianne Coleman and Jacky Lumby
Managing Finance and Resources in Education (2000)
  edited by Marianne Coleman and Lesley Anderson

Course books
Human Resource Management in Schools and Colleges (1999)
  by David Middlewood and Jacky Lumby
Leadership and Strategic Management in Education (2000)
  by Tony Bush and Marianne Coleman
Managing Finance, Resources and Stakeholders in Education (2001)
  by Lesley Anderson, Ann R.J. Briggs and Neil Burton

EDUCATIONAL
MANAGEMENT
DEVELOPMENT
UNIT

Managing Finance, Resources and Stakeholders in Education

Lesley Anderson, Ann R.J. Briggs
and Neil Burton

SAGE Publications

London • Thousand Oaks • New Delhi

SAGE Publications Ltd.
1 Oliver's Yard
55 City Road
London EC1Y 1SP

SAGE Publications Inc
2455 Teller Road
Thousand Oaks, California 91320

SAGE Publications India Pvt Ltd
B-42, Panchsheel Enclave
Post Box 4109
New Delhi – 110 017

Library of Congress Control Number: 2001132897

A catalogue record for this book is available from the British Library

ISBN 10 0-7619-7258-7
ISBN 10 0-7619-7259-5 (pbk)
ISBN 13 978-0-7619-7258-7 (hbk)
ISBN 13 978-0-7619-7259-4 (pbk)

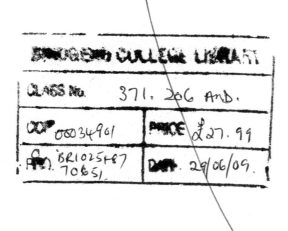

Typeset by Anneset, Weston-super-Mare, North Somerset
Printed and bound in Great Britain by Athenaeum Press Ltd., Gateshead, Tyne & Wear

Contents

The authors

Ann Briggs and **Neil Burton** both work in the Educational Management Development Unit (EMDU) at the University of Leicester, based in Northampton. **Lesley Anderson** was also a member of EMDU throughout most of the production period of this book. She now works in the Centre for Educational Policy and Management at The Open University.

Dr Lesley Anderson is a lecturer in educational management specialising in finance and resource management at The Open University. At EMDU she was Director of MBA in Educational Management by distance learning. Her publications include: 'A "third way": towards self-governing schools? New Labour and opting out', *British Journal of Educational Studies*, 2001, Vol. 49, no. 1; 'The move towards entrepreneurialism', in *Managing Finance and Resources in Education*, which she edited with Marianne Coleman (Paul Chapman, 2000); 'Farewell to grant maintained schools: the future of self-governing schools', *School Leadership and Management*, 2000, Vol. 20, no. 3; and 'Educational standards and grant maintained schools: perceptions of headteachers and chairs of governors', with Tony Bush, *Educational Management and Administration*, 1999, Vol. 27, no. 1.

Ann Briggs is a lecturer in educational management in the EMDU. She has considerable experience of secondary and further education, including a range of middle-management posts. She has researched and written on issues of resource management and accessibility to learning. She has contributed to both *Managing Finance and Resources in Education* (2000) and *Managing the Curriculum* (2001) in the *Educational Management: Research and Practice* series, published by Paul Chapman, and is a contributor and co-editor with Marianne Coleman to the forthcoming volume in the same series: *Research Methods in Educational Leadership and Management*.

Neil Burton is a lecturer in educational management with the EMDU of the University of Leicester on EdD and MBA courses and course leader of the BA (hons) in Primary Education. Neil has taught and managed in both the primary and secondary sectors as well as holding posts in initial teacher training and in a school curriculum advisory service. He has published journal articles and chapters on educational management (most recently in Brundrett, M. (ed.) *Principles of School Leadership*, Peter Francis, 1999) and is currently editing a second volume of case studies focusing on the experience of Beacon Schools with Mark Brundrett. He is co-editor (with David Middlewood) of and contributed to *Managing the Curriculum* (2001) in the *Educational Management: Research and Practice* series published by Paul Chapman.

Acknowledgements

Philip Buckle, Headteacher, Booth Lower School, Northamptonshire
Dr Steve Lewis, Dubai College, United Arab Emirates
John O'Neill, Massey University, Palmerston North, New Zealand
Tova Ron, The Centre for Educational Technology, Israel
Professor Mike Thurlow, University of Natal, Durban, South Africa
Vincent Chiu Shiu Yim, Senior Lecturer, Hong Kong Institute of Education, Hong Kong
The authors of the previous edition of this text: Dr Marianne Coleman, Professor Tony Bush and
     Dr Derek Glover
Academic and associate staff at the Educational Management Development Unit (EMDU), in
     particular, Joyce Palmer for her work on the manuscript and Tracy Harazdiuk for administrative
     support.

Introduction

This book is intended primarily for students studying for postgraduate courses in educational management such as the University of Leicester Educational Management Development Unit's MBA in Educational Management. It is therefore written as a teaching text. However, it offers much to the general reader, especially those working in education, in terms of providing an opportunity to increase their understanding and knowledge of, and develop their skills in aspects of, educational management.

The specific aims of this book are to:

- equip readers with a body of knowledge that will improve their understanding of financial and resource management as well as the role of stakeholders and how these groups can be managed;
- enable readers to reflect on concepts, theories and models of management in education;
- provide a range of analytical frameworks that can be applied by readers to their own working environments;
- provide opportunities for the improvement of their skills in the management of finance, resources and stakeholders through sited-based research; and
- enable readers to contribute to school or college improvement.

By the end of the book, readers should be able to:

- understand the link between finance and resources and the role of stakeholders in education;
- appreciate the opportunities that are provided through decentralisation to school/college level and be aware of the international trend towards self-management in education;
- understand the relationship between theory and practice in education;
- draw on knowledge about different levels of self-management and funding mechanisms in education in a variety of settings;
- analyse critically their own institution's current practice in managing finance, resources and stakeholders; and
- apply concepts of financial, resources and stakeholder management to their own management practice.

❏ Activities

Throughout the book you will find activities that ask you to:

- analyse and reflect on what you have read;
- examine and criticise practice constructively; and
- develop explanations to test the relationship between theory and practice.

These activities help you reflect upon what you have read and relate it to your own management practice, now and in the future. They may also assist you when you are considering a specific topic to investigate for a written assignment.

❏ Linked reading

This text is free-standing and contains ample material for the reader to be able to improve his or her management practice and produce a course assignment or project. However, additional reading is clearly helpful and, for students, is essential. There are three books to draw your attention to:

1. Coleman, M. and Anderson, L. (2000) *Managing Finance and Resources in Education*, London, Paul Chapman. All the chapters in this volume are relevant to your study and you will be asked to read certain chapters at specific points in the text.
2. Lumby, J. and Foskett, N. (1999) *Managing External Relations in Schools and Colleges*, London, Paul Chapman. As above, all the chapters in this volume are relevant and, as you work through this book, at various points you are asked to read specific chapters.
3. Bush, T. and West-Burnham, J. (eds.) (1994) *The Principles of Educational Management*, Harlow, Longman. The following chapters are particularly relevant to this book and you may wish to read them quickly before you start: Chapter 15 (Tony Bush) – 'Accountability in education'; Chapter 16 (Brent Davies) – 'Managing resources'; Chapter 17 (Brent Davies) – 'Models of decision-making in resource allocation'; and Chapter 18 (Marianne Coleman) – 'Marketing and external relations'. You may also like to note that a new version of this text, edited by Tony Bush and Les Bell, will be published in 2002 by Paul Chapman.

The references provide an additional source that may be helpful in preparing assignments.

❏ Structure of this book

Throughout the book, we focus on self-management as a policy approach that enables schools and colleges to take varying levels of control of the management of their own finance and resources and, thus, to put into practice, to some extent at least, the theories presented here. The relationship between schools and colleges and their communities is considered and from this we develop the link with stakeholders and the importance of managing relationships with them. Chapters 1 and 2 provide an introduction to the key concepts of managing finance, resources and stakeholders, as well as providing a context for them. Chapters 3 and 5 are concerned with the theory of financial management and the management of external relations – or stakeholders – respectively, whilst in Chapter 4 we consider the various levels of management responsibilities and the roles adopted by the key players in schools and colleges. In Chapters 6 and 7 we take a more practical approach to working with, and strategies for managing, the various stakeholder groups, including governors. We conclude in Chapter 8 with final thoughts on the over-arching concept of accountability.

1. The significance of finance, resources and stakeholders in education

---

This chapter considers:

- financial and resource management;
- managing stakeholders; and
- self-management.

Introduction

Changes in the structure of public education systems around the globe during the last two decades of the twentieth century have resulted in new responsibilities for many educational managers. In particular, the effective and efficient management of finance and resources is now crucial for the success of individual institutions. At the same time, these changes mean that schools and colleges can no longer (if they ever did) regard themselves as 'separate' from their local communities and the various 'stakeholders' who have an interest, and often an investment, in the provision of high-quality education. The shift to more open enrolment and formula funding brings with it the need for schools and colleges to compete to recruit and retain pupils and students. Educational managers operating within this environment must now be concerned with marketing their organisation and working with the different stakeholder groups in ways that maximise the potential for mutual support, both direct and indirect, between the school or college and its stakeholders. The management of resources, including finance, and the management of stakeholders, or external relations as it is sometimes described, are then implicitly linked and, thus, they are considered together in this text.

As a school or college manager you are likely to be involved in some, or all, of the following activities:

- Preparing a budget for your school/college, faculty, department or course.
- Considering and controlling the costs of certain educational activities.
- Deciding resource allocation within your school/college or department.
- Securing additional funding and/or resources for your school/college or department through entrepreneurial activities.
- Working closely with your governing body.
- Responding to the needs and concerns of parents.
- Developing and maintaining links with local businesses, industry and commerce.
- Preparing and implementing a marketing strategy for your school or college.
- Accounting for delegated spending and demonstrating value for money.

This core unit addresses these, and other, issues in the management of finance, resources and stakeholders. In this opening chapter we make the vital links between these aspects of management and the core functions of any educational organisation – those of learning and teaching. Additionally, we consider the policy context of self-management. We focus on this approach for two reasons. First, it has direct relevance for students working in a growing number of locations. Secondly, there is an implicit relationship between the level of autonomy experienced and the opportunity and flexibility to manage finance, resources and stakeholders. Thus we believe the development of knowledge and understanding about self-management is pertinent to all students of educational management as it will enable you to put your own experiences of management into context.

Financial and resource management

It is a basic premise that all educational institutions exist to enable learning to take place. To whatever extent they are held accountable, and by whatever means they are 'judged', their success, or otherwise, is based upon the 'effect' they have upon their students' learning. This effect is achieved in a variety of ways although it is always dependent, to some extent at least, on the resources available. Thus, there is an explicit link between the core purpose for which any educational organisation exists, that is, to promote learning and teaching, and the management of resources.

◎ **Reading and** Activity

Please read Rosalind Levačić's chapter, 'Linking resources to learning outcomes', Chapter 1 in Coleman, M. and Anderson, L. (eds.) *Managing Finance and Resources in Education*.

In this chapter, Levačić asks 'Do resources matter?' She goes on to provide a comprehensive framework for the analysis of resource management in educational organisations. As you read, try to summarise the key points of the chapter. Our summary is shown below, but please do not read it until you have completed the activity.

❑ Key points from the chapter

- Resources are necessary both for the operational core (teaching and learning) and for providing the environment within which learning can take place.
- The impact of the external environment on the educational organisation is crucial to its survival and success.
- The purpose of resource management and how it is, or should be, undertaken depends on the organisational perspective adopted.
- The rational model is predominant in the practice of resource management – official pronouncements on the subject are made from this perspective.
- The rational model conceives the link between resource inputs and learning outcomes as a production process.
- The concepts of effectiveness and efficiency are not easy to operationalise because of the highly diverse and intangible range of learning outcomes that are valued by educational organisations.

The second point in this list highlights the link between the management of resources, including finance, and the other aspect of this module – the management of external relations or stakeholders. As mentioned earlier, the two are implicitly connected as will be demonstrated throughout this core text. Therefore, we now move on to open discussion on why the management of external relations is important.

Managing stakeholders

The changes in the nature of educational systems have meant schools and colleges are now unlikely to succeed as 'closed' organisations that are unaware of, and unreactive to, their communities. As Lumby and Foskett (1999, p. ix) explain in the reader, *Managing External Relations in Schools and*

Colleges, schools and colleges are 'at the centre of a web of relationships with individuals and groups'. Exactly who these groups and individuals are, and how they can be managed, will be considered later in this volume. The point here is to highlight why they need to be managed and in doing this make the connection between finance, resources and stakeholders.

An implication of the basic premise that schools and colleges exist to enable learning must be that they require learners. Thus a fundamental reason for managing community links is connected with the recruitment of students and pupils. However, the reason is more than just one of viability. An implication of self-managing schools and colleges is that, alongside devolution of decision-making, the funding system applied to them is (usually) based on student/pupil numbers and the greater the number of students/pupils the college/school can recruit, the larger its revenue grant. There are, of course, limitations on the number any one institution can accommodate and educate but this figure falls at the extremity of a range within which it is in the school or college's interest to increase its recruitment. (This issue is considered in detail in Chapter 3.) Hence, the management of external relations is linked directly to the level of funding achieved.

Another way in which a school or college can generate income and/or increase its resources is by developing its relationship with other parties, either locally, nationally or even, possibly, internationally. Business, industry, commerce, the government, individuals are all possible sources of resource and it is important a school or college manages its contacts with them effectively. Thus, this is another reason why the management of external relations is important and *why* it is linked to financial and resource management. (Again, these matters are explored in much more detail in Chapter 5.)

However, perhaps the overriding reason *why* the management of external relations – or stakeholders – is important for schools and colleges operating as 'open' organisations is linked to their accountability. The move towards self-managing schools and colleges, as described later in this chapter, not only involves the devolution of financial and managerial control to more local levels but frequently also brings with it parental rights to choose schools. (There is an assumption that college students *choose* the college to which they apply.) Thus, schools and colleges are not only held accountable to their direct funding bodies, usually national and local government or a government quango, but need also to be responsive and responsible to a whole range of other stakeholders in the form of parents, industry and business, the local community and so on if they are to survive and be successful. Accountability, then, is an important dimension of this module and it will be considered in more detail in Chapter 5.

 Reading

Please read Tony Bush's chapter, 'The vanishing boundaries: the importance of effective external relations', Chapter 1 in Lumby, J. and Foskett, N. (eds.) *Managing External Relations in Schools and Colleges*.

In this introductory chapter, Bush explores reasons for the growing importance of managing external relations – or stakeholders – and among them he includes the impact of self-management. We have summarised the key points from the chapter below. When you have read the chapter, compare your own list with ours. Please do not look at ours until you have read the chapter.

❏ **Key points from the chapter**

- The emergence of school and college self-management in many countries has enhanced the importance of effective management of stakeholders.
- Educational institutions are now generally characterised as 'open systems' with permeable boundaries.
- Effective leaders and managers adopt a proactive approach, build partnerships with stakeholders, research so they can anticipate change and ensure that marketing is integral to their strategic planning.
- Successful schools and colleges adopt an inclusive approach to working with their stakeholders.

At this point it is important to state that, although schools and colleges have been coupled together in all that has been said so far, there are differences between the two that need to be considered. The management of finance and resources in colleges in the post-compulsory education sector differs in a number of ways. In scale, colleges are generally much bigger than schools; thus their budgets are usually of a different magnitude. They differ in nature because it is more usual, and possibly acceptable, for colleges to charge their students or their employers for the education they receive. Generally, government-provided education at school level is 'free'. Finally, there is a difference in the security schools and colleges experience – once a pupil has entered a school, mostly that resource is secured for a number of years. College students can, and do, leave at any time. Thus, as you work through this core text, you are encouraged to compare and contrast school and college management.

We now move on to consider self-management as a context for the management of finance, resources and stakeholders. We acknowledge that the concept of self-management has not been implemented universally and, indeed, where it has been introduced, its operational level varies considerably. However, it is of interest to school and college managers across the world in terms of providing a backdrop for the opportunity for the management of finance, resources and stakeholders at institutional level. In focusing on self-management we want to emphasise we are not trying to suggest that self-management is in any way *the* desired approach or that it is superior to other organisational policies. Indeed, we acknowledge the existence of counter literature (for example, Ball, 1990a; 1990b; Bowe *et al.*, 1992; Smyth, 1993; Ranson, 1996) in which it is argued that self-management is a fallacy and that even in schools that are described as self-managing, resource decisions may be relatively limited. In many countries schools do not have control of staff recruitment and staff rewards and, consequently, the percentage of the resources they are actually responsible for is very small. It is in this context that we present the rest of this chapter. We begin the discussion by considering what we mean by a self-managing school or college.

Self-management

The term 'the self-managing school' is generally associated with the Australian writers, Caldwell and Spinks. They used it first in 1988 as the title of their highly successful book in which they define a self-managing school as 'one for which there has been significant and consistent decentralisation to the school level of authority to make decisions related to the allocation of resources' (Caldwell and Spinks, 1988, p. 5). By the time they were writing their third book on self-management, Caldwell and Spinks' definition had been refined as a result of their work over the past decade as well as being influenced by the work of Bullock and Thomas (1997). This third book emphasises the centrality of decisions on resources in self-management:

A self-managing school is a school in a system of education to which there has been decentralised a significant amount of authority and responsibility to make decisions about the allocation of resources within a centrally determined framework of goals, policies, standards and accountabilities. Resources are defined broadly to include knowledge, technology, power, material, people, time, assessment, information and finance (Caldwell and Spinks, 1998, pp. 4–5).

The authors define the various components they identify as contributing to the resource allocation of a school or college as follows:

- *knowledge* – including the curriculum and the goals or purposes of education
- *technology* – the means of teaching and learning
- *power* – the authority to make decisions
- *materials* – the use of facilities
- *people* – the management of human resources
- *time*
- *finance* – the allocation of money (Caldwell and Spinks, 1992, p. 5).

Bullock and Thomas (1997, pp. 7–8) add four further items to this list. They are:

- *admissions* – decisions over which pupils are to be admitted to the school
- *assessment* – the methods of assessment employed
- *information* – the selection of data to be published about the school's performance
- *funding* – the setting of fees for the admission of pupils.

Bell (1998) adds one further factor:

- *school governance* – decisions over the power and composition of the governing body.

The inclusion of resource allocation in these definitions, the statement that resource management is broader than financial management and links with learning and teaching are all significant in the context of school and college self-management. On the basis that resources, as listed above, are essential to effective learning and teaching, and that the finance necessary to acquire them is limited, the careful and strategic management of finance by self-managing schools and colleges is essential. (It is, perhaps, important to point out here that although the definitions considered above refer to 'a school' they may equally be used for any educational organisation with the appropriate level of authority and responsibility.)

❑ An international trend

During the last decade and a half of the twentieth century, the restructuring of public education systems across the globe was endemic and there are many commentators on this trend (for example, Brown, 1990; Lingard *et al.*, 1993; Ball, 1994; Smyth, 1993; 1996; Bullock and Thomas, 1997). In 1992 Caldwell and Spinks wrote: 'everywhere, . . . large bureaucracies are collapsing in favour of a shift to self-management' (p. viii). 'There is evidence of . . . change in virtually every nation in the Western world with signs of major change in Eastern Europe and the Commonwealth of Independent States' (pp. 3–4).

In the UK, the Education Acts of the late 1980s and early 1990s moved schools largely out of local government control to operate in a quasi-market situation, responsible to central government agencies, although legislation at the end of the 1990s has modified that trend. In the same period in New Zealand, educational reforms moved responsibility for financial management and for educational outcomes to individual schools. In the USA, initiatives at state and district level increased both parental choice and school autonomy, and in Australia, decentralisation has 'spread like an epidemic across systems and state boundaries' (Angus, 1995, p. 8). In eastern Europe, the collapse of totalitarian regimes has led to a move towards increased autonomy for schools, notably in Hungary (Karstanje,

1999, p. 33) although, in some countries, for example Rumania, new systems of school management have been slower to develop (Radelescu, 1993, p. 85).

Although writers vary in the ideological perspective they adopt, there is considerable agreement over the economic factors stimulating the changes (Levačić, 1995, p. 2). Levačić (*ibid.*, p. 2) identifies the main economic factor driving educational reform as 'concern about the inability of the country's workforce and management to be internationally competitive'. This, in turn, has raised issues about standards and accountability (Dimmock, 1993) and has led many governments, particularly those of English-speaking countries, to dismantle their centralised educational bureaucracies and to create autonomous institutions with various forms of school-based management (Whitty *et al.*, 1998).

For Whitty *et al.* (*ibid.*) the international context of devolution is one theme in their book. They draw on comparative data about educational reform in five countries in order to 'illuminate the various ways in which governments in different parts of the world have attempted to remodel national and local systems of education and to increase the autonomy of individual schools' (*ibid.*, p. 8).

Other edited volumes are devoted to international comparisons of the restructuring of schools and education (Chapman *et al.*, 1996; Shapira and Cookson, 1997). For example, Beare and Boyd (1993) subtitle their edited collection *An International Perspective on the Movement to Transform the Control and Performance of Schools*. In their introduction, Beare and Boyd (*ibid.*, p. 2) suggest that 'the fact that school restructuring is an *international* trend should excite our curiosity'. They go on to set the context of their book by asking 'what is driving the movement, why is there such a consistent concern across the globe to improve schooling outcomes and school performance, and who typically are the prime policy actors?' (*ibid.*).

From the literature it is clear the restructuring of education through decentralisation and self-management can be viewed as a common response to similar problems or, indeed, needs, in many countries around the world. Although originally confined to English-speaking countries, Lockheed (1998) argues that the approach is now applied on a broader basis, although not universally.

❑ Terminology

A cursory glance at the literature quickly reveals the variety of terms that are used to describe the overall concept of educational devolution. For example, in a UK context the following terms are used:

- *self-management* (Davies and Anderson, 1992; Sherratt, 1994; Caldwell and Spinks, 1988; 1992; 1998)
- *self-governance* (Halpin *et al.*, 1993; Feintuck, 1994; Atkinson, 1997)
- *autonomy* (Bush *et al.*, 1993; Fitz *et al.*, 1993)
- *decentralisation* (Bullock and Thomas, 1997)
- *delegation* (Thomas and Martin, 1996)
- *incorporation* (Ainley and Bailey, 1997).

Internationally, the situation is even more confusing. Smyth (1993, p. 1) talks about the 'bewildering array of terms like "school-based management", "devolution", "site-based decision-making" and "school-centred forms of education" ' in the introduction to his edited collection on self-managing schools. Karstanje (1999) adds 'deregulation' to the list in the context of Europe. As Whitty *et al.* (1998) point out, the problem is that different meanings can be associated with just one of these terms – for example, to some school/college-based management is concerned with decentralisation and deregulation of school or college control while to others it is about shared decision-making within the school or college. They conclude that none of the terms 'lend themselves to precise definition' (*ibid.*, p. 9) and are 'open to semantic slippage' (*ibid.*, p. 10), a view that is also expressed by Thomas and Martin (1996, p. 18).

> ◎ Reading
>
> Please read Brian Caldwell's chapter, 'Local management and learning outcomes: mapping the links in three generations of international research', Chapter 2 in Coleman, M. and Anderson, L. (eds.) *Managing Finance and Resources in Education*.
>
> Like Levačić in the first reading, Caldwell highlights the importance of linking developments in self-management with learning outcomes. He draws on what he describes as third-generation research into self-management and argues that two earlier generations are discernible. However, according to Caldwell, it is only since the late 1990s that it has been possible to assess the impact of different levels of self-management on student achievement.

❑ Key points from the chapter

- Research into self-management has reached a third stage of development or third generation and it is now possible to link aspects of self-management and student learning outcomes.
- Illustrations from this third generation of research are provided.
- Based on work in Victoria, Australia, explicit links are mapped.
- A list of implications for both policy-makers and practitioners is provided.

❑ Self-management in education: degrees of autonomy

As has been indicated above, both the understanding of terms concerning self-management and the nature of the autonomy experienced by individual schools and colleges vary greatly. The following section considers some of the components proposed by Caldwell and Spinks (1992; 1998) referred to earlier in this chapter. It relates them to experiences of autonomy reported in various parts of the world. Further source material can be found in the appendix to this book. Both the discussion here and the vignettes will help you to assess what levels of autonomy you experience in relation to the different elements proposed.

- *Knowledge*: the decentralisation of decisions related to the curriculum, including decisions related to the goals or ends of schooling.
- *Technology*: the decentralisation of decisions related to the means of teaching and learning.

Degrees of autonomy concerning the nature and content of a school or college curriculum, the evaluation of institutional effectiveness in teaching it and decisions as to how it should be taught vary, relative to each other, as well as varying from country to country. Working within a national curriculum for schools, as in many Australian states (Ryan, 1993; Odden, 1995; Caldwell and Spinks, 1998; Whitty *et al.*, 1998), in Sweden (Lundgren, undated) and in China (Bush *et al.*, 1998; Ryan *et al.*, 1998), constrains the autonomy of individual schools to make decisions as to the content of what is taught. Similarly, working within – or moving towards – a framework of vocational qualifications, as in South Africa (Lumby and Li, 1998) and Hong Kong (Lumby, 2000a), may constrain the autonomy of colleges to devise their own curriculum, although it is likely there will still be choices for individual colleges to make from within the national framework. Indications of variations upon national 'conformity' can be seen in Sweden (Englund, 1993) and in England and Wales, where schools are encouraged to develop specialisms within the National Curriculum, which may indicate a degree of local autonomy.

A notable example of the freedom for schools to vary the curriculum according to the needs of the learning community, responding to market awareness, can be seen in the system of Charter Schools, legislation for which has been adopted in around half the states of the USA (Caldwell and Spinks, 1998). This legislation enables local groups of people to draw up a charter and operate a school, which is then vested with decision-making authority in terms of the curriculum, budget and staffing. Degrees of autonomy over the curriculum offered are evidenced more clearly in vocational and post-compulsory education. For example, in China where, in secondary schools, 'Teachers have little right to change the curriculum' (Principal, School 98, in Bush *et al.*, 1998), in vocational schools, there is evidence the state system can be modified in the light of the needs of local employers. A case study from Brazil (Gomez, 1991) indicates the capacity of local communities to establish their own vocational education in response to local need and, in Hong Kong, there is a move towards a more market-driven curriculum: 'Overall, the curriculum is planned to become broader, more integrated and more responsive to the learning needs of the range of students' (Lumby, 2000a).

This raises the interesting debate as to who is the more appropriate monitor of stakeholder needs: the state or the individual institution? The existence of systems of monitoring and evaluating the work of educational institutions at national and at federal state level indicates formal frameworks of accountability and an expectation of conformity to agreed standards. Examples of evaluation and monitoring of provision at state level in Australia – for example, through the *Better Schools* report in 1987 in Western Australia – in the USA (Whitty *et al.*, 1998) and at national level in Sweden (Lundgren, undated) and England and Wales indicate that even where schools have some freedom to vary the curriculum, monitoring of provision according to external standards is likely to be applied.

When considering the autonomy of a school or college in designing its own teaching methodology, a major influencing factor will be the prevailing culture within the country and the institution. In China (Bush *et al.*, 1998) the teaching teams – the *jaioyanzu* – meet regularly to discuss the course schedule, the teaching materials, pedagogy and subject knowledge. However, variations in pedagogy are constrained by the large teaching groups and low teacher contact time, which appear to be the norm. In Israel (The State of Israel, Department of Planning, 1997), the newly formed training centre for school principals includes sessions on learning styles and on resources for teaching and learning with the intention that variation in pedagogy within the schools will be encouraged. Following the launch of the 'Schools of the Future' programme in 1993, schools in the Australian state of Victoria are required to include statements in their charters about the distinctive nature of the school and the ways in which it addresses local priorities while, in Hong Kong (Advisory Committee on School-Based Management, 2000), school goals and policies for teaching and learning are set out by the school management committee. It is interesting to note that both these approaches, to some degree, set parameters for the teaching strategies adopted within the school.

- *Material*: the decentralisation of decisions related to the use of facilities, supplies and equipment.
- *Finance*: the decentralisation of decisions related to the allocation of money.

Autonomy over tangible resources such as money, facilities and equipment will enable a school or college to develop its own environment for learning within the constraints discussed above. The visibility of major purchases, or the state of the building, may in turn influence stakeholder attitudes to the school or college and become factors in its marketing, if the institution is operating within a market environment. At the very least they may influence the level of confidence students and parents have in the institution.

Research in schools in South Africa by the University of Leicester's Educational Management Development Unit indicates that, although the current policy is that the allocation of recurrent funding is on the basis of need, both schools and colleges depend upon parental and student contributions to maintain an acceptable level of funding and that, in deprived urban or rural areas, the lack of resources is a key issue. Local decisions about the allocation of funding or the use of facilities are in essence limited by the lack of resource, rather than a lack of autonomy.

A further constraint may be the collective willingness of principals to accept local financial autonomy. Movement towards self-management in Israel (Yonai, 1984; Foor, 1985; Resef, 1985), which proposed pooling all existing educational budgets and giving schools increased flexibility in conducting their financial procedures, has met reluctance from principals to subscribe to the accompanying bureaucracy and to accept greater financial autonomy (Friedman and Brama, 1998). Reforms in New Zealand in 1989 (Wylie, 1994) awarded considerable financial autonomy to individual schools and their boards of trustees. Although financial provisions were altered once more in 2000, the original reforms had been notable in the extent of local autonomy awarded and the degree of parental and community involvement in decision-making (Wylie, 1994).

A further indicator of financial autonomy rests on whether the school or college has delegated funding – or fee-generated funding – for staff salaries as part of a system where the funding follows the student, or as 'bulk funding' of the type introduced and recently withdrawn in New Zealand. Colleges in post-compulsory education, operating under autonomous conditions, would be likely to have control of budgets for staffing, as well as operational budgets. For example, in Pakistan, in 1989, in response to World Bank recommendations (1989), the Government of Punjab granted full operational autonomy, first to a few prestigious institutions, then gradually to other colleges. College boards of governors formulate the college budget, recruit and pay staff, acquire and dispose of property and set their own fee structure. However, the beneficial impact overall of these reforms is in question (Iqbal and Davies, 1994).

At the other end of the scale of autonomy of decision-making over finance and equipment is the system that operates in China, where local purchases, and the accompanying decision-making, are minimal, with educational supplies being selected and provided from a central source.

Chapters 3 and 4 of this book will deal in more detail with the management of delegated budgets: the brief overview provided here may help you to assess what degree of self-management your school or college has in this respect.

- *People*: decentralisation of decisions related to the allocation of people concerned with matters of teaching and learning.
- *Time*: decentralisation of decisions related to matters of time.

In many countries, schoolteachers are employed by a local authority or a state. Decisions as to their deployment are therefore taken at a level outside the control of the school. Headteachers in England and Wales may thus be in a minority in having considerable influence as to who is employed in their school. Independent, fee-paying schools, such as Dubai College described in the vignettes provided in the appendix, have the power to recruit and deploy staff as they see fit. Also, some of the Australian educational reforms, for example reforms in Western Australia under the *Better Schools* report (1987, cited in Whitty *et al.*, 1998, p. 23), gave schools responsibility for teacher selection. In South Africa, schools in wealthy districts can use parental and community donations to augment their staffing.

Once staff are deployed to a school or college, the principal may have greater or lesser authority to negotiate how they are to be deployed within the school, including their timetables. Research in case-study secondary schools in China (Bush *et al.*, 1998) revealed that although pupil:teacher ratios averaged around 13:1, classes observed typically had 50 children, and two classes of 75 children were noted. Teachers taught between 10 and 12 hours per week although, in vocational schools, there was a weekly rate of between 8 and 10 hours (Lumby and Li, 1998). In other systems, staff may be contracted to be in contact with students for an agreed number of hours per week, as in UK further educational colleges, or be given teaching allocations according to the culture and customs of the school. Changes in how staff are deployed can have a considerable impact upon the institution's ability to respond to student and community need. The success of a school or college may therefore depend upon the degree of innovation and responsiveness which can be achieved within the constraints upon its autonomy.

This inventiveness may also be applied to the timing of the school day, week or term, although often these are constrained by local agreements or by national custom and practice. In the UK, city technology colleges have autonomy in setting the length of the school day and term. Some opt for a longer day than usual, or for a school year of five short terms, instead of the customary three. Bray (1990) reports on the use of multiple shifts in schools in a number of countries, where there is high local demand for education. Bray (*ibid.*, p. 76) reports positively on this type of arrangement, noting that although the school day for pupils is shorter than average, and there is a narrowing of curriculum focus, the levels of achievement do not appear to suffer.

• *Power*: decentralisation of authority to make decisions.

All the above features of autonomy may be summed up through consideration of where the overall power lies to make decisions. As we have seen – for example, in the case of the Israeli principals' distrust of financial autonomy – authority to make decisions is not necessarily desirable. Nor is it necessarily permanent: the financial reforms in New Zealand were 'reversed' within the space of a little over a decade, whilst 'local' management of education – at a level between institutional and state or national – seems to be particularly vulnerable to shifting degrees of power, as evidenced in the Australian state of Victoria and in England and Wales. When imposed by national or state decree, the concept of autonomy might never be truly adopted, as may be the case with autonomous colleges in Pakistan.

Where the institution is set up by the local community, as in a vocational college in Brazil (Gomez, 1991), local autonomy is desirable and achievable, provided the necessary income is forthcoming. At the other extreme, within the highly centralised system of Chinese secondary schools, decision-making at school level is not necessarily carried out by the principal. In research reported by Bush *et al.* (1998, p. 188), one school principal comments on the location of power: 'A committee represents teachers chosen by election. Policy is made by the teachers' committee and implemented by the principal. The principal must carry out decisions and policy made by the committee' (Principal, School 98).

In 1994, according to Ogawa and White, three quarters of America's school districts had introduced local school management. However, given the limited role of the federal government in relation to education, Whitty *et al.* (1998, p. 26) point out that 'it is hard . . . to generalise about the nature and provenance of attempts . . . to enhance parental choice and devolve decision-making to schools'. They go on to add that 'the role of the federal Department of Education has had to be largely one of exhortation'. Cookson (1995, p. 409) suggests that, during the 1980s, President Reagan used it as 'a 'bully pulpit' for espousing his beliefs in school choice and local educational autonomy' while George Bush 'went further . . . in attempting to reorganise the public school system according to what he believed were sound market principles'. Diverse trends can thus be seen as to where power is located: the location of power may not be stable, and may be affected by the prevailing political agenda in the country concerned.

As we have seen, decisions concerning the content and delivery of the curriculum, the level of financial and staffing resource, the allocation of staff and their teaching contact time may all be centralised to a greater or lesser degree. The level of autonomy within any one institution may therefore be very small, and it is with this acknowledgement we discuss issues concerning self-management in the succeeding chapters.

Activity

The previous section has provided an analysis of degrees of autonomy and self-management in a range of countries. Try now to identify what levels of autonomy your own system operates under. How far is responsibility for the management of educational provision, finance and staffing delegated to the school/college? In doing this you should consider who has control of what and in what context.

❏ **Building on key learning points**

- The nature of the relationship between schools and colleges and their external environment is paramount to their success.
- There is an explicit link between the management of finance and resources and the management of external relations in educational organisations.
- School and colleges are accountable to a wide range of stakeholders.
- Since the 1980s, governments around the world have been restructuring their public education systems in an attempt to raise educational standards.
- Various forms of self-management and degrees of autonomy have been achieved by these reforms.

2. A UK perspective of self-management

This chapter considers:

- the nature of 'self-management' in schools in England and Wales;
- local management of schools (LMS);
- fair funding;
- other sources of state school funding;
- incorporated further education colleges;
- independent schools and the involvement of the private sector; and
- schools in Scotland.

Introduction

In Chapter 1, discussion of self-management in education included an analysis of the degrees of autonomy experienced in different educational systems around the world. In this chapter we focus on the nature of self-management and the related issues of funding education as they have developed in school and college systems in the UK in the final decades of the twentieth century. The purpose is to provide a context for the detailed discussion about the theory and practice of the actual *management* of finance, resources and stakeholders that follows in the remaining chapters. It is intended that this chapter offers an example of a framework for resourcing education which may be used for comparative purposes in your own studies.

The nature of 'self-management' in schools in England and Wales

The movement towards self-management in England and Wales implies that the extent to which schools are able to self-determine their operational and strategic decision-making is increasing. Such freedoms, in the particular model of self-management adopted for state schools in England (which also operates with some local variations in Wales), are not delegated to schools without compensatory checks and balances. The greater responsibilities given to schools to manage their own resources, personnel, strategic vision and external relations – all significant moves towards decentralisation – have been matched by the centralisation of other educational factors. Schools have for over a decade been required to follow a nationally imposed curriculum, with predefined educational standards for students to achieve by given ages; they are subject to regular, rigorous external inspections which examine the standard of pupil achievement, teaching and management structures on the basis of 'value for money'; quality thresholds for teaching staff and school managers have been imposed on them (through training requirements, frequently based on bidding processes); and budgets are externally audited. Schools have been given the freedom to operate within a very clearly defined envelope. They have been delegated the power to make decisions which affect the operational and strategic direction of the school, so long as that direction lies within the range of targets that have been imposed centrally. It could be argued the educational autonomy of teachers has been exchanged for the managerial autonomy of schools.

Local management of schools (LMS)

❑ The main principles

The LMS policy was introduced in the Education Reform Act 1988 with the aim of locating the main decision-making powers with those groups and individuals best placed to assess the impact of decisions on their pupils and students. It was seen as a means of ensuring a more effective and efficient utilisation of resources within schools for learning and teaching. A circular from the Department for Education (1993, para. 7) stated: 'The purpose of local management of schools is to enhance the quality of education by enabling more informed and effective use to be made of the resources available for teaching and learning. As such, LMS is a key element in the Government's overall education policies.'

Further clarification is provided by McAlister and Connolly (1990, p. 34):

> The principle underlying LMS is that responsibility for the management of resources should, as far as possible, be delegated to those who use them, in this case to schools. Delegated systems of management, including finance, are based on the claim that, if decisions about resource allocation are taken as close as possible to the operational part of the process, better quality decisions will emerge.

❑ Formula funding

Prior to LMS, schools were funded by the local education authority (LEA) on the subjective basis of perceived needs and historical budgets. In its 1994 LMS circular, the Department for Education (DfE) introduced formula funding with the stated purpose 'to bring about an equitable allocation of resources between schools, based on objectively-measured needs rather than historical spending patterns' (p. 7). Furthermore, the statement goes on to add 'within each LEA, schools with the same characteristics and the same number of pupils should receive the same level of resources under the formula' (*ibid.*).

It is significant the government did not determine the LMS formula but left it to each LEA to decide on the basis of local needs: 'The Secretary of State does not prescribe a uniform model formula. It is for each LEA to devise, and revise, its own formula having regard to local needs and circumstances' (DfE, 1993, para. 10).

In effect, LEAs constructed formulae to reflect the budgets schools had, historically, been allocated. It is clear this policy took power away from the locally elected representatives (LEAs) and redistributed it to both schools and central government. Levačić (1989, p. 137) highlights the impact of formula funding on LEAs which could 'no longer use detailed control of school . . . resources as the means of implementing their educational policies, they need to design the resource allocation formula so that it reflects, as far as possible within DES guidelines, their educational policies'.

Thomas and Bullock (1992, p. 217) identified four areas of discretion LEAs had in devising their formulae:

- protection for small schools;
- pupils with special needs;
- pupils with low socio-economic status;
- the weighting for pupils of different ages.

❑ LMS in action

Under LMS there were both 'winners' and 'losers'. Those schools that had benefited greatly from LEA discretionary budgets were 'losers' as were those with above-average staff salary costs because these were paid at an average, rather than actual, rate. Certain schools, however, particularly those with rising rolls or lower than average costs, were beneficiaries of the new system:

Stripped to its fundamentals, Local Management of Schools (LMS) is an organisational form which changes the way resources are allocated, the incentives and sanctions facing decision makers and the information to which they respond . . . The initial impact of LMS is to redistribute resources between schools (Levačić, 1992, pp. 16 and 24).

However, what was significant was the fact that the introduction of LMS greatly increased the scope for governors and managers to determine the school's educational objectives and to deploy resources in support of those objectives. Gilbert (1990, p. 16) emphasises the financial and managerial aspects of LMS:

LMS delegates the school's financial budget to governors. This is a major financial responsibility. At the same time, LMS delegates related managerial authority and responsibility for staff. Such financial and staffing delegation is intended to enable governing bodies and headteachers to deploy their resources in accordance with their own needs and priorities and to make schools more responsive to parents, pupils, the local community and employers.

In addition to LMS, the Education Reform Act 1988 also introduced a new category of school that enabled a more developed form of self-management. This school classification was described as grant maintained (GM). GM status offered the governing bodies of existing schools the opportunity to take over even more roles and responsibility from the LEA than under LMS, subject to appropriate approval and, indeed, ceased to make them accountable to the local authority. Thus, achieving GM status became known as 'opting out' (of local authority control) and no longer subject to the influence of locally elected political representatives. It has been widely acknowledged that GM status offered preferential treatment to schools in terms of additional capital funding and development funding. The position of these schools, effectively outside the influence of the wider local community, has been reversed, bringing them into a new relationship with their LEAs as foundation schools.

Fair funding

Fair funding, introduced in 1999, was designed to complement the new framework by establishing a single system of funding which aimed to reduce the inequalities between the funding levels of different LEAs and to remove the disparities in funding which accompanied grant-maintained status.

❑ The main principles
The system is based on seven principles:

- Raising standards in schools
- Self-management for schools
- Clear accountability of both LEA and school
- Transparency of school finances
- Opportunity for schools to take greater responsibility for management decisions if they want this
- Equity between the new categories of community, foundation and voluntary schools
- Value for money for schools and LEAs (DfEE, 1998, p. 8).

Moreover, it stresses the increased level of financial delegation and, indeed, describes a '100% delegation' model 'designed to allocate funds in a way which adequately reflects the respective roles of LEAs and schools' (*ibid.*, p. 1). The roles for LEAs are specified although, if a large majority of schools vote for it, there is also the provision for an LEA to retain funding and provide particular services.

The consultation paper on fair funding goes on to identify the difficulties with the arrangements for delegated budgets under LMS; it begins with transparency. The problems as seen by New Labour were that:

... over the years, a system of almost Byzantine complexity has built up. The series of acronyms is bewildering and daunting. Different LEAs appear to classify similar expenditure under different headings, making comparison between authorities very difficult. It remains far harder than it should be for heads, teachers, governors and parents to understand the reasoning behind their budget allocation as opposed to what other schools get and what LEAs retain. This lack of transparency can only hinder the crusade to drive up standards (*ibid.*, p. 6).

The second difficulty concerns value for money. In particular, the paper suggests the previous arrangements did not put sufficient pressure on LEAs to obtain value for money on their expenditure. There was suspicion that relevant expenditure can be 'hidden' in obscure parts of the authority's budget and LEA expenditure had not been submitted to any of the 'four Cs' outlined in the Prime Minister's paper on local government – comparison, competition, consultation or challenge.

Accountability was another concern, particularly with respect to division of responsibility between school and LEA under LMS. The government view was that (at that time) 'LEAs are left in the position where their critics can credit them for none of the successes in the education system and blame them for all the failures' (*ibid.*, p. 7). It was intended that the fair funding scheme would sharpen the lines of accountability.

Finally, there was concern that all these problems were compounded by the fact that 'previous policy on school structure led to a two-tier system in which GM schools enjoyed more generous funding than the schools that chose to remain within the LEA orbit' (*ibid.*, p. 7). The local partnership arrangements between schools and LEAs and the opportunity for greater delegation to all schools under the new framework were designed to remove the two-tier system.

❏ How the fair funding system works

Essentially, fair funding operates in four main stages.

Stage 1 – before the start of the financial year, LEAs decide how much they plan to spend on schools. This is known as the *Local Schools Budget* (LSB).

Stage 2 – Authorities are allowed to hold back funding in order to provide centrally for a number of tightly defined LEA *responsibilities*. These fall into five main categories:

• strategic management
• access
• school improvement
• special educational needs (SEN)
• grants-supported expenditure.

Under stage 2 of the fair funding process, LEAs decide how much funding they need to retain for these LEA responsibilities. However, the Department for Education and Employment publishes comparative tables on LEA expenditure and, from April 2000, required at least 80% of the LSB to be delegated to schools.

Stage 3 – The balance of the LSB left after deduction of centrally retained funds is called the *Individual Schools Budget* (ISB) and it is this budget that is delegated to schools via the LEA formula, which must allocate 80% of the ISB by age-weighted pupil unit. The LEA is allowed to allocate the remainder using other factors that best suit local needs and priorities. The share of funding each school receives is known as its delegated budget share and schools are free to spend their budget shares as they see fit, as long as it is 'for the purposes of the school'.

Stage 4 – Each LEA is required to produce a statement each year which shows the amount to be centrally retained, the budget share for each school, the formula used to calculate those budget shares and the detailed calculation for each school. These are known as *Budget and Outturn Statements* and are subject to audit. LEAs are also required to send a copy of those statements to each school they maintain. In addition, LEAs are required to draw up *Schemes for Financing Schools*. These schemes set out in detail the financial controls and arrangements that operate between schools and LEAs. The schemes may be revised if necessary.

❏ Increased delegation

Under the new system schools can take on wider responsibilities. These include:

- repairs and maintenance of school buildings (not capital works);
- the supply of school meals, including provision of free school meals and any subsidy for paid meals;
- provision of central support services, including payroll and other payments, obtaining financial and legal advice and dealing with recruitment and other staffing matters;
- ancillary services, including cleaning and grounds maintenance;
- advisory and inspection services;
- school library and museum services;
- staff costs; and
- insurance.

 Reading

Please read the chapter by Anne West and her colleagues, 'Financing school-based education in England: principles and problems', Chapter 4 in Coleman, M. and Anderson, L. (eds.) *Managing Finance and Resources in Education*.

❏ Key points from the reading

- The delegation of funding to schools from central and local government.
- The determination of school budgets.
- Funding special and additional educational needs at local government and school levels.
- Problems arising from the financing of education.

Activity

Under Section 52 of the School Standards and Framework Act, LEAs are required to produce a public document detailing the funding of the schools for which they have responsibility. If you are working in the UK (or have easy access to such information), get hold of a copy of this document from your LEA (and/or from other authorities) and identify the different levels of funding under each budget heading.

❏ Our comments

As indicated earlier, comparisons among LEAs reveal significantly different levels of delegation to schools. It is interesting to note the budget headings where the differences are greatest.

Other sources of state school funding

❏ The Standards Fund

The Standards Fund is the main source of funding to schools beyond fair funding. It was set up to provide financial support for specific projects that are identified and given priority by the government on an annual basis, thus centralising control over the priorities for school development. For some grants, LEAs are required to bid on a competitive basis; others are allocated on a formula basis.

❏ Specialist schools

This grant, available through the Standards Fund 'Spreading Excellence' heading, has two objectives. To:

1. support the implementation of development plans of secondary schools designated under the Secretary of State's Specialist Schools programme; and
2. enable schools to undertake additional responsibilities in relation to disseminating good practice.

Currently, the specialist schools programme encompasses technology, language, sports and arts colleges. Schools are required to put forward their proposals for ways in which they will adapt their learning and teaching in order to reflect the status they are seeking. Additionally, they are required to raise money for appropriate capital development to the order of £100,000, usually from the local community. Matched funding for capital development is provided by the DfEE for those schools that are successful, together with revenue funding from the Standards Fund for a period of three years. Schools must reapply after this time.

❏ Special educational needs

You have read a short passage on the funding of the education of pupils with identified special educational needs in the chapter by Anne West *et al.* The management of the education of pupils with special needs is complex; some pupils are members of mainstream schools while others attend special schools. However, the funding is all directed through LEAs and, as you have read in the section on fair funding, SEN is one of the categories for which LEAs are allowed to hold back funding from schools in order to provide central services (for example, educational psychology services).

❏ Entrepreneurialism

Supplementing school income through fund-raising activities has become a common feature of school life. In a small but useful way, it draws the school closer to its community, and the income generated may be substantial, depending on the wealth and degree of involvement of the local community. It is also possible to negotiate commercial support from companies, sometimes in the form of sponsorship of specific buildings, equipment or groups of children, in situations where mutual benefit can be established. The benefits achieved by the school through these efforts must be set against the time taken by staff and students in generating the income. The concept and practice of entrepreneurialism are discussed more fully in Lesley Anderson's chapter, 'The move towards entrepreneurialism', Chapter 3 in Coleman, M. and Anderson, L. (eds.) *Managing Finance and Resources in Education.*

Schools in Scotland

Although part of the UK, Scotland has a distinctive institutional history. The Act of Union in 1707 provides for the maintenance of certain separate institutions (including universities) and there has always been separate legislation for education in Scotland. The recently devolved status of the Scottish Parliament has served to underline differences in educational practice: for example, higher education students are not subject to the same fee requirements as those in England and Wales.

The move towards self-management in Scotland has been more piecemeal than in England and Wales, with parental choice being enhanced in 1981 (Alder *et al.*, 1989). However, school boards, the equivalent of governing bodies in England and Wales, were only brought about under the School Boards Act 1988. At this time these boards were marked by their difference from school governing bodies in England and Wales in that parents were in the majority from the beginning, although they were granted fewer powers than in the rest of the UK (Feintuck, 1994, p. 28).

Self-managing schools were introduced in Scotland in the same year, 1989, as in the rest of the UK, by the Self-Governing Schools, etc. (Scotland) Act. However, the opportunity to opt out was never popular with schools and there were, in fact, only ever three GM schools approved in Scotland and one of these never actually adopted the status. Feintuck (1994, p. 71) attributes this to a range of factors, including the relative newness of school boards with parents in the majority. It seems parents were unwilling to seek more than the basic powers granted to them (Munn, 1991, p. 73). At the time of writing (2000) the legislation that enabled schools to become grant maintained is about to be changed and the status abolished.

Interestingly, there is another unique school category in Scotland known as 'grant aided' and funded directly by the government. Just one school, Jordanhill, has this status although in theory other schools can seek to become grant aided. Jordanhill used to be a demonstration school attached to the teacher training college in Glasgow and was threatened with closure when it was no longer needed in this capacity.

Devolved school management was introduced in the early 1990s although there has been no statutory basis for it, simply the guidelines provided by the Scottish Office. Again, at the time of writing this is about to change by the forthcoming Royal Assent to the School Standards and Framework Act 2000.

Independent schools and the involvement of the private sector

In the UK the terms 'independent' or 'private' are used to categorise schools educating five or more pupils (DfEE, undated) that are not dependent upon local or central government for financial or other support. (The misleading term 'public schools' that historically has been applied to the major fee-paying schools and, in particular, to the boys' boarding schools whose headmasters are members of the Headmasters' Conference has largely fallen into disuse (Walford, 1991, p. 2).) Therefore, at a simple level, independent schools are self-managing in that they are privately run either by an individual owner or by a board of trustees/governors and their income is generated from the fees charged for the service provided (that is, the education of children). Most independent schools are registered charities and, consequently, they are non-profit making.

However, over the past decade or more, the distinction between state and independent schools has been becoming less clear (*ibid.*). Arrangements such as the Assisted Places Scheme and the Aided Pupil Scheme directed state funding into the private sector to support the education of specific children in private schools while many parents with children in state schools are expected to contribute to their children's education.

The situation is further complicated by city technology colleges that were introduced by the Conservative government in the Education Reform Act 1988 as part of their strategy to increase diversity in state education. City technology colleges operate outside the aegis of an LEA and provide free education to their pupils. Although the original intention was that they would be completely, or partly, funded by industry and commerce, they are now mainly financed by the state although individual colleges receive varying support from private organisations.

In recent times the distinction between the private and public sectors has been even more blurred by the increasing role of private companies providing educational services and, in a few cases, being contracted by an LEA or the DfEE to run individual state schools or an LEA in situations where the school or the LEA has been judged to be failing by the Office for Standards in Education (Ofsted). For example, in 1999 the company '3Es', which is the commercial wing of Kingshurst CTC in Birmingham, was contracted to run a failing school in Surrey and, from the same time, Cambridge Education Associates and Nord Anglia plc have each been running a London LEA. Furthermore, in 2000, the government announced a plan to create 'city academies' to replace seriously failing schools. The intention is that these academies will be built and managed by partnerships involving the government and sponsors from the voluntary sector, churches and business.

Incorporated further education colleges

Until 1993, further education (FE) colleges came under the aegis of LEAs and enjoyed little formal autonomy. However, in that year, FE colleges were incorporated and became self-managing. Thus, they lost their formal links with the local authorities and were conferred with a range of new powers.

These include the right to:

- employ their own staff
- enter into contracts on their own behalf
- manage assets and resources
- act as a legal body undertaking activities in the furtherance of their purpose as providers of education (Briggs, 1992, p. 62).

These changes to self-management were part of a desperately needed drive to improve the efficiency of FE which, at the time, was estimated to 'lose' 30–40% of students before they achieved the qualification for which they had enrolled (Audit Commission, 1993). So, in line with this move, shortly after incorporation both the level and methodology of funding were changed explicitly to achieve a political steer (FEFC, 1992). The new methodology was introduced by means of a document entitled *Funding Learning* (*ibid.*) which, with a title that focused on learning, was designed to convey the required message. As Gorringe (1994, p. 68) points out 'the methodology is the message'. However, alongside this message, there was still an emphasis on encouraging colleges to recruit more students through the funds made available for growth (Lumby, 2000c, p. 82), and through the basic funding formula which was dependent upon the recruitment, retention and achievement of students. Enrolments grew from 900,000 full-time equivalent enrolments in 1992/93 to 13 million in 1996/97 (FEDA, 1998). This growth was achieved by colleges using a range of tactics that enabled them to provide for additional students without increasing the resource allocation in the same proportion.

Inevitably, there has not been agreement about the success, or otherwise, of the system. A fundamental review (Kennedy, 1997) acknowledged a number of problems that resulted from the funding system and concerns expressed by colleges themselves and the Further Education Funding Council (FEFC) coincided with a change of government, all of which led to a major review (Lumby, 1998). The 1993/98 funding methodology was adjusted in 1999/2000 with a move away from market freedom, competition and transparent, equal funding for all colleges and a thrust towards nationally controlled growth, collaboration and some differential funding related to geographical and social disadvantage. Furthermore, from 2001 the FEFC and the Training and Enterprise Councils are to be replaced by a Learning and Skills Council with anticipated changes in systems and culture (Lumby, 2000c, p. 83).

❑ Key points from the chapter

- Vocational education is a topical issue internationally.
- In 1993, UK colleges of FE were incorporated as self-managing institutions.

- Significant changes in the funding arrangements have been implemented since 1993.
- These changes have resulted in the need for cultural change that has been achieved to varying degrees within individual colleges.
- There is still considerable scope for development of this sector.

 Reading

For a more detailed account of funding in UK further education colleges, please read Jacky Lumby's chapter, 'Funding learning in further education', Chapter 5 in Coleman, M. and Anderson, L. (eds.) *Managing Finance and Resources in Education.*

❑ **Our comments**

As has been suggested, both here and in Chapter 1, college principals have great autonomy of decision-making as to whom they employ, how they deploy them and on what type of contract. Provided there is trade union agreement, local flexibility can be enhanced by local decision-making. Chapter 3 offers further examples of this factor.

Colleges are bound by a complex web of formal contracts and local custom and practice as regards allocation of teaching duties, but are largely free to determine their own allocation of curriculum time, working day and termly patterns. This, in theory, enables them to respond flexibly to customer need.

The decentralisation of power differs between the school and college sector. Although schools have much freedom of decision-making, they are bound both by the National Curriculum and its inspection system, and by the funding framework, and this constrains much else. Subsequent chapters of this book will analyse ways in which the degrees of local freedom offered by self-management can be exploited to the benefit of the learner and the school. The nature and purpose of colleges demand greater flexibility and responsiveness to changing local needs, and college principals may have greater overall power to make decisions than school heads. However, the main constraint on colleges is the current funding mechanism, and the conformity to systems of provision and monitoring which it demands, and this may be seen as the main limitation on the local power of decision-making in colleges.

❑ **Building on key learning points**

- School and college self-management was introduced in England during the last decade of the twentieth century in an attempt to create competition between schools and colleges and, thus, raise educational standards.
- LMS applied to all schools although there was also an opportunity for schools to opt out of local control and take on a more extreme form of self-management known as GM status.
- LMS and GM (now called 'Foundation') status schools are now subject to fair funding, which provides more delegation to all schools.
- School funding in the UK is based on an age-weighted pupil unit.
- In recent times, the UK government has exerted more control over the level of funding that must be delegated to schools. It continues to increase this as well as now providing some funding directly to schools.
- A number of problems resulting from the funding methodology of further education introduced in the early 1990s when all colleges were incorporated have resulted in the establishment of Learning and Skills Councils from 2001. Further change in funding systems and culture are anticipated.

3. Financial management in schools and colleges: theoretical perspectives

---

This chapter considers:

- the resource management cycle;
- financial and real resources;
- effectiveness and efficiency;
- budgeting within educational organisations;
- costing in educational organisations;
- models of financial decision-making; and
- the economic realities of education.

Introduction

The premise underlying this chapter is that education must be financed and that it is the astute and effective management of this finance that will allow a quality educational provision to be delivered: 'A self-managing school is a school in a system of education where there has been a significant and consistent decentralisation to a school level of authority to make decisions related to the allocation of resources' (Caldwell and Spinks, 1992, p. 4).

Through this move towards the direct self-management of educational providers, it becomes apparent that to ensure local educational needs and priorities are met and satisfied, control of the management and internal allocation of finance (and thus the educational resources they can be converted into) must be devolved to individual schools and colleges. It follows that those in management positions within schools and colleges must be equipped with the financial skills and knowledge necessary to perform their management duties, and successfully accept responsibility for the power this brings with it. They must also be capable of handling the increased level of bureaucracy involved in managing devolved funding and bidding for extra funds, and interrogating the strategic direction of the institution with a view to maximising the funding available. A move towards self-management of funding by its very nature removes the institution from the support of the local or national authority that has previously controlled its financial affairs. For example, senior staff of newly incorporated further education colleges in the UK in 1993 found themselves in some cases managing multi-million pound budgets 'overnight':

> The complexities of managing large, multi-site technical and vocational institutions demand high calibre management skills, which in turn create training and development demands. Investment in improving the quality of institutional management is one of the most obvious ways of reducing the costs of technical/vocational education (Gray and Warrender, 1993, p. 143).

Essentially, education is a service industry focusing upon 'goal orientation where funding is an enabler' (Pettifor, 1974, p. 35).

An excellent discussion of the importance of resource management to the eventual learning outcomes of education can be found in the chapter by Rosalind Levačić 'Linking resources to learning outcomes', Chapter 1 in Coleman, M. and Anderson, L. (eds.) *Managing Finance and Resources in Education* (you may wish to reacquaint yourself with it at this point). We begin with a discussion of the resource management cycle, presented in Levačić's

The resource management cycle

The process of resource management in schools and colleges can be conceptualised as a simple figure or 'cycle'. Levačić (2000, pp. 11–13) identifies four distinct elements that collectively form the resource management cycle:

1) obtaining resources;
2) allocating resources;
3) using resources;
4) evaluation and review.

A simplified portrayal of the relationship between these elements is shown in Figure 3.1. Schools and colleges in England and Wales *acquire resources* from their sponsors, the local education authority (LEA), the Further Education Funding Council (FEFC) or the Learning and Skills Council (LSC). Schools and colleges may also derive income from fees, grants, donations or fund-raising activities. These organisations then decide how to allocate those resources to support the activities of the organisation and implement their decisions. Good practice suggests the effectiveness of these decisions will then need to be evaluated and their allocation reviewed for the next phase of the resource management cycle.

❑ Obtaining resources

Where the management of resources has been devolved to the school or college level, the main source of income will usually be a fee per student or pupil enrolled. In most instances any formula that has been developed to calculate the aggregate income from such universal fees will be adjusted to allow for the non-homogeneous nature of pupils/students, courses and accommodation. Other factors such as the age of the pupils/students, their financial background, local cost of living or political expedience

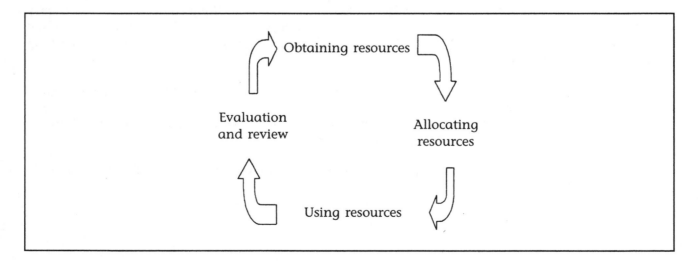

Figure 3.1 The resource management cycle

might also come into play. Such elements are likely to be influential whether the school is working within the state or private sector, the key difference being who actually pays the fees. For a discussion of funding mechanisms for schools and colleges in the UK, see Chapter 2 of this book.

Beyond this basic level of fees income, additional income may be sought by the school or college through fund raising, sponsorship or by making bids to charitable or governmental organisations. This aspect of educational resource provision is an increasingly important one leading to an entrepreneurial ethos permeating much of the education sector (both state and privately operated). As Caldwell and Spinks (1992, p. 83) suggest: 'a shift to self-management implies a refocusing of the work of teachers to replace funds which formerly came from government.'

 Reading

Further information and a discussion of additional sources of educational funding and educational enterprise can be found in Lesley Anderson's chapter, 'The move towards entrepreneurialism', Chapter 3 in Coleman, M. and Anderson, L. (eds.) *Managing Finance and Resources in Education*.

Financial and real resources

We noted earlier (p. 5) in Caldwell and Spinks' (1992) list of the resources available to schools and colleges that finance is only one of the seven resources they identify. Finance is particularly significant, however, because it provides the wherewithal to secure the other resources required to deliver high-quality teaching and learning.

There is, therefore, an important distinction between financial and real resources. *Financial resources* refer to the money available to purchase *real resources*. The latter are those human and material resources that are required to deliver educational services. Human resources include teachers, lecturers, support staff and, perhaps, unpaid volunteers. Material resources include buildings, equipment, furniture, books and teaching materials. It is the combination of human and material resources that largely determines the quality of education to be provided to pupils and students. The other factors mentioned – power to make decisions (leadership), knowledge and technology (staff development) along with time – are the factors that ensure the effective use of personnel and materials and are also made possible through the availability of funding. Financial management is significant primarily because this determines the extent and nature of these resources.

❑ Financial management in education as a cyclical system

Much of the management of education is treated as a cyclical system – the outputs from one cycle being used to determine the inputs of the next (e.g. plan–teach–evaluate/assess). Educational objectives are realised by the effective use of human and material resources, made possible through the availability of finance. Once combined, these resources lead to the meeting of educational outcomes through the provision of appropriate educational activities. These outcomes can then be evaluated in the light of the predetermined educational objectives to inform the planning (including the identification, allocation and organisation of resources) for the next cycle. This can be seen to be the basis of the priority-based budgeting system described in further detail below. A simplified model of the cyclical system is shown as Figure 3.2.

This model is a gross oversimplification of a complex phenomenon, providing an indication of the processes that are likely to take place. The delivery of high-quality education will always owe much to the presence of good, well led and motivated teachers and lecturers committed to their pupils or students. Figure 3.2 does not deal with these important qualitative variables: this comes within the

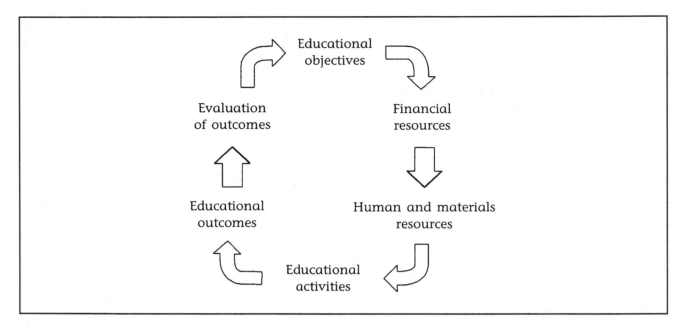

Figure 3.2 The cyclical system

sphere of human resource management. It does, however, reinforce the vital point that finance is important as a means of supporting *educational* objectives, such as high-quality teaching and learning (see Levačić in Coleman and Anderson, 2000).

Effectiveness and efficiency

❑ Cost-effectiveness

> Let no-one deride the word 'cheaper', there is no advantage in education being more expensive than it has to be (Knight, 1993, p. 15).

One of the key questions educational managers should constantly ask themselves is: 'Is there a less costly way of resourcing that will achieve the same results?' or, viewed another way: 'Given the resources available, can educational provision be improved or increased?' As Thomas (1990, p. 46) notes: 'Policy-makers require assurances that resources are being used efficiently as well as effectively: the cost-effectiveness of educational provision has to be demonstrated.' For this to be achieved there needs to be a commonly agreed understanding of efficiency and educational effectiveness – this is where notions of educational output are combined with the calculations of the cost of provision:

> *efficiency* – 'cheapest means of accomplishing a defined objective' (Rumble, 1987, p. 74).

Thomas (1990, p. 58) defines efficiency as 'aiming to produce the desired output in the cheapest way possible'. It is important that in defining efficiency the notion of achieving basic output criteria is retained; otherwise it might be the case that 'outputs that are actually produced do not contribute to the programme objectives; that is it may be efficient at doing the wrong things' (Atkinson, cited in Thomas, 1990, p. 50).

Knight (1993, pp. 19–20) defines and illustrates educational effectiveness:

> *Effectiveness* is the fullest possible attainment of the goals and objectives of the school . . .

Examples: Improved performance, possibly against performance indicators such as improved examination results or test scores; . . . improved student attitudes and behaviour; better parent and community relations; improved school environment.

Efficiency and effectiveness are alternative ways of viewing the same basic issue – the achievement of stated educational aims. Efficiency is a minimalist approach, focusing on the meeting of threshold standard at the lowest cost (price efficiency) or lowest combination of resources (technical efficiency) (Thomas, 1990, p. 47).

Effectiveness is concerned with maximising the benefits due to educational provision within the constraints of cost or resource availability. Mortimore *et al.* (1994, p. 23) rephrase this by stating that 'Cost-effectiveness . . . is concerned with selecting the least-cost alternative for securing the desired outcome'. Thomas (1990, p. 50) had expanded upon this by suggesting that 'The most cost-effective will be the least costly of the alternatives compared, which is not necessarily the cheapest possible method of attaining the objective'. This acknowledges that the decision is constrained by the limits of the knowledge the decision-maker is able to draw upon. Clearly the implication is that it is only possible accurately to compare the effectiveness of educational activities which have the same 'outputs'. This restriction on the use of cost-effective analysis is clarified by Levin (1983, p. 18): 'It is assumed that (1) only programs with similar or identical goods can be compared and (2) a common measure of effectiveness can be used to measure them.'

Woodhall (1987, p. 397) notes 'there are two ways of applying cost-effectiveness analysis': to maximise output in respect of a target cost or to minimise cost in respect of a given output. Both can be seen as being either operational or strategic, dependent upon the position of the decision-maker. At the level of the course leader, Woodhall (*ibid.*, p. 399) identifies five uses of cost-effectiveness analysis to support educational planning:

1. testing the economic feasibility of expansion plans or proposals;
2. projecting future educational costs;
3. estimating the cost of alternative actions;
4. comparing alternative means of achieving the same educational objectives;
5. improving the efficiency of resource utilisation.

Point 4 in the above list is one that deserves further discussion, particularly in situations where there is a drive to make greater use of educational technology. If we consider a teaching situation where the stated learning objective is in terms of the transfer of knowledge, the options might be for the teacher to tell the students, or for the students to research the information either from books in the teaching room or library or to use the Internet. Clearly each option has vastly different costs attached to it, not only in terms of the physical resources required but also in the infrastructure and the training that are required to make each option viable. Although the stated learning objective for each might be the same, the actual learning required, in terms of the associated skill base, is very different, potentially making more costly options more desirable on those grounds.

Mortimore *et al.* (1994, pp. 21–22) use the term 'cost-effectiveness' to link effectiveness and efficiency and argue it is an essential component of high-quality education:

> Cost-effectiveness in schools is concerned with the relationship between the learning of children and the human and physical resources which contribute to that learning. It should not be equated with parsimony and cheapness . . . if two schools which are comparable in every respect are equally effective in terms of performance, the one that uses the smaller amount of resources is the more cost-effective. A school that uses its resources more cost-effectively, moreover, releases resources which can be used to promote further development. Cost effectiveness . . . is highly desirable.

Similarly, the FEFC funding regime, under which incorporated further education colleges in the UK operated until 2001, 'was intended to refocus colleges on being more efficient, recruiting more students and raising the quality of achievement, all through a quasi-market mechanism that directly linked numbers of students and their success to income' (Lumby, 2000c, p. 81).

The notion of educational *benefit* requires further explanation. The benefits of an activity must be assessed as well as its costs if it is to be a cost-effectiveness analysis. These benefits will be in terms of educational objectives, so benefit may only be derived where the use of resources ultimately results in an improvement in teaching and learning within the school or college.

If these benefits can be expressed in quantitative terms, such as examination grades, Knight (1993) suggests a cost-effectiveness analysis will allow a comparison of alternative goals or programmes. Where resources are limited and fixed within any one time period, alternative ways of deploying those resources can be compared in terms of the benefits that might accrue: 'This monetary expression of benefits allows comparison of different programmes, but it also involves the problem of setting financial values on non-financial benefits' (*ibid.*, p. 186).

The English school inspection body, Ofsted (Office for Standards in Education), requires that schools be judged by:

- the extent to which resources are used to maximise the achievement of the school's aims and objectives;
- the extent to which the school aligns its spending priorities with its educational priorities;
- the cost-effectiveness of programmes, procedures and practices; and
- the quality of the educational outcomes which result.

◎ **Reading and** Activity

Please read Tim Simkins' chapter 'Cost analysis in education', Chapter 10 in Coleman, M. and Anderson, L. (eds.) *Managing Finance and Resources in Education*.

Focus your reading to consider the following situation. Your institution has identified the standards of student/pupil literacy as being an educational priority. Alternative strategies have been identified:

- retraining existing teaching staff;
- employing extra teaching staff to reduce teaching group size;
- employing teaching assistants to work alongside the teaching staff;
- employing a literacy specialist to support and guide teaching staff and offer student/pupil withdrawal provision;
- purchasing computer-based learning support facilities for the students/pupils; and
- purchasing paper-based resources aimed at students/pupils.

What further information would you require to carry out a cost/benefit analysis of the alternative proposals? How would you hope to 'sell' your findings to your management and teaching colleagues?

❏ **Our comments**

So much depends upon the individual circumstances of the institution and the availability of resources – employing an extra member of teaching staff may be the cost-effective solution, but it is highly dependent upon being able to appoint an appropriate person to the post. However, to determine the efficiency you would need to ascertain the potential benefits of each of the alternative strategies along with the attached costs of each. It is quite likely you will conclude that the different solutions to the problem are just that – different – rather than being better or worse. In terms of the costs of the alternatives you will need to look beyond the direct costs (such as salaries or purchase price). Will there be any initial 'start-up' costs (recruitment of staff), or ongoing costs (consumable paper resources), and what is the likely availability of these resources (do the required training courses exist)?

Although an examination of the costs and benefits of alternative strategies might narrow down the range of possible alternatives, other factors will also influence the decision-making process. The following two sections examine the different approaches to examining and accounting for the use of financial resources in education: 'Budgeting and costing are two different approaches to determining the necessary funds for educational activities. Budgeting focuses on the allocation of available funds; costing on the funds that are required to allow certain educational activities to take place' (Burton, 1999, p. 129).

Budgeting within educational organisations

Why budget? Because:

- resources are 'scarce' – you can't do everything you want to;
- you are accountable for the funding you receive;
- you want to ensure the things you need to do are properly resourced; and
- you want to plan ahead.

Internal or departmental budgeting within an educational organisation is one of the most important activities in the resource management cycle. The budget is the tool for ensuring the resources required for the educational activities that lead to the achievement of educational objectives are made available. The budget is much more than a spreadsheet itemising income and expenditure under different section headings. It should be used as a means of expressing school or college aims and educational priorities in financial terms.

At its most effective, budgeting is an integral and flexible component of the educational planning cycle. It goes beyond pure monetary analysis to ensure the resources necessary for the educational activity of the institution are made available. Also it will contain both short and long-term planning elements to allow for both immediate and future resource investments over a number of years to be accounted for: 'The literature reflects a general consensus that effective practice requires the integration of financial, staff and curriculum planning and that the aims and objectives of the school as reflected in the curriculum should drive the budget rather than the other way round' (Levačić, 1992, p. 26).

 Reading

Please read Kevin McAleese's chapter, 'Budgeting in schools', Chapter 8 in Coleman, M. and Anderson, L. (eds.) *Managing Finance and Resources in Education*.

❏ Our comments

Much of the budgetary process is best understood by reference to an example of an educational budget. Understanding of the applications of the perspective offered above can be best appreciated when approached through a particular context. Consider any budgetary system in terms of five key elements:

1. Integration within the overall management planning cycle (are the activities of the institution costed and if so by whom?).

2. Ability to facilitate both long and short-term financial planning (contingency funds and the constraints on long-term planning).
3. The level of consultation and participation within the process (how are conflicting calls on funding prioritised and resolved?).
4. The degree of decentralisation of the decision-making process (defining the 'cost centre').
5. Sufficient flexibility to encourage innovation and to allow for change (the degree of virement allowed to sub-budget holders).

Activity

Obtain a copy of the budget for the current year from your department, school or college. After familiarising yourself with the structure of the statement, seek to interview a member of the management team responsible for the budget to ascertain how the five points listed above are integrated into the budgetary system. You will need to be diplomatic in your approach to the interview and structure the questions carefully beforehand to avoid any ambiguity.

❑ The budget as a resource management tool

 Reading

A series of articles in *Managing Schools Today* by Kevin McAleese, during 1997 and 1998, focusing upon creative budgeting and planning within schools, provides an excellent practical background to the use of budgets as a management tool within education; these can be used to supplement your reading from Chapter 8 in Coleman and Anderson (2000), again by McAleese.

Levačić (1993) claims that the budget has four functions that enable it to transform finance into real resources. These functions are:

1. planning and decision-making;
2. control;
3. accountability and stewardship; and
4. motivation.

These functions are discussed below.

❑ *Planning and decision-making*
Preparing the budget for the next financial year is a key part of planning. In this respect the budget is forward looking – it is made up of expectations about future revenue and expenditure.

◎ Reading and Activity

Please read Derek Glover's chapter, 'Financial management and strategic planning', Chapter 7 in Coleman, M. and Anderson, L. (eds.) *Managing Finance and Resources in Education*.

Consider the models of financial management he proposes in relation to your own financial context.

❑ **Our comments**

Ideally, the decision-making process should be strategic to ensure the educational objectives of the organisation are supported by appropriate resources. As Glover suggests, there are several models through which the educational and financial priorities of an organisation can be combined. The following sections examine the potential for this in greater detail. You will probably derive greatest benefit from being able to compare the theoretical perspective, offered by Glover, with your own financial context.

❑ *Control*

The purpose of control is to ensure decisions are implemented. It necessarily restricts the ability of individuals in the organisation to vire funds or spend money as they wish. Budget information for control purposes can be either backward looking, from a record of past transactions, or forward looking, based upon a record of monthly expenditure intentions. The control of the political structures within a school or college through the budgetary processes is discussed below in the section entitled 'Models of financial decision-making'.

❑ *Accountability and stewardship*

Budget holders present accounts to governing bodies or other relevant groups to demonstrate the money has been used for the purposes intended. This limited form of accountability shows probity but it is more difficult to show the spending has been effective. The British government's controversial decision to publish 'league tables' of various performance indicators represents an attempt to judge educational effectiveness, though these measures of 'output' are presented in isolation from the funding information. Within the inspection parameters, Ofsted is required to make judgements concerning 'value for money' which might be perceived as an extension of 'cost-effectiveness analysis' as discussed above.

❑ *Motivation*

Budgets can be used to motivate and empower staff. This delegation of financial authority, called 'intrapreneurship' by Caldwell and Spinks, is an approach to management that 'encourages individual initiative when it is not possible to formulate a coherent and integrated organisational response' (Caldwell and Spinks, 1998, p. 199).

Levačić (1993) suggests that teachers may be motivated through participation in decision-making, by being budget holders in their own right, by receiving more real resources or by being paid more.

❑ **Approaches to the budgetary process**

There are three main approaches in the preparation of budgets. These are:

1. incremental budgeting;
2. zero-based budgeting (also referred to as ZBB); and
3. priority-based budgeting (PBB), sometimes referred to as programme planning – budgeting system (PPBS).

The *incremental* approach treats the previous year's budget as the starting point for the preparation of the new budget. There are marginal or 'incremental' changes but the budget remains largely unaltered from the previous year. The budget holder does not have to justify the whole budget and can confine the discussion to marginal increases or reductions which are likely to be determined largely by the general financial position of the institution rather than an assessment of the value of the programmes provided by the sub-unit under review.

An example of incremental budgeting would be a decision to increase departmental budgets by a fixed amount, say 2%.

Advantages
- The budgetary process is relatively predictable and secure.
- Debate and discussion are limited: a feature that may be welcomed by busy practitioners.
- The prospect of conflict between sub-units is avoided, especially if resources are allocated on the basis of general increases or reductions (as in the example given in the previous paragraph) rather than by discriminating amongst activities to determine spending levels (Davies, 1994, p. 348).

Disadvantages
- Inappropriate budget allocations of the past will be reinforced.
- There is little opportunity to plan for changes in priorities or in the educational climate.
- There is an implicit assumption all costs are rising at the same rate.

Zero-based budgeting offers a very different approach from budget setting. It begins with the assumption all categories of spending should be scrutinised. Budget holders must justify all planned expenditure, not just new initiatives or those at the margin of existing provision. In other words, budgeting starts from a zero base and is determined by a decision-making process.

Advantages
- It allows for new initiatives to be incorporated into budgets.
- It should prevent inequalities of the past from continuing.
- It enforces an evaluative or reflective element into the financial planning process.

Disadvantages
- It can be a very time-consuming and therefore costly process.
- There is no consistency between budgetary periods, making year-on-year comparisons difficult.
- Some sub-budget holders will be better at the bidding process and justifying their costs than others.
- As many costs are fixed, year on year, a true ZBB is not really possible.

For example, at least some staff are likely to be on permanent contracts and will be retained whatever the outcomes of the ZBB bidding process.

The *priority-based* budgeting system attempts to match the stated aims and priorities of the school or college with that allocation of funding. Clearly, certain priorities will need to be regarded as implicit (e.g. to work in a dry, well lit environment), but the educational priorities, which drive the process, should be arrived at through informed educational debate.

Advantages
- It makes costs an issue at the point of educational debate rather than an afterthought.
- It allows changes in national and local priorities to be adequately resourced.

Disadvantages
- The budget may 'lurch' as priorities change.
- The basis on which the priorities are ranked becomes a key issue in the decision-making process.

Activity

It is quite possible for all three systems to co-exist, e.g. within a department which receives a general funding on a historical basis, but then must justify this allocation and any extra funds in addition to this on a ZBB basis, referring to the predetermined educational priorities. For your department, school or college, investigate the institutional and departmental budgetary approach. List the advantages and disadvantages of incremental, priority and zero-based systems in your local context.

Costing in educational organisations

Effective financial management in schools and colleges requires an appreciation of the significance of costs. It is not possible to make judgements about competing claims on resources without knowledge of the costs of all the activities under consideration. In this section, we consider the nature of costs in education and different ways of classifying costs.

Educational costing is well established in the USA where 'the activity of costing is best defined in terms of its purpose or outcomes' (Burton, 1999, p. 129). According to Hans (1996, p. 93), costing systems can be 'descriptive, telling administrators how much a given activity or process costs, and second they can be predictive, suggesting how resources ought to be combined in the future for cost effective use'.

In the past such systems have often not been applied because funds have simply been allocated to the school or college – the formula and incremental budgeting approach of the funding agency encouraging a similar approach from schools and colleges. What indeed is the incentive, as Kedney (1993, p. 1) suggests, 'if provision is up and running, the quality is judged to be at least adequate, life is generally thought to be reasonable and will stay that way, so why bother with costing'? Clearly as resources diminish it becomes more imperative to cost activities, otherwise a short-term 'cut now and put back later' policy (turning lights off, restrictions on photocopying) will develop.

Although costs can be defined ultimately in financial terms, not all costs are obviously monetary. They may also include time and intangible resources like teacher morale, health, motivation and energy. As Knight (1993, p. 9) illustrates, the costs of educational decisions may have both financial and non-financial elements:

> The closure of a small village school is proposed. Financial costs saved include the extra teaching staff necessary for a small school, the maintenance costs of the premises and the financial return foregone on the capital value of the building – offset by some additional transport and meals costs. Non-financial costs include the effect on the community of the loss of its social centre, and time spent by children travelling – offset perhaps by educational gains of children in a larger school.

This example illustrates the point made earlier in this chapter about the need to consider costs and benefits when making educational decisions.

❑ Types of cost
The significance of educational costs can be appreciated by classifying them in several different ways.

❑ Direct and indirect
Direct costs are those which can be identified with a sub-unit or 'cost centre' (department or faculty) within the school or college. *Indirect* costs (or overheads) cannot be attributed to a particular activity or unit within the school or college and so cannot be accurately apportioned. Frequently it is a case of how the budget is determined and arranged – if the library is funded via departments or faculties it can be classified as a direct cost; if it is centrally funded, it will be an indirect cost. Unless administrators, clerical and technical staffs work exclusively within particular cost centres their salaries will be categorised as indirect costs.

❑ Variable, stepped and fixed
Variable costs are those that change as the level of activity increases or decreases. *Fixed* costs remain unchanged despite fluctuations in the level of activity. These can be represented by the cost 'curves' in Figure 3.3.

Stepped costs are fixed over a range of activity – for 18–38 children, one classroom and one teacher

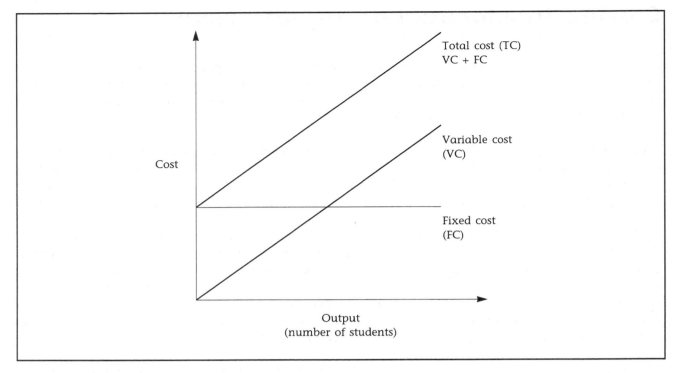

Figure 3.3 Fixed and variable costs

may be sufficient, but beyond 38 there is a need for two of each (costs have suddenly and dramatically increased in one large step). The distinction between fixed and variable is very dependent upon the time period in question. The longer the time period the more variable the costs are. Costs, which are generally accepted as fixed in the short term, such as premises costs and the salaries of teaching staff, can be varied in the long term – using more efficient energy supplies, increasing (or decreasing) the number (or pay) of teaching staff. Diagrammatically this can be shown as a cost 'curve' with discontinuities showing that different cost levels are possible for the same level of activity.

For example, in a situation where there are increasing student numbers, a class may be allowed to rise to 35 students – one class, 35 students. In a school with falling rolls, where the student numbers have fallen to 35 from, say, 60, the students may still be split between two classes – two classes, 35 students. This make two levels of cost possible for a class of 35 students (output O_1 on Figure 3.4). In the first case the students are taught at the cost of one classroom and one teacher (cost C_2 on Figure 3.4), while in the second it takes two of each to perform the same outcome (cost C_1 on Figure 3.4).

The distinction between fixed and variable costs over time is particularly important for schools and colleges experiencing expansion or contraction of enrolment. During periods of growth, fixed costs are unchanged in total, but fall per head of the expanding school or college population. Conversely, fixed costs per head rise during periods of falling rolls, adding to the many problems of contraction. In the long run, all costs become variable (personnel, even buildings can be changed) but there may be a substantial time lag before fixed costs can be adjusted in line with levels of activity.

❑ *Average and marginal costs*
Average costs represent the total costs of a school or college divided by the number of pupils or students. This gives an indication of the cost of educating one pupil or student. It is simplistic because it does not discriminate between categories of student, on the basis of age, needs or course, for example.

A more useful concept is that of *marginal* cost. This indicates the extra cost of educating one more student. If there is room in a class, the marginal cost might be relatively low and certainly well below the marginal revenue receivable for that pupil through formula funding. However, if a new class has

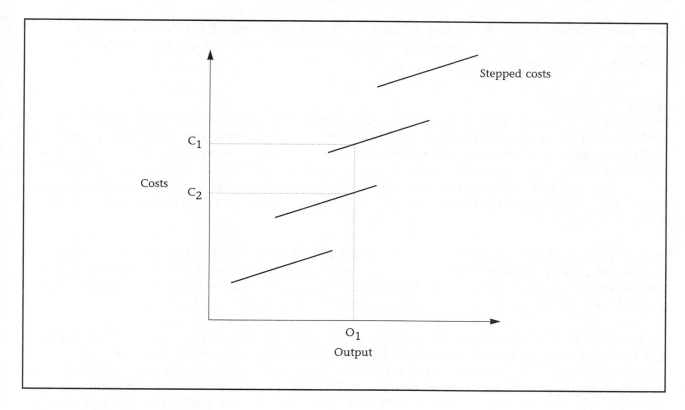

Figure 3.4   Stepped costs

to be created, the marginal cost will certainly exceed marginal revenue, the point where it is necessary to move up from one stepped cost curve to the next, and may lead to a decision not to admit the extra student. The concept of *marginal cost pricing* is to increase production (enrol extra students) until the fees obtained (the price) of that last student are equal to the extra (marginal) cost of that student.

❑ *Costing new initiatives*

Whenever a decision needs to be made whether to create a new reception or kindergarten class or offer a new subject at examination level, the cost of such an initiative needs to be carefully considered. Sometimes it may be possible to make use of currently under-utilised resources – an empty classroom, a member of the teaching staff with a less than fully committed timetable. On other, more costly, occasions it will require expenditure on new accommodation, new teaching resources or staff. Once the expected costs have been established the number of extra pupils or students required to cover those cost (through the revenue obtained from their fees) must be calculated. That number will be the 'break even' point – any greater enrolment than that figure will bring in greater revenue than expenditure,

---

Activity

Active recruitment is now a feature of many schools and colleges. Take two examples. In an underperforming secondary school, which is in competition with a neighbouring school with a better academic reputation, the director of studies is under pressure to run a course on law in the coming year. In a general vocational college, which has an agricultural college nearby, there is pressure to run small-scale courses in animal care. Taking either case, what would be the elements in the calculation of the viability of the course, and what criteria would determine whether the course should operate?

any less and there will be a net loss to the school or college. Even if this break-even point is not achieved, the initiative may still operate as a 'loss leader', where it leads to greater enrolment elsewhere in the school or college.

❑ *Opportunity cost*

Every decision to use or deploy a resource should involve a consideration of alternatives. In the rational model to be discussed later in this book, the most appropriate option is chosen in terms of the objectives of the organisation: a 'monetary orientated' definition being that *opportunity cost* is 'concerned with the "value" of the best alternative use to which the resources can be put' (Kedney and Davies, 1994, p. 455). This implies that alternative outcomes can be valued. A decision to purchase more computers, for example, may mean fewer new books can be afforded. The opportunity cost of the computers is the books forgone.

Levačić (1993, p. 6) distinguishes between on-budget and off-budget opportunity costs: 'On-budget costs involve purchasing resources with money. The monetary value is equivalent to what else could be bought with the opportunity cost. Off-budget costs involve a use of resources that does not have a direct monetary cost and so does not show up on the school budget.'

Knight (1993, p. 12) suggests that schools more readily appreciate the significance of certain on-budget opportunity costs than those that are off-budget: 'Schools are quick to see that the opportunity cost of high fuel bills is the books they would have liked to buy, but slower to see that the traditional ways they have deployed teachers can often mask substantial opportunity costs for meeting students' learning needs in other ways.' Levačić (1993, p. 5) also refers to staff deployment in illustrating the concept of off-budget opportunity costs:

> If it is decided to give the existing staff more non-contact time and to employ no more teachers then class sizes have to rise. There is no additional monetary cost, so no on-budget cost of increasing non-contact time. But there still is a cost: the educational benefits pupils would have experienced had they been taught in smaller classes.

Activity

Consider alternative means of delivering a unit of teaching in your own school or college (small group, large group, distance learning, computer-based learning, etc.):

- What are the main cost elements for each?
- What are the main educational benefits for each?
- Why might students choose one mode of learning over another? (This will be a decision based upon perceived costs.)
- Why did *you* choose to study for an MBA via distance learning rather than through a classroom-based course?

❑ **Our comments**

Hopefully, the links between this activity and the section on 'cost effectiveness' will have been apparent. The use of opportunity costs allows the manager to incorporate wider perceptions of the costs of any decision. While the costs that appear on the balance sheet are clearly of importance, it is also necessary to recognise that costs may be transferred elsewhere. The student may receive less personal support (a cost to the student) in a large group teaching situation; the teacher may have to spend more time preparing materials for a computer-based course than a face-to-face course (a cost to the teacher).

❏ Cost centres – managing the budget within the institution

Cost centres refer to any parts of the organisation which have budgets allocated to them, a 'cost centre' being an arbitrary gathering together of costs for management purposes; in education this will usually be a department, course or phase (Lucey, 1996, p. 111). Crisp *et al.* (1991) distinguish between 'central cost centres' and 'academic cost centres'. In secondary schools and colleges, the latter will often be academic departments or faculties. Central costs refer to all costs that are not attributed to departmental cost centres.

Crisp *et al.* (*ibid.*) argue that budget holders must operate within a well defined and clearly understood system of control and act in ways which serve corporate objectives. They state that budget holders are expected to:

Use their delegated powers to further the objectives of the institution as set out in the college strategic plan;
Provide the information necessary to enable the institution to monitor their financial decisions and actions, and be ready to justify these decisions and actions if called upon to do so;
Exercise their discretion within the total resources allocated to them and do nothing which commits the college to on-going expenditure above that agreed in the budget;
Act lawfully and abide by the terms of national and local agreements and other contracts entered into by the college (*ibid.*, p. 5).

Schools may classify their expenditures in terms of 'pay' and 'non-pay'. The non-pay costs can be further subdivided by subject department or centralised costs (such as lighting and heating). Once costs are known they can be managed more effectively and the activities that give rise to cost be held to account.

Central costs, those which cannot be directly attributed to particular courses or cost centres, such as the costs of maintaining the grounds (other than sports fields) or the salaries of the senior management and their administrative staff, do need to be linked in some way to the level of educational activity within the school or college. An approach that is increasingly being applied to manage educational finance is *activity-based costing* (ABC). By accurately costing activities that are performed centrally within the school or college (such as the act of cataloguing a new library book or logging on to the Internet), many central costs can be charged to cost centres. This encourages a more efficient use of resources as those who use it are charged for it. To appreciate the principles, attempt the following activity.

Activity

In both schools and colleges one of the usual central costs is the library service because it is difficult to attribute to any one department. How are these library services costed in an institution known to you? What would be the problems inherent in attempting to cost library facilities to the academic departments or subjects? How might this lead to greater fairness and more efficient and effective use of the resources?

❏ Our comments

Frequently, central costs tend to be shared between the income-generating elements of the institution. This may lead to inequalities appearing if all cost centres are charged similarly for services used more by some than others. The history department may feel it is inappropriate for them to be 'charged' the same as physical education for grounds maintenance (mainly sports fields), whilst PE may feel they are unfairly subsidising the history department's use of the library facilities. Taking an ABC approach to the problem would suggest those who use it most would pay the most out of their budgets. An ABC approach, based on the cost of the act of cataloguing or borrowing a book from the library, or the cost of marking a football pitch, will allow those who make the greatest use of particular facilities to bear the greatest cost of their provision.

Within the general approach to ABC, as proposed by Hans (1996, p. 92), it should be recognised that 'full costing of activities and processes is not always necessary or appropriate'; in effect the costs of the process of costing must be allowed for. Managers must use their judgement to decide when ABC should be used and when simpler, cheaper approaches (such as incremental budgeting) can be more appropriate.

As it reaches the modelling phase, activity-based costing can become very complex, with the potential for subjectiveness as the choice of production activities (cost drivers such as having a whole-school assembly or recruiting students by contacting employers), and the means by which indirect cost is attributed, is made. (Indirect costs being those 'costs that are related to the cost object but cannot be traced to it in an economically feasible way' – Horngren *et al.*, 1994, p. 28.)

ABC has been warmly welcomed by financial managers in many sectors of the general economy as a means of effectively controlling and managing costs of production with much greater precision than was ever possible before. Many costs that were incurred by companies using 'modern production methods' were simply aggregated and assigned to 'fixed cost overheads', their true source not being able to be linked to any particular products. Innes and Mitchell (1991, p. 22) point out that 'ABC highlights the fact that many overheads, conventionally classified as fixed cost, are in fact susceptible to variation, not in respect to volume changes, but in respect to changes in activities which cause their occurrence'.

Given the high levels of 'top slicing', many educational institutions apply to cover centralised costs which are not normally directly linked to courses or classes. DeHayes and Lovrinic (1994, p. 82, emphasis added) observe that 'ABC provides a method to trace financial inputs through various production activities . . . to a variety of outputs of . . . *education*'. In this way the 'true, long term cost of a product or service' (Howson and Mitchell, 1995, p. 65) can be established and that cost allocation can be made as 'a fair distribution of overheads to cost centres' (*ibid.*, p. 64) allowing 'policies on top slicing and cost allocation to be devised' (*ibid.*, p. 68).

There is a significant departure in the underlying approach of ABC compared with previous models, at least according to some of its proponents. According to DeHayes and Lovrinic (1994, p. 83, emphasis added): 'current budgetary processes portray the cost of inputs such as personnel, rather than the cost of outputs, such as . . . *courses*.'

The emphasis here is clearly on the cost of achieving or producing something tangible. With ABC, all costs must be linked to the end products. To assess and judge fully the value added by various educational processes, DeHayes and Lovrinic claim the relevant cost components must be included for a fair comparison to be possible. Self-study units may appear to be a more cost-effective alternative to teaching small groups of students – but the cost of producing, storing and managing the materials must be included.

Probably the most damning inadequacy that pre-ABC techniques are accused of is product cross-subsidisation or, as Horngren *et al.* (1994, p. 114) describe it, 'peanut butter costing', where the costs of resources are uniformly assigned to cost objects. Decisions as to which courses, schools or classes are financially viable can only be made where the information regarding the cost of those courses is accurate and clearly distinguishable from the cost of other courses. It is crucial, in the view of Stone (1992, p. 6), that 'reasonable criteria' and 'defensible methods' are employed in the apportionment of costs.

Alone, ABC is purely an accounting system that is as clear and accurate as the information that is put into it. The choice of cost drivers, those easily measurable indicators (such as staff:student ratio) which are used as a basis for determining the scale of costs to be attributed, is absolutely crucial and, potentially, could be manipulated to give a range of different 'answers' to the same question. It is with this point in mind that Hans (1996, p. 179) suggests that school or college 'budgets probably represent . . . the result of an overwhelmingly political process'.

❑ Costing and pricing

The true value of ABC is really achieved when the costs, derived from the use of ABC, are applied as constraints and parameters to resource allocation decisions whilst comparing equally beneficial alternatives. The viability (or non-viability) of courses and the most efficient enrolment numbers can then be identified along with the most efficient mix of resources. It will also be possible to identify the point where, although a course may not be covering the full costs, it will be returning more than the marginal costs and so be making a contribution to the centralised fixed cost overheads. This will ensure courses that might otherwise be dropped as uneconomic continue to a point where they are no longer able to cover the marginal costs. Turney (1996, p. 39) calls this avoiding 'the death spiral', in which, using full costs, uneconomic lines are dropped leading to overheads being spread over a smaller production base, making those products, in turn, uneconomic.

Although we need to be clear that costing does not equal pricing, the influence of costs must be recognised in any educational pricing structure. Using the approach offered by Turney above, there is the implication of marginal cost pricing – the income obtained from an additional student must cover the costs incurred due to that extra student. Another approach is to charge sufficient fees to cover the total cost of the educational provision – average cost pricing. In a commercial context this will often become 'average cost plus' pricing – where all costs of provision are recouped though the fees, plus an additional charge is made to realise some element of 'profit' from the educational provision. Clearly, in any pricing structure, an awareness of costs is essential for an accurate assessment of viability, though there are situations where a course or other educational activity may well be offered as a 'loss leader'. An 'after-school club', for example, may be operated at a financial loss in order to entice more parents to send their children to the school. An 'introductory learning skills' course may be offered as a loss-making enticement by a college to get students on the premises where they are more likely to enrol on subsequent courses.

In reality, pricing is often based upon a range of factors, often not directly linked to costs. A further non-cost determinant of price is the perception of 'what the market will bear'. Although it is sometimes assumed that the price, determined by this means, will be in excess of cost, there is no rigorous process to ensure this will be the case. It is an appropriate and defensible means of determining the level of profit in a cost-plus approach, but it would be wholly inappropriate to base price entirely on the prices charged by competitors. There is significant flexibility about this point as the prices charged by different educational providers may well have a high degree of similarity, leaving it to the customer to decide upon the comparability of quality.

❑ Privately funded education

There are many examples throughout the world where the state plays no or little part in the funding of education. In such circumstances, these education institutions are entirely dependent upon the fees received from student enrolment or income from a sponsoring body (such as a large company or charitable body). Clearly in such situations price becomes an important determinant, though not always 'cheapness'. In some cases, high-profile schools are seen as being desirable from an attendance perspective – they have 'snob' appeal. It is the high level of fees that is perceived as being a particular 'selling point'. Additionally, these schools and colleges are able to offer differential fees on the basis of student desirability – they may reduce fees (offer scholarships) for those students who are particularly academically able or have particular sporting talents that are likely to bring kudos to the institution.

In many private educational establishments there may be a very interesting balance demonstrated in the actual fees asked of a student between how much the student wants the school, and how much the school wants the student. Such issues need to be determined through a pricing system that allows the fees from 'less desirable' students to subsidise the lower fees of 'more desirable students'.

❑ **Key factors in the costing process**

Davies (in Bush and West-Burnham, 1994, p. 335) identifies eight factors as being crucial to the costing process, namely:

1) Scale of operation
2) Time frame
3) Fixed costs
4) Variable costs
5) Total costs and economies of scale
6) Average costs
7) Marginal costs and thresholds
8) Cash flow.

These should be considered in any attempt to cost an educational activity. Frequently, educational establishments either lack the ability or systems to identify and account for costs accurately. Even where such information is collected and collated, it is often seen as being highly confidential and not made available to those outside the senior financial management level. For these reasons it is often very difficult to cost activities within a school or college accurately. Coombs and Hallak (1987, p. 191) clearly know the value of accurate financial information: 'good educational cost analysts can literally be worth their weight in gold – provided they ask the right questions and arrive at responsible answers, and provided the decision makers understand the answers and take them seriously'.

Additionally, Pyke (1998, p. 79) comments: 'For costs to be managed economically, efficiently and effectively it is necessary to have a costing system which identifies where costs arise and who was responsible for incurring them.' Even within higher education Palfreyman (1991, p. 26) continues this line of argument noting that 'Most institutions of HE have poorly developed management accounting systems and hence are not at all well placed when it comes to providing accurate, timely and relevant financial data for management decisions on the costing and pricing of self-financing activities'.

Activity

Using Davies' (1994) format (Figure 3.5), attempt a costing of a scheme under consideration in your own school or college, or one known to you. List the fixed and variable cost elements you have used.

Year	Fixed cost	Variable cost (to date)	Total cost (to date)	No. of students	Average cost	Cash flow
1						
2						
3						
4						
5						

Figure 3.5   Costing educational schemes

Quite clearly, the availability of the financial information is the key enabler in the process. Frequently the information simply is not available, or the form or the data makes it very difficult to extract the precise information you require.

Models of financial decision-making

The allocation of resources in schools and colleges is one of the most significant aspects of financial management. There are several alternative models of financial decision-making to be considered.

Bush (in Coleman and Anderson, 2000) discusses four theoretical models of educational management. These are as follows:

1. rational
2. political
3. collegial
4. ambiguous.

Bush discusses the impact of these management styles on internal resource allocation in Chapter 6 of Coleman and Anderson (2000).

 Reading

Please read about these processes in detail in 'Management styles: impact on finance and resources', by Tony Bush, Chapter 6 of Coleman, M. and Anderson, L. (eds.) *Managing Finance and Resources in Education*.

❑ **Our comments**

The extent to which decisions are made as the result of some rational process is starkly brought into question, a particular difficulty being that decisions often need to be taken in the absence of adequate information. Other, non-financial, factors can be brought into the process to fill this vacuum, thus resulting in decisions that are politically acceptable rather than financially justifiable.

❑ **Rational models**

Levačić (2000, p. 8) chooses to express the rational model in these terms: '[The rational approach] has clear aims and goals, which are pursued through formal structures and rational decision making.' All these phrases may be problematic. First, the notion of organisational goals is contested by those who believe that only individuals can have goals (Greenfield, 1973), or that they will be the subject of disagreement between members of the organisation. Secondly, information for decision-making may not be freely available or be unambiguous. Finally, 'optimal use' of resources may not be clear cut but depend on judgement and negotiation.

Simkins (1989, p. 154) argues that the rational model should be underpinned by three key principles:

> The budgetary process should reflect organisation-wide objectives and priorities and an awareness of the longer-term implications of particular resource commitments;
> The process should embody a thorough consideration of alternative patterns of expenditure, and in particular an awareness of opportunity costs. Budgeting should involve an adequate consideration of options, including some 'zero-basing';

The budget should represent an optimal allocation of resources in terms of the organisation's objectives. This means that there should be some ongoing evaluation of the performance of the organisation's sub-units in terms of their effectiveness and efficiency.

Simkins (*ibid.*, p. 155) concludes that there is a strong case for a rational approach to financial management but points out this does not mean it happens in practice:

> The case for making both management in general and budgeting in particular more rational is a strong one, especially at a time when educational institutions are faced by increasing demands on scarce resources . . . Yet to argue for rationality is not necessarily to ensure its occurrence . . . The rational model . . . becomes intrinsically problematic where goals are ambiguous, contested, or conflicting, or where the relationship between means and ends is unclear.

❑ Political models

The *political* model is the main alternative approach featured in the literature on financial management in education. Davies (1994) identifies three key factors that influence the persistence of traditional or political budgeting processes:

1. *Incrementalism* links decisions to the previous year's budget with only minor 'incremental' change to the budgetary process.
2. *Micro-political forces* relate spending decisions to the relative powers of groups and individuals in the organisation, a process which is likely to be resolved by conflict.
3. The *organisational process approach* relates budgetary considerations to wider organisational issues. It may be preferable to keep the main interest groups happy rather than produce a radical budget that upsets certain constituencies.

Simkins (1989, p. 158) argues that the political model focuses on three variables which are relevant to an analysis of budgetary processes:

1. Differences in **values and interests** among individuals and, particularly, groups. This is most likely to result from different discipline groups. It is understandable that members of science or languages departments, for example, disagree about the relative importance of their subjects in the school or college curriculum;
2. The **power** that individuals and groups can bring to bear upon the decision-making process of the organisation. Sources of power include the individual's formal position in the organisation or their level of expertise. The power of groups may be influenced by their ability to mobilise external resources and by their perceived centrality to the aims of the organisation. For example, departments hosting core subjects within the English and Welsh national curriculum are likely to hold more power than those responsible for the less significant foundation subjects;
3. The processes through which power is brought to bear on the **decision-making situation**. In budgeting, emphasis is likely to be on persuasion through the marshalling of expertise and the control of information, or upon the use of bargaining and exchange strategies to reach acceptable compromises on resource allocation.

At times the players within a financial management situation may exert power in a way that attempts to use a rational planning process for their own ends. Much depends upon the power complex of the organisation but what sets out to be rational may be affected by a battle for the control of resources.

The rational and political models differ in that rational approaches are largely normative, reflecting an *idealised* model, difficult to achieve in practice, while political approaches describe many *actual* school and college situations.

Activity

Consider an area of financial management within a school or college known to you, for example, the allocation of funds for a vocational course, the introduction of a revised reading scheme for 5–7-year-olds or funding a staff development programme needed for enhancing information technology skills.

- How far does the management accord with rational or political models?
- What evidence have you found to suggest 'the political might subvert the rational'?

❏ Collegial models

During the 1980s and 1990s, collegial models were increasingly advocated for schools and colleges (Campbell, 1985; Wallace, 1988). Their main features are as follows:

- Decisions are made through a process of discussion leading to *consensus*.
- Staff have *formal representation* within the decision-making bodies or, in smaller schools, all staff are members of the appropriate groups.
- Collegial models are particularly appropriate for professional bodies such as schools and colleges where *expertise* is distributed widely within the organisation.

Within collegial models, budgetary decisions are likely to be made through a participative process involving many staff and all the main groups, as well as senior staff and governors. This process should lead to wide acceptance or 'ownership' of the decisions because it gives so many people the opportunity to take part. In practice, however, the collegial setting may well become the focal point of political activity rather than leading to consensual outcomes. What begins as a collegial process eventually produces political outcomes (Bush, 1986). Simkins' (1986, p. 27) research in secondary schools demonstrates that these political pressures tend to limit the applicability of collegial models in financial management:

> [There are] problems of role conflict for middle managers which arise in any move towards greater collegiality. And this probably explains why no school in the sample operated entirely according to collegial principles in the complete sense that senior management had removed from themselves the final right of decision.

❏ Ambiguity models

Ambiguity models assume that turbulence and unpredictability are dominant features of organisations. There is no clarity over the objectives of institutions and their processes are not properly understood. Participation in policy-making is fluid as members opt in or out of decision opportunities.

In this model, budgetary decisions are likely to be characterised by a lack of clarity. Organisational goals are inconsistent or opaque, making it difficult to relate resource allocation to the aims of the school or college. The organisation is fragmented with the powers of groups and individuals unclear and subject to change. Bureaucratic process may have developed to a point where it has become unclear at what point or which group has decision-making authority. It may be a case where activity has been delegated to a lower stratum within the hierarchy, but not the ability to act or make decisions.

A further source of ambiguity is the fluid participation in decision-making. Individuals vary in the amount of time and effort they devote to the organisation and participants also vary from one time to another. Hence outcomes may be uncertain and unpredictable. Choices somehow emerge from the confusion. In this model, budgeting is anything but a rational process (Bush, 1986).

Activity

To what extent are the budgetary control processes in your school or college a reflection of the institutional culture? To what extent are budgetary processes employed to *impose* a particular management culture? Consider the budget as a means of political control within your institution.

The economic realities of education

State-funded education is a political entity with the funds directed towards it competing with other politically desirable outcomes. The perceptions and value of state-funded education vary from country to country. These range from a highly desirable investment in the human capital of the nation to a necessary expense to ensure that a minimum level of state control can be employed.

Small, rural schools tend to be less technically efficient than larger, urban schools that are able to benefit from economies of scale – for example, having one building to heat rather than several, smaller buildings for the same number of pupils in rural schools. The value to the community of these rural schools goes beyond simple measures of educational efficiency. Similarly, the economic and environmental costs of allowing parents a free choice of where they send their children to school in England have resulted in more car journeys and less use of chartered buses as students are no longer able to be grouped together so efficiently for transport purposes.

A further education college may be faced with a combination of the factors mentioned above: a large, technically efficient main site, together with a number of small local 'outreach' centres. These latter provisions may not be economically efficient, but the importance of the provision to the local community may result in the outreach centres being subsidised by the relative efficiency of the main site. Nevertheless, when funding is scarce, the continuation of the outreach provision will be questioned.

Even in state-funded systems where each student is funded to the same amount, inequalities will become apparent (Burton, 1999). It is possible to alleviate these inequalities to some extent by targeting resources to meet particular needs. Those students requiring additional educational support can be identified and targeted with additional resources to ensure any extra cost of educating particular groups of students can be met without depriving other students within the school or college of their share. Clearly the onus is on the identification of the need in the first place that will enable this extra funding to be released, so in those institutions where the identification is managed more effectively a greater level of overall funding will be achieved.

In educational systems where it is possible to 'bid' for additional funds in line with state-sponsored initiatives and aspirations, it is quite easy to see how these funds may go to the institutions with the 'best bid' rather than the greatest need.

In some countries, for example China, the funding of the institution will partly depend upon its capacity to generate income from its own commercial activities: 'School enterprises are now found in every mainland province and recent estimates [1993] set their number at 730,000 nationwide, producing 60.5 billion yuan of business and providing 440m yuan of profits for the education establishment' (*South China Morning Post*, 1994, quoted in Fouts and Chan, 1997, p. 38).

This situation – found in both academic and vocational schools in China – will be familiar to those working in further education. UK further educational colleges derive income, for example, from the commercial activity of their training restaurants and hair and beauty salons. They also set up trading companies to handle enterprise activities, such as certain elements of their vocational training programmes.

As has already been found in the publicly funded schools in the USA, where, to a large extent, local taxes support local schools, more affluent areas tend to have better funded schools. Local variations between schools and colleges, dependent upon the affluence of parents or students, are found in other state-funded education systems. Schools in South Africa can 'request', based on the outcome of a parents' meeting, that parents make specific donations to the school funds; in the UK local fund raising is very dependent upon how much parents can afford to give. At the post-compulsory level, the costs of 'state education' are being increasingly shifted to the individual who will ultimately benefit, in salary terms, from the education.

When exploring the nature of school or college finance, all these contextual issues need to be addressed and accounted for in order to place decisions and recommendations into a clear perspective.

❑ Building on key learning points

- This chapter has demonstrated that the main difference between financial and real resources will often be revealed in terms of flexibility. While money can be turned into a form of resource that is most appropriate for needs, existing resources, such as teaching rooms, restrict the potential learning possibilities.
- Efficiency and effectiveness are, in some respects, different sides of the same coin. While efficiency focuses on meeting baseline objectives for least cost (or resources), effectiveness attempts to surpass these objectives by the greatest margin within resource constraints.
- The significance of budgeting, as a means of controlling and enabling educational activity, is evident whatever the level of delegation. On a national level, governments are able to direct and refocus the aims of education in much the same way it is possible for schools and colleges to do so on a local level. Educational priorities can be determined and controlled through the provision of funds to support them.
- The concept of 'cost' in an educational sense is still regarded as an emotive issue in many sectors. This chapter has demonstrated that 'cost' is a rational means by which alternative ways of producing the same educational outcome can be effectively compared.
- Following such comparisons, decisions will be made to allocate resources. An examination of these processes leads to the establishment and use of particular decision-making models, such as the rational and political one, as a means of describing the inherent processes using a common set of terminology.

---

4. Delegated financial and resource management

This chapter considers:

- managing the delegated budget;
- managing the staffing resource;
- management of accommodation; and
- management of learning resources.

Introduction

The situation of self-management – as described in Chapters 1 and 2 – brings with it a delegated responsibility for financial and resource management, allocation systems for which were described in Chapter 3. In countries and systems where there is little or no self-management, budgets may still be devolved from a central or local authority to educational managers, to be used for specific educational purposes.

In this chapter we introduce a framework of responsibilities which we consider are present – to a greater or lesser extent – across this spectrum of systems. Whether the responsibilities are taken up by senior or by middle managers will vary according to the degree of delegation, which is in turn influenced by factors ranging from the political system and culture of the country, through the size and nature of the institution to the personal management styles of the individuals in post.

In some colleges and schools there will be a finance department, a bursar or simply the head who deals with the financial matters that concern the institution as a whole. In others, there is a delegated role for middle managers – departmental heads, year group leaders and subject leaders – in managing the resources of subsections of the institution. Chapter 3 has considered in some detail ways in which the internal allocation of the school's or college's budget can be analysed. In this chapter we take an overview of resource management, considering how the responsibilities of delegation can be approached and how the linking of resources to learning can be achieved.

These 'resources' can be seen as assets in terms of:

- the delegated budget
- the staff
- physical resources.

Management of the budget itself may be a simple affair where the amount of delegation, or the allocation itself, is small, or it may involve the monitoring and evaluation of spending very large annual sums, for example in a big secondary school or a 'resource hungry' department of a further education college.

Management of staff in terms of human resource management – selection and recruitment of staff, monitoring the capabilities of individuals, supporting them and meeting their professional needs – is covered in other texts in this series: Middlewood and Lumby (1998a) *Human Resource Management in*

Schools and Colleges and Bush and Middlewood (1997) *Managing People in Education*. This section considers staff simply in terms of their resource value: as the vital factor in translating the school's or college's income into a successful learning experience for the pupils and students.

Management of physical resources can involve pre-existing 'stock', such as classrooms or capital equipment and resources purchased in previous years, and considerations about purchases and resource allocations to be made within the current year's budget.

Delegation of the budget and its responsibilities for decision-making within the school or college may be seen as a manifestation of *delegated leadership*, where 'leadership density' (Sergiovanni, 1987, p. 122) is spread through the institution rather than being concentrated in a single leader, or *teacher leadership* (Leithwood *et al.*, 1999, p. 116) where individuals formally or informally carry out a wider range of functions than would be normally undertaken by a classroom teacher. Both concepts attempt to describe ways in which the experience and expertise of the individual are harnessed for the benefit of the whole institution.

Activity

Consider one subdivision of your school or college: this could be a subject department or a school grouping based upon the ages of the children. Try to work out what its 'assets' are, in terms of:

1. the money allocated to it this year;
2. the number and roles of people who work in it (you may have to deal with 'fractions' of people where their role is shared across the institution); and
3. the rooms and equipment allocated to it (include what you feel is 'your share' of any shared resources).

- How independent is this subsection from the rest of the school or college, with regard to its assets?
- What level of flexibility do you feel the section leader has in allocating and reorganising those resources?

❏ **Our comments**

Although the subsection may have an annual budget it can spend, you may feel the rest of its resources are inextricably tied up with those of the rest of the school or college. Any innovations will therefore involve liaison and negotiation with other section leaders. On the other hand, you may feel the section is quite independent in terms of its resources. Does that mean its leader can go ahead independently with innovations?

Managing the delegated budget

McAleese, in his chapter 'Budgeting in schools' in Coleman and Anderson (2000), emphasises the fact that when budgets are substantially delegated to schools and colleges, the benefits of that delegation permeate through to the middle managers – the heads of department: 'Heads of department found themselves with annual budgets for books and equipment which could actually be *managed*!' (*ibid.*, p. 133, emphasis in original).

In UK schools, this delegated budget would be less than 5% of the total institutional budget. In UK further education colleges, the delegated budget would be likely to be larger, and to include an allocation for staff pay: an increasingly important factor with more than half of the lecturer workforce being employed on some form of casual contract (Shain and Gleeson, 1999, p. 451). In more centralised systems, the delegated budget would remain the responsibility of the head, principal or senior managers only. In this section we look at the role of the senior or middle manager in managing this delegated budget.

Levačić, in her chapter 'Linking resources to learning outcomes' in Coleman and Anderson (2000, p. 4), emphasises the 'great responsibility in the hands of school and college managers to allocate resources to the best possible effect'. If senior managers retain a proportion of the budget for whole-institution needs, and delegate a portion of the budget to the cost-centre heads by systems such as those described in Chapter 3, decisions on spending are being made at a point as near to the end-user (for example, the teacher and student) as possible.

Levačić describes the four key processes of financial and resource management in terms of *planning*, *obtaining*, *allocating* and *using* resources, represented in Chapter 3, Figure 3.1. If resource allocation is to be linked to learning outcomes, departmental spending needs to be linked to departmental planning, which should in turn be consistent with the strategic planning of the school or college (Glover, 2000, p. 121), a system which potentially involves both senior and middle managers. This process would introduce a further element, that of *evaluating* past use of resources into the cycle, between the *using* and *planning* elements.

Both resource evaluation and resource allocation would be carried out in the light of the departmental and whole-institution plan, which in turn would pay attention to levels of student satisfaction and achievement. However, Glover (2000), commenting on his investigation of practice at 25 large UK secondary schools, found the extent to which this happened varied. Even when a school was involved in whole-institution planning, prioritising areas for development and allocating budgets accordingly, this did not necessarily address the problem of dealing effectively with finite resources and linking resources to particular learning initiatives: 'It might mean that we know all spending is on school priorities, but it does little for those little schemes which we might want to try in the department' (*ibid.*, pp. 122–23).

Some institutions may find themselves in the situation reported in FE colleges by Ainley and Bailey (1997, p. 57), where middle managers were not involved in the strategic decisions and whole-college target-setting, but were 'allocated some budgetary responsibility for implementing the consequences of these decisions . . . they then have to gain the agreement of the teachers in their areas to meet those targets'. Heads and principals operating in systems of limited delegation could equally find themselves in this situation, with funding 'earmarked' to initiatives decided upon by local or national government.

Whilst 'it is neither manageable, possible nor a good use of teachers' time for everyone to be involved in the fine details of development planning' (Stoll and Fink, 1996, p. 63), the devolution of both the implementation of the plans and the management of the associated budget requires good communication systems within the school or college, and training for both senior and middle managers in understanding the principles of the planning process and in managing delegated budgets effectively.

This need for understanding the whole process, and one's own part in it, is graphically illustrated by an FE college finance manager reported in Lumby (2000c, p. 90): 'It is the *Titanic* that is sailing along. Moving the deckchairs around is not going to make any difference. If you are going to avoid the iceberg you have got to move the ship.' As a result, Lumby reports that, on the whole, college managers have recognised their mutual dependence and their willingness to get together to find whole-college solutions to difficult financial situations (*ibid.*, p. 93).

A helpful summary of the skills required by middle managers in managing budgets effectively is provided by interviewees in the study of middle managers by Glover *et al.* (1998). They reported the need for help with:

- financial competence so that zero budgeting from a new start point each year is less onerous;
- problem-solving against a background of constantly declining resources and an expectation that we can find alternatives;
- recognising that if we do something to help one area of work we are denying help to another colleague or area within the faculty; and
- the development of techniques and time management so that monitoring and evaluation are real and yet not intrusive for our colleagues.

This range of knowledge and skills is of even greater importance in senior managers. Financial competence, whatever the budgeting regime, and the skills of dealing with limited resources, whilst developing and maintaining an effective learning environment for all students, are essential attributes of successful educational managers.

Managing the staffing resource

Staffing costs typically constitute around 80% of the whole institution's budget and are thus the major resource to be managed. Decisions for the selection and recruitment of new staff may be taken at a senior level – or may be taken outside the institution – existing teachers and lecturers may have permanent contracts, and have job descriptions that historically assign them to particular departments and roles. However, senior and middle managers are well placed to influence decision-making at the 'next level up' and, within a continuously evolving institution, there is scope for innovative deployment of staff in order to achieve new curriculum goals or to establish new modes of learning and learning support.

Hall (1997) suggests six key stages at which the staffing resource can be managed:

1. recruitment and selection
2. induction
3. deployment
4. development
5. promotion
6. exit.

Managers with responsibility for a subject area, for a group of qualifications or a stage of student progress are accountable for the effectiveness of the teaching and learning within their own section of the school or college. They should therefore have a voice at all the above stages and may have direct influence over many of them.

For example, an audit both of staff skills and teaching needs within a manager's area of responsibility can provide essential detail for the strategic planning of the institution, which can influence recruitment and deployment of staff. The development of staff skills, and the deployment and promotion of staff within an area of the school or college, can lie within the hands, or at least within the influence, of the middle manager, who is generally the person best placed to assess the needs of the curriculum and the skills of the staff. Senior and middle managers can then work together to provide the most effective learning experience through appropriate staffing strategies.

If well accepted systems of staff appraisal and the monitoring of teaching effectiveness are in place, middle managers will have both cultural and procedural support for their staffing decisions. However, the constraints of the school day – at least 80% of the time of the UK heads of department studied by Brown and Rutherford (1998) was spent teaching – and the constraints of school cultures where heads of department may be very reluctant to monitor the work of their colleagues (Turner, 1996) may cause these decisions to be made on a more subjective basis, and at a more senior level.

◉ **Reading and** Activity

Please turn to Les Bell's chapter, 'The management of staff', Chapter 11 in Coleman, M. and Anderson, L. (eds.) *Managing Finance and Resources in Education*. Read from page 186 up to the end of the section on page 193, noting the key stages for decision-making in managing the staffing resource.

In your experience, are staffing decisions at these key stages based upon *effectiveness*: where the focus is on creating conditions where pupils of all abilities achieve to their full potential, or *efficiency*: where the most cost-effective use is made of the available resources to achieve the targets set by the school or college?

❑ Our comments

If your focus is on *effective* recruitment and deployment of staff, you will have due regard for the quality of the learning experience for the students, but you may be surprised at the benefits which a focus on *efficiency* can bring in eliminating wasted spending and thereby having the funding to create 'something extra' for the students or staff. If your focus is on efficiency, this may be because your senior managers feel the institution is under-resourced, and decisions need to be dominated by issues of cost.

For example, in UK further education colleges, large numbers of teaching staff are employed on a temporary basis, often hired through lecturing agencies that act as the employers. This strategy can enable a college to recruit staff quickly where an additional need for staffing is caused by unexpectedly high student recruitment, or where a subject area is being offered on a trial basis to test the student market. In both these instances, permanent staffing might not be cost-effective. Some lecturers are employed on a 'term-time only' basis, on the grounds their services are not needed when the students are not in college.

However, there is concern both for the quality of course delivery, where a lecturing team lacks stability and continuity or even the opportunity to meet as a group, and for the quality of working life for the lecturers concerned.

❑ Innovative use of the staffing budget

Where there is a budget that can be allocated to part-time staffing, or to teaching and non-teaching assistants, the possibilities for additional support for learning and for teachers are increased. Mortimore *et al.* (1994) examined case studies in schools where non-teaching staff had been innovatively employed as, among others, welfare assistants, classroom assistants and in a range of technician roles. Sometimes the innovation came as an addition to a more traditional role, such as instances where a school nurse and a librarian both acted as tutors. The common theme of the innovations was a desire to 'free up' classroom teachers to carry out their teaching role – or in one case to 'free up' management time for the head – and in many cases the experience of the students in the classroom was enriched by giving them contact with an additional supportive adult.

Mortimore *et al.* (*ibid.*) presented costings for the innovations, both in terms of what was gained and the opportunities forgone through adopting the innovation. Figure 4.1 is an example. Innovations such as this depend upon an audit of the skills and responsibilities of existing staff together with an

Cost-effectiveness data (figures include on-costs)		
Posts	Two classroom assistants	*Source of funds* School budget. Preferred to materials or part of a teacher
Salaries	£20,070 p.a.	*Benefits* Enrichment of practical work in the curriculum. Teachers have become more adventurous in their design of practical work. Allows more flexible classroom organisation
Premises Equipment Supervision	£240 p.a. £300 p.a. £1,110 p.a.	
Total recurrent costs	£21,720	

Figure 4.1   Assessing cost-effectiveness
Source: Mortimore *et al.*, 1994, p. 23

audit of the current role, unused skills and adaptability of associate staff (*ibid.*, pp. 210–11). The change needs careful management and may not be replicated in successive post-holders. The initial responsibility for identifying and matching needs and skills, and the support for implementing the change and settling staff in to the new arrangements, may lie either with senior or middle managers, depending on the size and structure of the organisation.

In England and Wales, specific funding is now being provided for the employment of extra support staff, for example to support children in schools with special educational needs, and to underpin classroom work on literacy and numeracy. However, funding may not always be available for the specific purpose identified, and an audit such as that demonstrated by Mortimore *et al.* (*ibid.*) will hopefully enable a school or college to improve the learning environment in the specified area.

◎ **Reading and** Activity

Now read the remainder of Les Bell's chapter 'The management of staff', Chapter 11 in Coleman, M. and Anderson, L. (eds.) *Managing Finance and Resources in Education*, from page 193 to the end.

What innovations in the deployment of associate staff might be appropriate for your school or college?

❏ **Our comments**

We hope you have identified some areas where there might be an untapped resource within your existing staff, or areas where associate staff might be employed to enable teachers to spend more time teaching. Remember five of the points made here by Bell:

1. Many classroom assistants are involved in work that previously would have been the domain of teachers. Where this is so, supportive training needs to be in place for the assistant and the teacher, and both need to be clear about their respective responsibilities.

2. The innovation should pass the test of 'fitness for purpose': the focus should be on meeting the needs of the children or students and the objectives of the school.
3. A staff audit is an essential tool when planning innovatory deployment of staff.
4. The proposal should be properly costed: this includes the *opportunity cost* – the awareness of what will be forgone in order to carry out the proposal.
5. Although institutions and individuals have reported benefits from the deployment of associate staff in classrooms, no direct link between pupil performance and additional staffing has been evidenced in research.

Management of accommodation

If the largest portion of the budget of an educational institution is spent on staffing, the next highest expenditure is on the buildings, and the building itself is a significant capital asset. This part of the budget will largely be spent on maintaining the fabric of the building, and paying the charges of public utilities. However, the building exists as a learning environment for the students and a working environment for staff, and its appearance and ambience will also have an impact upon the marketing of the institution to potential students and staff. Some schools and many colleges will have a manager in charge of premises or estates, and decisions to make extensive changes to the building would need to be taken at a senior level. Decisions about the day-to-day management of accommodation, and suggestions for improved use of existing space, may lie with the middle managers or the class teachers. Murphy (1994, p. 53) warns that improving and rationalising the use of accommodation may be a 'daunting, messy and long-term task' and innovation may be hampered by notions of 'territory', ignorance of 'ownership' and a general acceptance of the status quo.

Managers at all levels have a role to play in enhancing the learning environment for students and for their staff teams. Where a suite of rooms is allocated to a subject or a year grouping, a particular ethos can be created through the quality and configuration of furniture, the type of floor and window coverings, the decorative state and the use made of the wall and storage areas. This may entail use of the whole-school or college maintenance budget, and may also involve allocation of a portion of the devolved budget to enhance the learning environment.

In a secondary school investigated by Briggs (2001), heads of department, under the leadership of the deputy head, designed subject-based areas for team teaching and resource-based learning to support curriculum innovation, created through amalgamating pairs of classrooms with portions of corridors and cupboards: 'We try to create learning environments which we call curriculum learning centres in each major curriculum area, which are light, airy, spacious, well-furnished, well-equipped, with good artefacts or appropriate manipulatives, for whatever subject it is, within sight and easy to get at' (secondary school deputy head).

The adapting of accommodation will often be precipitated by a particular learning need. In a primary school in the same study, one initiative came from the staff in a particular year grouping, following earlier whole-school initiatives proposed by the headteacher:

> We had a real 'glory hole' which was our kiln room: people used to just close the door on it, it was an absolute waste of space really. As the numeracy and literacy initiatives have come into the school, my staff in Key Stage 2 asked if we could set in those subjects. To enable us to do that, we needed a sixth teaching area. So by getting rid of the sliding partitions, and building partitions of nice wood, with pine doors, and carpeting half the room, and putting up shelving and making sure that there was the right storage, we've created a teaching space for about 20 children (primary school headteacher).

A successful learning environment can depend upon the culture of the department and the motivation and collegiality of the individuals within it. In two examples of the work of departmental heads researched by Brown and Rutherford (1998, p. 82), devolved money had been spent on accommodation for staff:

> The department had its own staffroom for which the head of department had purchased a large oval table and matching chairs . . . we observed the collegium in action when members of the department gathered around the table in the staffroom during their free periods and at lunch.

> Another example was observed where the head of department had spent a significant amount of the departmental monies on the establishment of a departmental staffroom, furnished with individual desks and workspaces for staff. She had purchased good quality pictures to hang on the walls, to enhance and improve the appearance of what otherwise would have been a rather barren environment.

In both cases the decision had been made to improve working conditions for staff: in the first example the improvement also encouraged discussion of departmental issues and in the second it provided an encouraging environment for preparation, marking and administration. The impact upon teaching and learning in the department would not be measurable, but it would be discernible by the staff involved.

Activity

Try to identify one area of your school or college that could be better utilised, either for teaching or for staff accommodation:

- Who 'owns' it?
- What collaboration would be needed in order to change its use or simply to improve it?
- What budgets could be accessed in order to improve it?
- Who would benefit?

❏ Our comments

The most difficult problem here is often with the micro-politics of perceived 'ownership'. Schools and colleges can be very territorial places, even with regard to junk-filled storage rooms. Conversely, sometimes it is not possible to identify who has an interest in a space that has gradually fallen out of use. Kedney (1992, p. 146) identify the following barriers to improved use of accommodation:

- Lack of accountability
- Lack of information
- Too much information
- Inappropriate territoriality
- Short-term thinking.

In order to overcome some of these barriers, the benefits to the whole institution of the enhanced facilities and improved learning environment can be argued, even when the primary purpose is to enhance one area of the curriculum.

Both whole-school and departmental decisions may have to be made to forgo the purchase of certain materials or equipment for the current year. In some cases, holders of non-devolved budgets will contribute whole-school or college funding to the initiative, dependent on some 'matched funding' from the budget of the department involved. Hopefully the benefits will be far-reaching enough to justify the expense, and the initiative may 'spark off' other similar innovations elsewhere in the building.

Further examples of whole-school and college initiatives on improving the learning environment can be found in the reading that follows.

◎ **Reading and** Activity

Please read the chapter by Marianne Coleman and Ann Briggs, Chapter 13 in Coleman, M. and Anderson, L. (eds.) *Managing Finance and Resources in Education*.

Compare the ideas that are presented with practice in your own school or college. Make a list of the ways you think these ideas could be developed in your own school or college.

❑ Key points from the chapter

- Increased autonomy has enabled educational managers to explore the innovative use of buildings.
- The state of buildings and use of both buildings and space are related to the school/college culture and the quality of learning.
- The learning environment is a significant factor in school effectiveness in the literature.
- The impact of ICT on schools and colleges raises questions about the continuation of traditional educational buildings.
- The argument that schools and colleges make poor use of space in terms of occupancy over the year is well rehearsed.
- Various approaches to making more use of space over the years have been tried.
- Inadequacy of information and micro-political factors inhibit educational managers in their attempts to be cost effective.

Management of learning resources

In a very small school, or an institution operating in a very centralised system, the head or principal may make all the decisions about the purchase of learning resources, or they may be selected, purchased and supplied by an external government agency. Where there is delegation of purchasing power, the middle manager often has a devolved budget for the purchase of learning resources appropriate to a subject or to an age group of children. This will probably have been allocated according to one of the models described in Chapter 3, and may have involved a certain amount of 'bidding' or micro-political activity by the middle manager in order to secure the share which is felt to be appropriate to the needs of the department. The management of this budget will hopefully follow a pattern similar to that in Figure 3.2 both at whole-institution and departmental level, with the cost-centre holder contributing to the overall assessment of how well the institution is matching resources to learning outcomes through monitoring and evaluating the departmental spending process.

Within a small department, this may involve informal group discussions to determine effective allocation and assessment of previous spending. In a larger department, it may involve subdivision of the budget to course leaders, subject leaders or class teachers so that appropriate purchasing decisions can be made as near to the teaching activity as possible. This process involves the cost-centre holder in another 'layer' of monitoring and evaluation of the spending process. Given that the proportion of the budget being considered here is small – once the staffing and premises allocations have been made – this process can seem onerous, considering the sums involved. Glover *et al.* (1998, p. 287) comment: 'The administration of departments or cost centres is the most readily understood function of middle managers. Our evidence is, through this work, for example in managing finances, producing lists and auditing stock, middle managers justify most of the pressures on their time.'

❑ Accessibility of learning resources

Like the buildings, the learning resources, whether they are significant capital purchases or sets of textbooks, are part of the assets of the school or college. If best use is to be made of those assets, decisions about their accessibility to staff and students need to be made. Schools and colleges often have difficult decisions to make about the institutional purchase and management of such resources as computers and audio-visual equipment. It makes sense to have a whole-school or college policy and a cross-institutional budget for the purchase of such equipment, but the day-to-day responsibility for the booking and maintenance of the equipment may need to be taken on by an appropriate head of department, who then becomes the perceived 'owner' and gatekeeper of the resource.

Similar issues can arise over the accessibility of learning materials. In Figure 4.2, learning resources held near the top of the diagram are more accessible to pupils and students; as they near the bottom, the access by the tutor becomes more favoured. Interestingly, however, materials placed on an intranet may be more accessible to the tutor than those in the filing cabinet, as they can be accessed at a range of computer points around the building.

The increased accessibility as one travels up the diagram is dependent upon there being someone to manage the resource base and, in general terms, the management becomes more expensive the more accessible the resource. In the top two layers, the resources become accessible to the whole institution or beyond: the senior managers have 'gained' a whole-school resource, but the middle manager and classroom teacher have potentially lost 'ownership' and control of its use.

This illustrates the reluctance middle managers and their teams might feel about making 'their' resources available to staff and students beyond their department. They will have to contribute in some way financially to their management, and teachers may wish to make their own decisions about which students access their resources at which point in their programme.

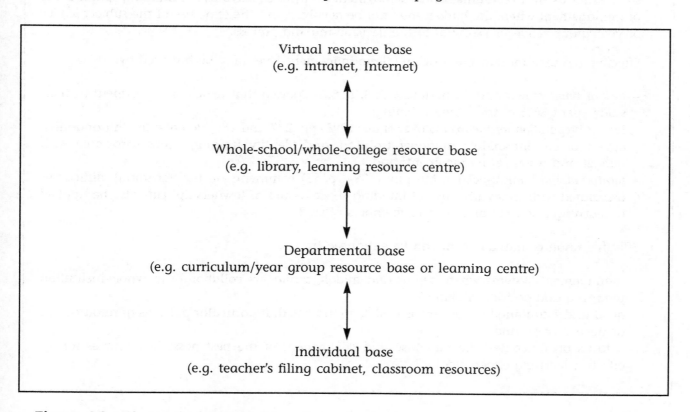

Figure 4.2   Choices for location of learning resources

Where the teaching strategy of a school or college is learner centred, based on individual or group investigations managed by the teacher, an accessible resource base is essential, with materials provided in a range of media and at different levels of understanding. Resources shared across a department, or across the whole school or college, with managed student access, become a preferred model, with mutually beneficial decisions being made by senior and middle managers about the level of accessibility of resources. The learning resources manager quoted in Coleman and Briggs (2000, p. 226) sums up the benefits of extending the accessibility of learning resources:

> Having a learning resource centre which is open for 57 hours a week, with specialist tutors and librarians offering study support, is invaluable when the time spent in the classrooms is at a premium. The demands of most subjects are such that the classroom lecturer cannot present a wide enough range of experiences solely within the confines of the classroom.

❏ Managing information as a resource

All the areas of resource management detailed in this chapter could be enhanced through effective management of information. Easily accessible and manageable data sources – both internal and external to the institution – for managers to use when making decisions on budgets, staffing and accommodation are an increasing necessity if schools and colleges are to be both efficient and effective. For an extended consideration of this subject, please consult Ed Baines' chapter 'Managing information as a resource', in Coleman, M. and Anderson, L. (eds.) (2000) *Managing Finance and Resources in Education*.

❏ Building on key learning points

- The focus of this section has been on the accountability of senior and middle managers for the proper expenditure of devolved funding and the subsequent use of the resources purchased.
- Senior and middle managers may also expect to collaborate over whole-school decisions on such issues as staff recruitment and deployment and the effective use of building space: areas of management where the budget may not be devolved, but the expertise of the subject leader or year group leader is essential to the decision-making process.

- Effective resource management at middle management level may be impeded by:

  - *lack of time*: Brown and Rutherford (1998, p. 83) reported that heads of department in their study spent 80% of their time teaching;
  - *lack of preparation for the role*: Glover *et al.* (1998, pp. 287 and 289) describe the 'hit and miss' aspect of current middle manager training, and identify training needs associated with budget and resource management; and
  - *territoriality and micro-politics*: Murphy (1994, p. 53) comments on the 'territorial' difficulties associated with innovative use of building space. Issues of 'ownership' can also be applied to learning resources and even to members of staff.

- Effective resource management can be enhanced by:

  - management systems where senior and middle managers collaborate in whole-institution planning and decision-making;
  - good understanding by teachers as well as managers that particular patterns of resource can achieve success; and
  - a focus on outcomes: the purchase and deployment of the best possible resources for an effective learning experience.

---

5. Managing external relationships: theoretical perspectives

> **This chapter considers:**
>
> - the increasing influence of stakeholders upon schools and colleges;
> - schools and colleges as 'open' organisations;
> - schools and colleges as 'accountable' organisations; and
> - marketing and external relations.

Introduction

The move to self-management of schools and colleges not only entails the local management of finance discussed in the previous chapters, but also puts a changing emphasis on the ways in which external relationships are managed. Both developments arise out of the school or college operating as an 'open' organisation, accountable not only to central government but also to the community it serves.

This chapter explores the nature and extent of that open relationship and the levels of accountability under which schools and colleges operate. External relationships are then examined from a marketing perspective, which presents marketing – implicit or explicit – as being central to the management of external relations. Although managers working in many areas of education may be uneasy applying marketing terms to educational provision, nevertheless this framework of thought is useful in analysing the school's or college's interaction with its internal and external community as part of a holistic philosophy of meeting the needs of its learners. Underpinning the whole chapter, therefore, is a consideration of who the institution's stakeholders are and how – in broad theoretical terms – the school or college can address their needs. Chapter 6 will build on this theoretical discussion to consider the practical management of relationships with individual stakeholder groups.

The increasing influence of stakeholders upon schools and colleges

As we saw in Chapter 1, during the 1980s and 1990s certain major worldwide trends were evident within educational systems. The variety of terms which can be used to describe these movements away from centralised decision-making was also discussed; these terms included *decentralisation* – the assignment of decision-making tasks away from centralised government to local council or school level - and *deregulation* – where the institution makes decisions within parameters set by the government (Karstanje, 1999, pp. 29–30). Both these trends can lead to greater autonomy for the individual school or college.

Increased autonomy, especially when accompanied by greater parental or student choice and a funding system which depends upon numbers of pupils or students enrolled, has in many countries led to a changing relationship between the educational institution and its community. An awareness of the needs of the 'customer' and the nature of the 'market' is becoming increasingly essential. Schools and colleges have also taken on more direct contact with outside agencies than was formerly the case.

With the move to an increasingly consumer-led economy, the 'monastic tradition' of education in the first half of the twentieth century, where the concept of external relations was hardly relevant (Sayer, 1989, p. 4), has been replaced by a closer relationship of schools and colleges with their communities, and by parents and external professionals becoming increasingly involved with the work of the institution. Having made their choice in the educational market-place, parents will often work hard to maintain and advance the reputation of their chosen institution (Kenway and Fitzclarence, 1998, p. 670).

❏ Customers and clients, partners and stakeholders

A variety of terms is used both to define and explore the relationships of a school or college with its client groups. They have definitions and interpretations that overlap, and the situation is complicated by the terms being used interchangeably, both in writing and in speech. The definitions offered below may help you to identify who are your customers, clients, partners and stakeholders – four of the most-used terms. This in turn may help you to consider where the main priorities of the school or college lie: clearly not all stakeholders can be at the forefront of consideration all the time, but none can be totally ignored. It may therefore be useful to consider them in turn before moving on to consider the issues of openness, accountability and marketing which affect the relationship of schools and colleges with these groups in their community.

❏ *Customers and clients*

These terms are virtually interchangeable, though a manager may be more comfortable with one term than the other. These are people who seek a service, and they may be internal to the institution or external. Just as a student is a client of the school's educational service, a teacher may be a client of its reprographics or caretaking service. Clients can be direct, as in the above examples, or indirect – for example, the future employers of students at a college – and here the situation becomes complex. For example, are parents the direct or indirect customers of a school? Are present employers the direct or indirect customers of a college? This web of relationships can be seen as situational; in a school context it can be represented as follows: 'Thus the child is the customer in the classroom, the parent is the customer for reporting procedures, the [local and national government authorities and inspectorate] are equally customers in context' (West-Burnham, 1992a, p. 57).

❏ *Partners*

Support is required from partners if the work of the school or college is to succeed; likewise, a local community can be dependent upon the successful work of its school or college: there is a situation of mutual accountability. Partners might be local sources of funding and resources, such as local education authorities or businesses – but would educational institutions regard the national government as a partner? Parents once again feature strongly as school partners: the school/parent partnership can be seen as essential for the well-being and progress of a child's learning. Are parents similarly the partners of further and higher education institutions?

The nature of partnerships can, however, be seen as problematical. For example, Macbeth (1995) argues that parent/teacher relationships are often more administrative than educational and do not fulfil the definition of partnerships offered by Pugh (1989): 'a working relationship that is characterised by a shared sense of purpose, mutual respect and the willingness to negotiate. This implies sharing of information, responsibility, skills, decision-making and accountability' (quoted in Macbeth, 1995, p. 17).

It would be interesting to analyse how many other partnerships entered into by schools and colleges fully correlate with this description.

❑ *Stakeholders*

Stakeholders can be defined as 'all those who have a legitimate interest in the continuing effectiveness and success of an institution' (Waring, 1999, p. 180). This definition leads us to considering all clients and all partners as stakeholders, together with others who may have a 'legitimate interest'. For example, higher education institutions and employers, who may be considered as indirect clients of schools and colleges, clearly have a 'stake' in the quality of student they receive.

Stakeholders can also be seen as those who have an 'immediate and direct effect' (Hoy and Miskel, 1987, p. 88) on the institution, perhaps through control of its finance and aims. This definition may help us to define 'legitimate interest' but, when set with the earlier definition, it serves to demonstrate the interdependency of the institution and its stakeholders.

As in the case of clients, stakeholders can be internal or external: see Table 5.1 for one suggested categorisation. Of the two categories, the internal stakeholders are by far the most influential on the character, performance and perceptions of the educational institution. Not only do they have a significant impact through their individual and team performance within the activities of the institution, but they are also crucial in the communication of the institution and what it stands for to the wider community; they are the stakeholders most closely responsible for the formation and transmission of the institution's reputation. The external stakeholders will have to rely, to a very large extent, on past experience or on the information communicated to them by internal stakeholders for their information about the institution. This relationship can be considered within the context of organisational 'openness' – and, later in the chapter, in terms of marketing.

Schools and colleges as 'open' organisations

Because the school in most communities is the central social agency, it is in a unique position to create a partnership 'web' with all the individuals, groups, organisations and institutions which share responsibility for the growth and development of pupils (Stoll and Fink, 1995, p. 134).

Organisations can be viewed as either open or closed. The closed system is concerned principally with its own internal operations, setting rigid boundaries between itself and its external environment. The

Table 5.1 Internal and external stakeholders

Internal	External
Senior management	Potential students, parents (and staff)
Teaching staff	Ex-students, parents (and staff)
Associate staff	Local community
Current students	Local business and commerce
Parents of current students (in compulsory education)	Local regulatory and finance bodies (school boards, education authorities)
Governors	National regulatory and quality assurance bodies
Regular visitors	Other educational institutions Funding bodies

quotation above emphasises the open nature of many schooling systems today. Some independent schools and elite universities may retain the image of being closed systems, yet even these must be responsive to the society in which they operate. Underlying the whole educational system is the guiding philosophy that schools and colleges exist to serve their community – however 'community' is defined – and operate in response to that community's needs:

> The open-system concept highlights the vulnerability and interdependence of organisations and their environments. In other words, environment is important because it affects the internal structures and processes of organisations, hence, one is forced to look both inside and outside the organisation to explain organisational behaviour (Hoy and Miskel, 1987, p. 86).

The organisation itself has little effect on, or control over, the wider general environment, which may be undergoing cultural, social, political and technological changes. The specific environment is more amenable to management by the individual organisation and includes the stakeholders, those who have 'an immediate and direct effect on the organisation' (*ibid.*, p. 88). However, groups in the specific environment are also subject to the influence of the general environment, and the effect of this influence may, in turn, impact on schools and colleges. Stoll and Fink (1995, p. 137) illustrate this cumulative effect as follows:

> Pupils are not only a part of schools and families; they are part of community groups, neighbourhoods, clubs, gangs, teams and other social, economic and political units. Partnerships mean recognising all these influences and attempting to bring some coherence to the multiple messages pupils receive. It may mean involving the community in developing school development plans, as is done in Denmark (Kruchov and Hoyrup, 1994). It may also mean . . . working hard to separate the school from the negative features of the surrounding community.

Activity

Think about the specific environment of a school or college known to you. The following introductory paragraph from an Ofsted inspection report on a British school may help you to identify salient features:

> The school's intake comes from an area characterised by high unemployment and socio-economic disadvantage. 21 percent of the school population comes from ethnic minority backgrounds. These pupils' home language is often not English. The school is a community school with youth work, adult education provision and a community nursery.

- Using your knowledge of the local environment, prepare a similar contextual introduction for your school or college.
- Try then to identify ways in which the specific environment influences the organisation or management of your institution.
- List the ways in which the institution is similar to, or differs from, others in the local area.
- On the whole, are the institution's responses designed to mitigate or to celebrate features of the local environment?

❏ Our comments

The contextual introduction will differ for every individual school and college and this will, in its turn, influence the answer to the final question. Looking at the response of your institution to its specific environment, and comparing it with others in the locality, will have enabled you to identify the particular features of 'openness' your institution has.

❏ **The open organisation: a resources perspective**

An open organisation can be viewed in terms of the resources it receives from, or shares with, its environment. Resource theory (Hoy and Miskel, 1989, pp. 36–37) focuses on the need for an organisation to obtain resources from its environment, and Chapter 1 of this book explores a wide range of resources that are potentially involved. The relative autonomy of schools and colleges throws this situation into sharper relief, as needs are not 'buffered' by a mediating agency such as a local education authority. The resource lists identified in Chapter 1 can be simplified as follows:

* fiscal – financial resources
* people – students, parents, governors
* information and knowledge
* products and services.

❏ *Fiscal*

A school or college may gain funding from its local community indirectly, through formula funding for pupils and students enrolled or directly through fees. Increasingly, the institution is becoming financially dependent upon its stakeholders for additional funding. This may come in the form of gifts or regular voluntary payments by parents, or as part of a sponsorship deal by local business.

A college or school may generate its own income by entrepreneurial activity within the local and wider community. This may involve both staff and students in activities that can be seen both as vocational training and as essential income generation. A good example of this is the work-study programme in China, reported by Fouts and Chan (1997), where technical and vocational schools:

> must launch work-study programmes and, in conjunction with their specialities, operate small-sized factories, farms, stores, or service enterprises. In this way the students will be enabled to learn, through practice, some vocational or specialised skills, and the income generated can also help improve the school facilities (*Guanyu*, 1986, in Fouts and Chan, 1997, p. 37).

In other countries, the wider commercial environment may impact upon the school through such schemes as the collection of vouchers by members of its local community or through spending at certain supermarket chains, which the school in turn can exchange for educational materials. 'Free' schemes such as this can come at a cost: one Australian study revealed that 589 teacher hours were spent over six months in processing such vouchers (Harris, 1996). An example of a more ambitious attempt at sponsorship, the scheme for the setting up of city technology colleges in England in the 1980s primarily through private sponsorship, had to be 'rescued' when only 20% of funding was obtained in this way, the shortfall being met by public funds (Power and Whitty, 1999).

❏ *People*

Pupils and students are, of course, the *raison d'être* of the school or college. Where each one represents a proportion of the income, whether through formula funding or through fees, they also become a unit of resource. Importantly, they are a means by which the institution is judged and marketed. Kenway and Fitzclarence (1998, p. 671) comment on the value of 'good' students to the schools in their Australian study: 'Value-added students, those with *face value*, are those which lift the school's academic, sporting or cultural performance – only the good are good for the school.' These students, in their turn, can attract more 'high value' students to the school.

The particular needs of students may cause the school to become a centre for community services, as in the following example from a school named in publications as Central Ontario Secondary School (COSS):

> With a lot of our programmes, we use a lot of resources from the community. We have addiction services in the school, we have family life counsellors in the school, we have social services . . . The [welfare] worker still comes into the schools so we don't have to have the students spend the day going over to [town]. We

have them come in and we call them out of class and they are serviced (teacher, quoted in Leithwood *et al.*, 1999, p. 95).

The close involvement of community workers with the students at COSS has led the staff to reassess their role, in line with the school culture, to be more student centred and less curriculum focused. In both the above examples, students, whether successful or needy, are the agents by which resources are brought into the school. In special schools for students with learning difficulties and disabilities, the number of external links is increased. Here all the 'usual' stakeholders would be involved but, in addition, liaison to establish resource would be needed with local health authorities, social services, the voluntary sector, pressure groups and national organisations for people with disabilities.

Parents are potentially a valuable resource for a school, but they may be ambivalent about their position: 'That parents have been on the periphery of schooling for so long, that this position is generally accepted by most parents, and that teachers, whose views are respected, reinforce this assumption – all these make a change of attitude difficult to achieve' (Power and Whitty, 1999, p. 197).

The involvement of parents as governors (see Chapter 7), and the implementation of home–school contracts by some schools, are attempts to formalise the partnership of parents with teachers in their children's education. Parents are used as a resource when acting as paid or unpaid classroom assistants, or by contributing specialist skills and knowledge to supplement the school curriculum.

The contribution of governors will be discussed more fully in Chapter 7, but the make-up of school and college governing bodies is usually designed to involve parents, staff and representatives of local businesses and community groups in the management of the institution. Once links have been established through the activities of governance, these individuals and the groups they represent may be more motivated to support the school or college in other ways, such as facilitating access to specialist knowledge, work experience or resources.

❏ *Information and knowledge*

Some information may be provided as a matter of course by central and local government agencies (for example, directives about the content of the curriculum and the structure of qualifications, or local population data). The response of schools and colleges to this type of influence may be largely reactive, except where predictions can be made and strategies adopted – for example, in response to local demographic and labour-market trends.

Knowledge about the local community and its culture will largely be gained through the 'people' links outlined above. The cultural and social make-up of the community is likely to be addressed through the culture of the institution, its extracurricular life and the local 'flavour' it gives to its prescribed curriculum. In extreme situations, the culture of the school may be devised to mitigate negative forces in the culture of the surrounding community.

Knowledge to be gained from individuals and institutions in the local community can provide valuable enrichment to the curriculum. Warwick (1989, p. 21), reviewing the benefits for schools of links with business, identifies six such areas of enrichment:

social – extending the students' knowledge of society to include industry and business;
economic – enhancing economic and industrial understanding, perhaps through enterprise education;
vocational – preparation for the world of work including careers education;
affective – learning 'through' industry rather than about it; the development of skills such as communication and team work through simulated activity;
pedagogic – drawing relevant examples to enliven the curriculum from local industry;
instrumental – 'passing on knowledge, experience and practical skills'.

This 'openness' enables guest speakers and pupil mentors to come into the schools and colleges from the local community, but also for students to go out, as in an elementary school in Texas, 'using the community as a classroom. They believe that schooling without walls is both motivating to the students and pedagogically sound' (Sergiovanni, 1998, p. 19).

❏ *Products and services*

The local and national commercial community can be a source of products for use in the school or college, with commercially sponsored resources ranging from wallcharts to computer labs or, even in the case of the Public Finance Initiative (PFI) in Britain, the school itself. Whilst the products may be a useful, even essential supplement to existing resources, and in some colleges and schools may be the visible element of a lively working partnership between local business and education, there is a concern that 'curriculum materials can also be used to portray a partial, and inaccurate, account of business interests and impact' (Power and Whitty, 1999, p. 20). In Britain, this concern has led to the publication of a good practice guide for parents, teachers and governors by an independent consumer-protection organisation (National Consumer Council, 1996).

In the case of services, there can be a useful integration of response to need. The case-study school COSS referred to earlier is a good example of a school that has 'opened its doors' to local services:

> Here the need is so great that they bring the community services to the school. They have social services coming here twice a week. They have a health nurse who comes in if kids are pregnant. We have a girl from the family health centre . . . [which is] for kids who are over sixteen or over eighteen who have to move out of their home (teacher, quoted in Leithwood *et al.*, 1999, p. 95).

Personnel from these services are invited in for the good of the students, who in turn can receive a better education because their pressing social needs are being addressed.

Activity

Consider some of the ways in which your educational institution obtains resources from its environment. Try to think of examples of all four types of resource: fiscal, people, information and knowledge, products and services:

- Who carries out this activity?
- Who co-ordinates it?
- Is the interaction mutually beneficial?

❏ **Our comments**

The 'people' section was probably the easiest to think through, but those people can often bring the other resources: fiscal, information, knowledge. Would your institution need a change of culture in order to maximise these last three benefits?

This section has largely focused upon a one-way benefit – the resources the school or college gains from its environment. Try also to bear in mind that the institution is also accountable to its community (see below: 'Schools and colleges as accountable organisations') and that communities should benefit from their schools and colleges, with resources flowing in both directions. If a school or college is not serving its community, thus establishing a two-way benefit, then the systems described above are unlikely to flourish.

❑ **Implications for the management of open organisations**

The management of external relations, like any aspect of management, will be in the context of the values and mission of the school or college, but 'Individual schools cannot begin to meet the needs of pupils in this complex and diverse world without help from other sources ... Schools require togetherness with their various stakeholders to ensure coherence in the lives of children, and to continue to develop as organisations' (Stoll and Fink, 1995, p. 149). In this context, stakeholders external to the school or college will also have an *impact on the development of the vision and mission* (West-Burnham, 1994) *and culture* of the institution (O'Neill, 1994).

Secondly, schools and colleges may *take a proactive role in making links* with other organisations, or bringing in representatives from external groupings to be part of the educational organisation. For example, representatives from local business and industry are commonly invited to be members of the board of governors.

The educational institution may also make arrangements to *absorb demands from the external environment* and to protect the 'technical core' of teaching. In order to do this, certain people in the school or college may be given responsibility for handling the relationships with particular external groups, parents or local industry:

> The overall implication for practice is that school organizations do not have to be simple passive instruments of the external environment. Both internal and external coping strategies can be used to buffer environmental influences and actually to change the demands. Structures, programs, and processes can be developed by educational administrators to manage the environments of their school organization (Hoy and Miskel, 1987, p. 103).

The effectiveness of the organisation may depend on a *'match' between the organisation and its environment*. In an unstable environment, an organisation that was 'informal, flexible and adaptive' (*ibid.*, p. 98) could be most effective, while a formal 'mechanistic' model could be most effective in a stable environment. An open organisation operating in a market environment may *enter actively into the marketing* and the management of the image of the school or college in the community (see below, p. 65).

Schools and colleges may respond to external demands through planning and by forecasting where likely changes and future pressures may occur. The move towards having *an institutional development plan* may be seen, in part, as a response to the demands and influences from outside the institution.

Schools and colleges as 'accountable' organisations

The concepts of decentralisation and deregulation introduced at the beginning of this chapter, together with the concept of open organisations, lead us to consider the situation of *accountability* in which schools and colleges operate. For example, if decision-making is assigned to the institutional level, within parameters set by government, using funding largely devolved from public funds, a situation of *public accountability* exists. Later in this section we shall examine other ways of defining accountability. First, we shall examine accountability as a concept:

> At minimum, accountability means being required to give an account of events and behaviour in a school or college to those who may have a legitimate right to know. One of the central aspects of accountability relates to establishing which individuals and groups have that legitimacy (Bush, 1994, p. 310).

❏ Our comments

You may decide that the principal, perhaps in conjunction with the governing body, is accountable, or you may feel all those working within the school or college share this accountability. According to the circumstances of your institution, you may feel that its professionals are accountable to central or local government, the local community, parents and students, to each other and to any one of a range of stakeholders.

Accountability of an institution may be for *outcomes* and results. Alternatively, it can be understood as 'adherence to codes of practice' (Bush, 1994, p. 314), with the focus being on the *process*.

In Kogan's (1986) definition of the term, accountability implies that *sanctions* can, and will, be applied for the failure to satisfy those to whom the organisation is accountable. More positively, accountability may be seen in terms of *responsiveness* and *responsibility*. Responsiveness can be seen as 'the capacity to be open to outside impulses and new ideas' (Scott, P. 1989, p. 17), whilst responsibility carries overtones of moral duty, which may stem from professional and cultural obligations.

Later in the chapter you have read, Scott draws on the work of Halstead (1994) and considers five models of accountability:

1. the central control model
2. the evaluative state model
3. the quasi-market model
4. the professional expert model
5. the partnership model.

These models are closely argued by Scott, and you may find it helpful to read the summaries that follow here before reading the chapter itself. An alternative model is offered in Chapter 8 of this text.

❏ Central control model

In the first model Scott proposes, schools and colleges 'are accountable for delivering a service which is defined by the state'. The government may prescribe the curriculum and set down how the process of 'delivery' is to be evaluated. Although at first sight this may look like the system at present in operation in the UK, Scott argues that, in reality, 'those in positions of power rarely operate with such a coherent view of policy', and policy will be interpreted and implemented in different ways by the different actors within the system. The central control model fails to acknowledge the influence of other stakeholders, particularly the teachers themselves who, in order to create an effective learning environment, will feel they need some control over curriculum content and delivery.

❑ Evaluative state model

This more nearly describes the system of public accountability in the UK at present. Here the state depends for policy implementation upon semi-independent bodies that have a role, for example, in defining the curriculum or assessing quality. Schools and colleges are controlled through the operation of these bodies (Whitty *et al.*, 1998), which are in turn answerable to government ministers. Scott comments that this model, like the first one, can be seen as 'deprofessionalising' teachers and, consequently, as potentially lowering the standards it aims to promote.

❑ Quasi-market model

In this model Scott (1989) introduces the concept of market accountability into the equation. Schools and colleges are funded on a per capita basis, and parents and students are offered freedom of choice as to which institution they select. Selection may be influenced by the publication of inspection reports and 'league tables' of examination and test results, the parameters for which have been set by government policy. Institutions deemed to be successful or failing are publicised, which impacts on their ability to attract students – and staff. Scott comments that this model reinforces social and economic inequality, as parents and students from some socioeconomic groups will have greater ability to access the more 'successful' schools.

❑ Professional expert model

Here Scott considers an application of the principle of professional accountability: decisions are seen as being made by the professionals at different levels of the system, according to their role and particular expertise. Each level is then accountable for its outputs to the 'next level up', from the classroom teacher to the government minister. Scott argues this model largely excludes parents and that accountability cannot be neatly allocated to particular levels. Also, there is disagreement on who are the 'experts' on curriculum development and pedagogy: the policy-makers and researchers or the practitioner teachers?

❑ Partnership model

The final model proposed by Scott is values-based: since values cannot be weighed against each other, the different stakeholders within the educational system have to negotiate with each other and work in partnership to agree solutions. Since the views of all partners are equal, teachers cannot plead privilege through professionalism – any more than government can wield power through policy-making.

◎ **Reading and** **Activity**

Now read the remainder of David Scott's chapter, 'Accountability in education systems: centralising and decentralising pressures', Chapter 2 in Lumby, J. and Foskett, N. (eds.) *Managing External Relations in Schools and Colleges,* from the bottom of p. 25, in order to deepen your understanding of the models summarised above.

As you read, consider the various ways in which your own educational system demonstrates features of the five models. Then think about the five bullet points at the end of the chapter: do you feel these strategies are available or appropriate to you or your colleagues?

❑ Our comments

You will probably have found it difficult to place your educational system neatly into any one of the models of accountability. However, the reading will have enabled you to consider what the priorities of your system are: whether for public control, professional accountability or for a system based upon market forces or values-based consensus. It will also have been useful to think through how proactive you can, and need to be, in influencing change in the system in which you operate.

Reading

For further discussion of issues related to accountability, you may like to read Chapter 5: 'Schools and the state', by Keith Foreman, and Chapter 6: 'The state and colleges', by Jane Helmsley-Brown, in Lumby and Foskett (1999).

One important dimension of accountability is that of *market accountability* – the obligation of the school or college to respond to the needs of its clients and stakeholders. In the next section, we consider various ways in which market relationships of the school or college can be managed.

Marketing and external relations

Australian governments have spent the last decade redesigning educational institutions and educational systems . . . They have been steered towards 'free' market mores, manners and morals but within the tight rein of state and federal government policies.

A range of practices . . . have encouraged schools to see themselves as free-standing entrepreneurial small businesses. They are increasingly competing with each other for 'clients' – parents and sponsors and the money which flows from them (Kenway and Fitzclarence, 1998, p. 662).

By the next century, we will have achieved a system characterised not by uniformity but by choice, underpinned by the spread of grant-maintained schools. There will be a rich array of schools and colleges, all teaching the National Curriculum and playing to their strengths, allowing parents to choose the schools best fitted to their children's needs and all enjoying parity of esteem (Department for Education, Welsh Office, 1992, p. 64).

These two perspectives on the 'marketisation' of schools during the 1990s give us a flavour of both the openness and constraints of the situation. The situation where 'free market mores' operate within the 'tight rein' of state control in the Australian example displays the same tensions as those that underlie the rhetoric of the Welsh Office, where schools are 'all teaching the National Curriculum', but are also 'playing to their strengths, allowing parents to choose . . .'

The section that follows considers the application of marketing techniques, both to the strategic planning processes of schools and colleges and to their relationships with customers. The concept of the customer and customers' needs, which lies at the heart of marketing, fits well with the desire of the school or college to identify and provide for the needs of its pupils and students and to satisfy a range of stakeholders in the wider community. Since schools and colleges are operating in a market environment, marketing is crucial to the way in which external relations are managed.

❑ Marketing and its relationship to strategic planning

Marketing actually combines many activities . . . designed to sense, serve, and satisfy consumer needs while meeting the organization's goals (Kotler and Armstrong, 1994, p. 223).

⊙ **Reading and** Activity

Please consult Nick Foskett's chapter, 'Strategy, external relations and marketing', Chapter 3 in Lumby, J. and Foskett, N. (eds.) *Managing External Relations in Schools and Colleges*. Please read the section titled 'Strategy, management and external relations', which begins on p. 39, up to the top of p. 42.

Think through the activities of strategic analysis, strategic choice and strategic implementation as you think they might apply to your school or college. How far do you think your institution is adopting a marketing approach to strategic planning?

❏ **Our comments**

The strategic analysis focuses on the fact that the school or college is unlikely to be operating in isolation and encourages its managers to identify both competitors and customers. The school or college development plan will have more coherence if it takes account of customer needs and behaviours, particularly those of the student and parent, but also those of other stakeholders. In an environment of competition between institutions, those that consider the needs and decision-making processes of the customers will survive and prosper.

In situations where the overall nature of the curriculum is prescribed by government or constrained by external assessment criteria, it is important to identify what it is that makes an institution distinctive, and to know what elements of the market will value that distinctiveness.

Finally, the strategies adopted should be robust enough to address the issues outlined above, and to evaluate whether the needs of the market are being met.

❏ **Marketing strategies**

It is useful for the school or college to consider what its broad strategies are in relation to marketing and provision. Murgatroyd and Morgan (1993) suggest four categories:

1. *Broad open strategy* – Here the institution aims to satisfy the need of all potential students and pupils in its locality: this might be the strategy of a village primary school or a general further education college.
2. *Enhanced open strategy* – The provision is still broad, but the school or college has extra provision that is deemed to enhance its attractiveness, such as extensive extracurricular activities or links with colleges in other countries.
3. *Basic niche strategy* – The school or college has a particular curriculum expertise, which is promoted to customers, such as excellence in sport or success in students gaining admission to universities.
4. *Enhanced niche strategy* – Here the 'niche' is the primary focus of the institution, for example a school being named as a technology college.

Once the broad strategy has been established, a more specialised strategic analysis may take place to enable further aspects of provision to be considered. For example, the activity below invites educational managers to make use of the General Electric 9 Cell Matrix as part of an overview of provision. Despite concern about the appropriateness of the application of models from the commercial world to education, many such models can usefully be applied to educational organisations.

This matrix provides a decision tool for managers to evaluate provision – or proposed provision – at their school or college in terms of its market value. Consideration of the internal appropriateness of a course or provision is balanced against its external attractiveness. For example, it may seem internally highly appropriate to offer evening classes in Russian to local adults – due to the availability of an enthusiastic part-time teacher and a strong tradition of language teaching at the school or college – but if the proposed course is of low attractiveness to the local community, the provision would need to be evaluated carefully. Conversely, there might be a strong local demand for specialist music provision, but if the school or college focus – and therefore its funding and resources – had successfully been established as technology-based courses, then music might not have a strong enough internal appropriateness to become a priority for specialist provision.

Activity

Consider the detail of Figure 5.1 and then fill in the cells in Figure 5.2 with examples from your school, department or college. You can use the grid to assess non-mandatory courses, extracurricular provision, facilities for the students and community, and even elements of the school or college ethos.

- To what extent were you able to apply this analysis?
- Is such an analysis of any value within your sector of education?
- Is Murgatroyd and Morgan's broad analysis of strategy more useful in your situation?

❑ Our comments

Where the school is limited in the choice of courses it can offer, it might be more useful to consider the analysis offered by Murgatroyd and Morgan when linking marketing to strategic planning. In any case, this analysis will help institutions with a more potentially diverse provision to identify their overall direction.

Whilst the label 'General Electric' may sit uncomfortably within the language of education, this framework for decision-making can be usefully applied to schools and colleges. For example in the

	High	Moderate	Low	
	H	H	M	High
External attractiveness	H	M	C	Moderate
	M	C	C	Low

Internal appropriateness

Figure 5.1 General Electric nine-cell matrix: adapted version

H = high-priority investment
M = medium priority: evaluate provision
C = consider cutting

Source: Adapted from Hill and O'Sullivan, 1999

	High	Moderate	Low	
	H	H	M	High
External attractiveness	H	M	C	Moderate
	M	C	C	Low

Internal appropriateness

Figure 5.2 Evaluating your own provision

UK, there has been a steady growth in GNVQ (now VCE) courses in schools at sixth-form level, encouraged by the government's 'Curriculum 2000' initiative, which aims to combine vocational and academic provision. Many schools, seeing these courses both as matching the internal aspirations and teaching strengths of the school, and as responsive to community needs and government requirements, are *investing* in these courses as an addition to their traditional academic A-level structure.

You may be aware of situations in your own institutions where carrying out the General Electric analysis would lead you to consider discontinuing a course. This could be where a market for a non-mandatory course is declining, the college or school does not have the resources or expertise to adapt it to meet new needs, and the best action is to withdraw from that area of work.

Through these examples, we can see how marketing techniques can help educational planners to recognise the situation they are in and enable policy to be linked to development planning. Within the context of the priorities of the development plan, commercial practice can also be used to inform *promotion* of the educational institution.

❑ Marketing mix strategy

The activity of promotion involves the school or college in decision-making about how it wishes to be seen by its client groups. The concept of marketing mix strategy offers a useful framework for promotion planning. This analysis comes from the world of business, but is readily adaptable to an educational setting. Decisions focus upon a number of factors beginning with P; descriptions of the marketing mix strategy may therefore refer to 'the four Ps' – or five or seven: see below.

Foskett and Helmsley-Brown (1999, p. 213) describe the whole mix as in the description that follows. The first four Ps, identified within business settings, are as follows:

* *Product* – the particular features of the product or service that is being offered.
* *Place* – the location of delivery of the service.
* *Price* – the 'price' (in monetary or other terms) demanded for the product or service.
* *Promotion* – the promotional strategies selected to present the product or service.

In 1984, Cowell, when considering the marketing of the service sector – of which education is a part – added:

* *People* – the staff delivering the service.

This highlights the importance of internal marketing, which ensures the values and purpose of the institution are being consistently represented by the staff. In this context, Gray (1989, p. 53) points out the synergy within the service sector between the product – or service – offered and the people involved in delivering it: 'Any service is dependent on the staff who deliver the service to a degree not normally associated with the manufacture of products. The service is to a very real extent the people who deliver it.'

In the context of marketing education, two more Ps were added by Kotler and Fox (1995):

- *Process* – the ways in which processes such as teaching, administration and student support are carried out.
- *Physical facilities* – the nature of the facilities for teaching, student support and extracurricular activities.

Managers operating in post-compulsory education, or in schools operating outside state provision, may actively consider their marketing mix when considering how best to communicate what the organisation offers – or to plan improvements in what it has to offer. Managers within the compulsory education sector, in areas where there is little competition for pupils and places, may only consider it implicitly, but it is likely they will be aware of factors within the mix when communicating with potential stakeholders.

❑ Marketing – the promotion of the school or college

Although schools and colleges in many countries are operating within a market environment, the concept of marketing can sometimes be difficult to apply to public service institutions. The 'product' – for example, the long-term benefits of education – may seem intangible, and marketing may have in the past been seen as unethical, compromising the relationship of the provider with the client (Cowell, 1984). However, the openness and accountability of schools and colleges discussed earlier, together with recruitment strategies governed by systems of allocating pupils and funding, ensure these institutions operate within a market environment.

Internal marketing can be seen as the heart of the marketing process. Internal consultation serves to generate a vision, which all understand and can take part in sustaining and promoting. The school or college staff are key players 'since their activities define the quality of the organisation, and they represent a key stakeholder group with whom management must manage relationships with great care' (Foskett, 1999, p. 37). They are also essential to the 'word of mouth' process which is of primary influence on prospective parents and student, both as providers of quality education and promoters of its worth.

Foskett's 'marketing triad', reproduced as Figure 5.3, illustrates the tension between the various factors at work in marketing education. Foskett explains that, whilst all three elements should be present at all times, the balance between recruitment, community and quality responsiveness will vary according to the 'micro-market' conditions existing at the time. A school that has been criticised for its quality of teaching may have the top sector of the triad as its main focus, hopefully with beneficial effects on its marketing image. A college with declining numbers of students will put a great deal of effort into recruitment, though maintaining the quality of provision will be essential for retention and further recruitment of students. In the open market described above, all institutions will need to keep alive their lines of community communication, though these may be more apparent at particular phases in the recruitment cycle.

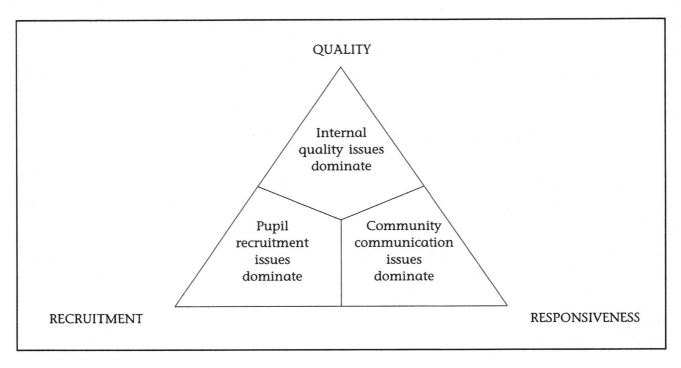

Figure 5.3 The marketing triad model

Activity

Consider Foskett's marketing triad model: you will find a more detailed account of it on pp. 37–38 of Nick Foskett's chapter, 'Strategy, external relations and marketing', Chapter 3 in Lumby, J. and Foskett, N. (eds.) *Managing External Relations in Schools and Colleges.*

- Which of the three main factors dominate the management of external relations at your school or college at present?
- Why do you think this is?
- How does this affect the promotion of your school or college?
- Try to list ways in which activities in one sector of the triad will have an effect on the other two.

❏ **Our comments**

As indicated above, the focus of the school or college on one sector of the triad will depend upon its primary concerns at that stage in its development. It could be important to consider how long term this focus will be, and whether it means that activities in other sectors will suffer. We hope that carrying out the exercise has shown you the interdependence of the activities in each sector: effective communication between the people carrying them out is therefore essential.

Some managers, whilst responding to the influences outlined in Figure 5.3, may not see their activities as marketing and therefore may not consider marketing to be influential in their recruitment strategies. In his study in UK primary schools in the early 1990s, Bell (1999, pp. 66–67) found that many of the headteachers in the survey denied the importance of marketing in their school decision-making. However, the comments they made about their schools would seem to contradict this:

> I do give a lot of time to parents that are interested in looking round the school. We set out to be attractive to parents. You can't disregard parents any more.

Our school prospectus I know needs to be good.

We try to be genuinely open door. We use the grapevine rather than the *Birmingham Evening Mail*.

One head, having spoken of the time taken to build his school's good reputation, the positive attractions of its academic success and its 'inordinate number' of extracurricular activities, and of his policy of informing the local press on a regular basis about pupil achievements, stated 'I have never advertised the school in any way, shape or form' (*ibid.*, pp. 66–67).

This study demonstrated a sound underlying awareness of marketing principles among the headteachers: note that all three areas of the marketing triad model are referred to in the above quotations. The marketing activities that were taking place were viewed as part of the good practice of managing the school, and there was a reluctance either to acknowledge the market culture or to take a strategic view of the school within the market-place.

None of the schools in Bell's study had a *marketing* plan. This document places the promotion of the school or college as the *outcome* of a process that identifies objectives and analyses the market.

In research carried out by Bagley *et al.* (1996, p. 265), a reluctance to respond to parental concerns was noted in some of the UK case-study schools: although consultation with parents was carried out, it was acted upon selectively. Furthermore, there was evidence in one school of what might be seen as aggressive promotion: 'We talk to our parents and we convince them that that's what they want . . . people are malleable. If you've got a product to sell you can mould people into receiving the product' (deputy headteacher, Newcrest).

Bagley *et al.* (*ibid.*) conclude that:

Attention to scanning and interpretation in relation to parents is not a high priority for the case study schools. Indeed our fieldwork suggests that, in the case study areas, much less attention is given to this than to promotional activities, and that school managers are much more concerned to monitor the actions of competing schools than to discover the preference of users directly.

 Reading

To understand more about the process of market analysis, read Stephen Waring's chapter 'Finding your place; sensing the external environment', Chapter 12 in Lumby and Foskett, and consider the activities he describes in terms of your institution. You will be asked to consider this reading in more detail in the next chapter of this book.

Within the promotion process itself, some methods are more appropriate than others. Whilst some forms of promotion such as advertising may be successful in obtaining the interest of the potential customer, once the attention has been gained, other forms of promotion may be more appropriate. Gray (1991) argues there is a kind of 'hierarchy' and that, within this hierarchy, some types of promotion are more successful than others.

For example, the *attention* of potential customers may be captured by attractive web sites, glossy brochures circulated round the feeder schools or advertisements on prime-time television to attract university applicants, but these methods of promotion will not be likely to lead directly to committed *action* on the part of the customer. They may simply arouse an *interest* in customers seeking this kind of provision. Between the raising of interest and the commitment to action, a potential customer might have his or her *desire* encouraged and maintained by other methods of promotion, such as by a visit to the institution for a social event or an open day. Commitment is likely to be achieved by the one-to-one conversation with a teacher at an open day, or by the friendly student who shows prospective students round the college or university. These one-to-one encounters are more successful in strengthening the initial interest, increasing the desire to participate in the life of that educational community and committing the customer to the *action* of enrolment.

The sequence for the promotion process – known as AIDA – can be seen as follows:

- Customer *Attention* - gained through advertising and publicity materials.
- Customer *Interest and understanding* – nurtured through information offered in web sites, prospectuses or promotional videos and captured by promotional activities.
- Customer *Desire* for the benefits – which is best achieved through personal contact and 'selling'.
- Customer *Action*, or commitment – where personal contact is the most successful.

The model is shown in Figure 5.4.

Activity

Complete the promotion process grid for your school or college indicating where each of the methods of promotion fits in to the sequence. Some activities may meet the needs of more than one part of the process. How do you think this might be developed to attract parents or students who are new to the area? Our comments are shown below, but please do not read them until you have completed the activity.

❑ **Our comments**

You will have considered the use of printed material such as brochures and newsletters and where these might be distributed. You may have also considered the placing of advertisements and the preparation of a web site or video. However, the importance of personal selling in the promotion process emphasises the need for all those involved with the school to be aware of their marketing power: 'There are few, if any, schools where all teachers do not at various times have direct contact with parents. The messages transmitted in these contacts project a reality which is more influential than many of the overt advertising activities' (Cave and Demick, 1990, p .78).

Intended customer response	Publicity materials	Promotional activities	Personal contact
Attention *Awareness* of the benefits			
Interest *Understanding* the benefits			
Desire *Wanting* the benefits			
Action *Obtaining* the benefits			

Figure 5.4   The 'AIDA' promotion process

Internal marketing within the institution, whereby all staff and students are involved in an understanding of its vision, a commitment to the processes at work and a real sense of the value of what is being attempted and achieved, is thus an integral part of marketing.

❏ **Building on key learning points**

- Self-management of schools and colleges has led to an increasing awareness of external relations: with customers, clients, stakeholders and partners.
- As open organisations, schools and colleges are interdependent upon their environment.
- The external environment is a source of resources: fiscal; people; information and knowledge; products and services.
- Self-management leads to a greater degree of accountability, for both the processes and outcomes of the institution.
- Marketing is an essential part of strategic planning.
- Marketing – including internal marketing, and sensing and responding to the needs of the external environment – is central to the management of external relations.

6. Managing relationships with stakeholders

This chapter considers:

- the nature and purpose of relationships with different stakeholder groups;
- customer relationships;
- competition and collaboration between educational establishments;
- managing relations with the local community; and
- education and the state.

Introduction

When managing relationships with individuals and communities, it is important the nature of the relationship be carefully identified so appropriate strategies can be adopted. In the previous chapter these issues were addressed from a variety of theoretical perspectives, including a consideration of customers, partners and stakeholders. The nature and management of these relationships will now be examined in more detail.

The nature and purpose of relationships with different stakeholder groups

As we have seen from the previous chapter, the term 'stakeholder' can be used as a convenient way of categorising 'all of those who have a legitimate interest in the continuing effectiveness and success of an institution' (Waring, 1999, p. 180). This definition includes all those groups and individuals who come into contact with the institution through any means. Inevitably, the form and extent of the contact will vary considerably according to the situation and the group; on each occasion there will be management implications or a management response. Effective communication among these groups is essential to ensure stakeholders share the same vision and interact to the benefit of the students. This chapter aims to examine these relationships and to suggest ways in which the strategic leadership and operational structures of the institution can lead to improved communication.

Managing relationships can be perceived, in certain circumstances, as a form of social manipulation. The line between an honest and open exchange of information and blatant advertising based on a careful selection of the available data is one that is often perceived as being blurred and subject to the particular points of view of the various stakeholders.

The importance of the effective management of these relationships does vary considerably as a consequence of the educational system and phase, the stakeholder group and the specific circumstances of the situation. Most 'western' educational systems, which are typically described in terms of open enrolment and public accountability, have a particular need to focus on the nature and strength of these relationships in order to ensure student numbers and the resultant financial support. Other educational systems, whilst their student numbers and finances may be ensured, may wish to emphasise and strengthen these relationships for the tacit support they encourage. Different institutions may focus on different stakeholder groups (e.g. parents in primary education and students and employers in the tertiary phase) due to the nature of their clients or their perceptions about which stakeholders have the greatest influence over their operations.

Where the educational system is subject to open enrolment, the importance of maintaining and enhancing stakeholder relationships has become well established: 'Several studies across a variety of national contexts indicated that more involvement from a variety of stakeholders in decision making is characteristic of higher-producing schools . . . the principal [acts] as a boundary sponsor, constantly seeking ways to involve community members' (Hallinger and Heck, 1998, pp. 13–17).

Taking a holistic stance towards educational provision, McCreath and Maclachlan (1995, p. 69) comment on a Partnership in Education project in Strathclyde, Scotland: 'in order to improve opportunities for children, it is necessary to work with all the people who surround them and who can have an influence on their lives.' This particular project brought schools into partnership with 'health visitors, pre-five staff, librarians, speech therapists, social workers, educational psychologists, community workers and the voluntary sector' (*ibid.*, p. 69).

❑ Managing the boundaries

'Where do the boundaries fall, and how permeable are they?' (Glatter, 1989, p. 3). It will be apparent from the previous chapter that all members of a school or college operate at the boundaries at some time; hence the need for internal marketing and vision sharing if interactions are to be managed effectively. Communication of the institution's culture and aims can be through documents or the spoken word, through staff and student behaviour, through actions done and left undone. In order to clarify this situation for managers, Clark (1996, p. 101) offers three roles for communicators:

1. boundary managers
2. para-intermediaries
3. people-linkers.

The *boundary managers* are those whose roles include operation inside and outside the institution. These might be senior managers or pastoral heads who deal regularly with parents. The *para-intermediaries* have professional roles that operate at the boundaries all the time. They would include governors, guidance workers, student admissions officers and marketing managers. The *people-linkers* are the 'natural networkers' at any level, including the students.

Through such instruments as job descriptions and policy statements, the roles of the first two groups can, to a certain extent, be formalised. The ways in which the role is carried out by all three groups will largely depend upon the openness, 'health' and culture of the institution.

There is a danger of conflict between the formal and informal role holders in this area, displaying tensions between staff as to what messages are being conveyed, and by whom. In research in a further education college reported by Ardley (1994, p. 7), one senior lecturer commented:

> The college has employed a marketing team – the perceptions of those people are not those shared by the professional educators within the establishment, and there is a considerable mis-match, and I feel that we, as educators, have been done a very great disservice by the people who market the college.

❑ Communicating the message

The key to the whole process, for the educational leader, therefore, is to find the right message and express it in the most appropriate terms for the different stakeholder groups. It should be recognised that the message to each group may not be exactly the same but it must be consistent. Different groups will have different priorities, and the vision the institution presents to those groups will need to be tailored accordingly. Students may be particularly interested in the nature of staff/student relationships; parents in exam results or educational costs; teachers in resource levels; and the local community may be concerned about the way the students arrive at and leave the establishment – each will have a specific issue. It is the role of the leader to combine these issues within the overall vision and find the most appropriate means of communication for each case. In this way the leader or his or her delegate is instrumental in communicating the image of the institution and embedding or enhancing the perceived reputation.

Activity

Ask yourself the following questions about your school or college. Try to list the activities taking place at each stage:

- How do we communicate with our stakeholders?
- How do they communicate with us?
- How much common ground is there?

❏ Our comments

It is possible for a great deal of communication – in either direction – to be one-way. For example, a school or college may send out reports – both to government offices and to students – publicity materials and community newsletters. They may receive information from government departments, application forms from potential students and information about local community events.

Whilst these activities are important, opportunities where dialogue can take place are also crucial (for example, progress evenings or cultural events shared by students, parents and staff, employment-focused events involving employers, students, parents and staff, and written communication which indicates constructive response to student feedback). Without multidirectional communication, the messages 'crossing the boundaries' may not achieve effective response.

Communication of all types, whether through formalised channels such as those referred to above or the multitude of day-to-day interactions among the interested parties, needs to be shared with others so that the issues arising from them may be discussed. It is one role of the boundary managers to facilitate this sharing of information and opinion.

The message can thus be communicated in a variety of means, some more effective, some more prestigious than others. Foskett and Helmsley-Brown (in Lumby and Foskett, 1999, p. 218), in a summary of research evidence, claim that 'word of mouth' is the single most important means of communication, particularly to current and prospective clients. It is for this reason that the internal stakeholders need to be fully aware and in support of the vision the institution is attempting to communicate.

 Reading

Please read Nick Foskett and Jane Helmsley-Brown's chapter 'Communicating the organisation', Chapter 14 in Lumby, J. and Foskett, N. (eds.) *Managing External Relations in Schools and Colleges*.

Pay particular attention to the ways that, and the reasons why, institutions may choose to focus their attentions on particular potential client groups.

❏ Our comments

The AIDA approach (pp. 216–20) is an important way of understanding the communication processes involved here, and you will find further discussion of it in this book (Chapter 5). Although the 'sales' aspects of the approach are emphasised, this can be used as a way of analysing any communication where there is an attempt to influence and convince another party. Relationships communication (pp. 220–23) is a function of the different relationships that exist within an educational organisation. We will now proceed to investigate these relationships with individual stakeholder groups in more detail. Relationships with staff are explored in Bush and Middlewood (1997) *Managing People in Education*, and managing relationships with governors follows in the next chapter.

❏ Marketing reputation

In Chapter 5 we considered the internal and external stakeholders of the school or college and noted that the internal stakeholders have a crucial influence on the way external stakeholders view the institution. The internal stakeholders are instrumental in creating and communicating what the external stakeholders see and respond to; this communication activity is an essential feature of marketing.

In the words of Davies and Ellison (1997, p. 4): 'virtue does not bring its own reward, but virtue with marketing may!' Those elements within the institution that are effective and worthy of praise should be publicised and held up to public scrutiny so that they might be valued more widely. This will act as a motivational factor within the institution as it begins to benefit from the praise as a whole. As Gray (1991, p. 175) suggests: 'Where marketing becomes integrated as a central aspect of the school management, the other elements of management are improved.'

Marketing in this sense is seen as a means of enhancing the position and value of departments or the organisation as a whole. In this way the institution begins to make a more proactive attempt to develop a reputation within the wider community. In this sense marketing is 'The means by which the school actively communicates and promotes its purpose, values and products to the pupils, parents, staff and wider community' (Davies and Ellison, 1997, p. 220).

Although the reputation of an institution may vary from stakeholder group to stakeholder group, it will always be based on the perceptions they hold. These perceptions may have very little basis in fact or may be outdated or biased, but they must still be recognised as the views these particular groups hold. Marketing then becomes a clear task of communicating information that will lead these groups of stakeholders to develop a better and more accurate picture of the institution. In strategic terms it is essential the senior managers have a clear appreciation of the perceptions held by different stakeholders. Essentially the senior managers need to determine the answers to three key questions about each stakeholder group:

1. What are they saying?
2. What do we want them to be saying?
3. How do we get them to say that?

Although stated in simple terms these are three crucial stages in the process of strategically managing and enhancing the reputation of the school through proactive marketing. These three stages are:

1. *intent*
2. *analysis*
3. *implementation*.

(Note the different order from the questions above.)

The first stage of this approach focuses on intent – the direction in which the school or college leader wishes to take his or her institution. This intent will usually be given form through the expression of a 'vision' or mission statement for the institution, reflecting the core educational values and ethos. To ensure the vision is appropriate for the institution, it needs to be based upon a clear understanding of the current situation, in particular the aspirations of the key internal stakeholders. So a prerequisite for the vision is an analysis of the current situation and stakeholder aspirations (hence the note about the order of the process). The analysis does need to be inward looking. It needs to evaluate the curriculum that is being delivered to the students – what does it contain? How is it resourced and organised? It also needs to examine how the curriculum is delivered – through the relationships with teaching and administrative staff, through learning and teaching styles and through the ethos of the institution.

◎ Reading

Please read Stephen Waring's chapter 'Finding your place: sensing the external environment', Chapter 12 in Lumby, J. and Foskett, N. (eds.) *Managing External Relations in Schools and Colleges*.

Pay particular attention to the range and sources of information about perceptions of performance the chapter identifies.

❑ Our comment

Note the range of sources of information concerning the perceptions of stakeholders and the performance of the institution. The extent to which these are freely available and shared among the stakeholders will vary not only from country to country but also among individual institutions. It is also important for the educational manager to balance the cost of obtaining information from particular sources against its relative usefulness. Information is only as valuable as the purpose to which it is put – it is up to the decision-makers to recognise the importance of the information.

Activity

How is it possible to discover the perceptions of the institution held by these different stakeholder groups? Ask them! The internal stakeholders are the easiest to access and do have the greatest influence on the actual performance of the school or college. Identify and approach an internal stakeholder group within your own institution. What do they perceive to be the strengths and weaknesses? What do they see as being the core values of the institution? To what extent is this view held consistently?

Armed with such information the educational leader should be able to identify key strengths, weaknesses and desires amongst the various stakeholder groups that can be used as a basis for strategic development and a vision for the school or college. The importance of identifying strengths in an educational system based upon open enrolment is articulated by Davies and Ellison (1997, p. 7): 'There is no point in having a quality product and having belief that it is desirable if the message is not communicated and the school does not continue to exist.'

Any reputation an institution attempts to present to the external stakeholders must be based upon the reality of the situation. As 'Webster's Law' (1985) states: 'No organisation can sustain a reputation that it does not deserve.' A key reason for this is that the internal stakeholders are constantly experiencing the realities of the institution and it is through them the reputation is communicated to the wider community. As part of the management of these relationships it is vital the vision and core values either reflect the aims and aspirations of the key internal stakeholders or can be effectively shared with them for them to have ownership of it. As Davies and Ellison (1997, pp. 18–19) suggest:

If those working in the school cannot articulate the purpose and aims, its core values and its achievements and demonstrate their belief in them, then many of the marketing techniques and approaches will be seen as superficial and may be ineffective as the clients could be faced with a discrepancy between the image of the school and the reality of their experience when coming into contact with the school community.

Although the internal stakeholders are key constituents, external stakeholders also have a significant influence on the nature of the institution. Often these are expressed in the form of constraints or externally imposed expectations. In England, the main influences are in terms of:

- a curriculum – imposed by the state or a national professional or trade body;
- finance – accountability to a funding body (or bodies); and
- quality – often presented in terms of student achievement and collated on a national basis.

Clearly these imperatives significantly influence the direction the institution will want to take. Any national regulations must be adhered to, but it is also important for the school or college to acknowledge the local educational environment. Locally there may be particular needs and aspirations that will need to be taken into account, from social and educational deprivation to over-inflated expectations of educational outcomes. It is also likely other educational establishments in the area will also require analysis, particularly where client choice is possible. The distinctiveness of the other organisations, particularly at the same phase, needs to be identified. This will aid the institution in identifying its core student base and help to ensure it is in a position more effectively to target resources to meet student needs.

❑ The image of the school or college in the community

Beare *et al.* (1992, p. 235) make the point that the image of the school, and indeed of schools in general, is vital in influencing levels of resourcing and ultimately therefore, the quality of the education offered to the student:

Image begets public esteem; esteem creates public support; public support begets political attention; and political influence begets finance and staff numbers and governmental priority. There is no magic in the formula. Education can win tangible public support and finance when respect for its operations and output are high, but kill community regard and in the same process one kills the supply of resources.

In their study of schools in a provincial Australian city, Kenway and Fitzclarence (1998, pp. 667–68) identify, through the comments of students and their parents, the features that would attract or deter them from choosing a school. For example, students commented positively about the provision at some of the schools (SG indicates a male student and SB a female student):

SB: I am going to Hall High because we went there with the school . . . and they had some good stuff there. The dark room where they do the video and the cooking and they have got a big library – for when you do projects . . . And they have got this room where when you want a job you can go and ask . . . they can look for a job for you.

SG: I decided to go to Brandon Heights because they've got everything set out . . . It's a smaller school and you won't get lost. And they've got tennis courts and basketball courts and they've got a big gym and they've got good stuff.

Other features observed on visits acted as a deterrent to students or their parents:

SB: I went to Johnston Park open-day . . . you looked sideways and you got into trouble.

SG: I didn't like the teachers at the other schools, and the classes were out of control. I expected to see the teachers in control.

SG: My parents didn't want me to go to McRobbie because when they went there they saw girls spitting on the table and rubbing it in.

SG: Parents don't like a school with no uniform.

SB: They think no uniform, no discipline.

SG: I'd rather have the uniform. We seem too scruffy when we're out and about. It's feeding the reputation (*ibid.*, p. 668).

The students here have identified issues such as resource provision, school layout and positive and negative features of discipline all as influencing their choice of school. They are also aware of the contribution they and other students make to the reputation and attractiveness of the school. The issue of internal marketing clearly applies to all within the school or college community.

Activity

Consider these questions:

- Do the schools or colleges within your area demonstrate a range of different strengths and weaknesses?
- Are they perceived as being different in nature?
- Into which niche does your institution fit?
- How does this affect or influence your client base (your students)?
- To what extent are you responding to the real or perceived needs of your 'clients'?

◎ Reading

Please read Jacky Lumby's chapter 'Achieving responsiveness', Chapter 13 in Lumby, J. and Foskett, N. (eds.) *Managing External Relations in Schools and Colleges*. Focus on the author's perceptions of why responsiveness is important.

❑ Our comments

One of the key issues here for the manager is prioritising. The manager needs to be keenly aware of whom to respond to and when. The extent to which conflicting demands from different stakeholders need to be addressed is one which effective leaders manage well (you can't please all the people all the time!).

The implementation phase of this process is dependent, to a very large extent, on the effectiveness of proactive staff – summarised in 'the seven Cs' by Crego and Schiffrin (1995, p. 78):

CLOSENESS	to customers (a full and clear appreciation and understanding of the needs and aspirations of students and parents)
CLARITY	of vision and strategy (to enable the clients to gain and share ownership of the core values)
COURAGE	on the part of senior managers (to make the difficult decisions and act upon them to work towards long-term, strategic aims)
CREATIVITY	to think 'beyond the box' (through research to go beyond the obvious and familiar to identify the 'right' solution for the situation)
COMPETENCIES	within the school (and the staff in particular) which are distinctive and continually developing beyond immediate needs
COMMITMENT	to persevere with strategies for deep, long-term gains, rather than focus on short-term superficial targets
CONSISTENCY	of words and deeds.

In summary, we suggest it is important that a strategic approach be taken in which senior managers:

- analyse the current situation;
- identify strengths;
- look to research for potential solutions;
- communicate the vision and enthuse staff;
- involve, activate and focus the key stakeholders; and
- monitor and review.

Customer relationships

❏ Who pays for education?

Clearly the answer will differ from nation to nation and from phase to phase but, generally, in the case of compulsory state education, the answer will be 'we all do, through general taxation'. Does that make the whole population customers? In a way, yes. At a national level, through long-term investment in the education of the population, there will be benefits as a more educated, knowledgeable and skilful workforce enters the labour market. However, education is much more than a prelude to employment and the social and cultural benefits of education may also be a high priority for both government and community.

In most transactions where a service is rendered, the relationship between the provider and the recipient can be described quite simply and accurately using a market model – the provider offers a service in return for a fee; the recipient, who is willing to pay the fee, receives the service: a typical customer/provider relationship. 'A market-orientated organisation', according to Foskett (1999, p. 35) has 'its emphasis on satisfying customer requirements.' The international perspective of home–school relationships is addressed by Johnson and Davies (1996) in a themed edition of *International Journal of Educational Research*.

Such relationships do exist in education but generally only within adult further education (self fee-paying) situations. In most other educational situations the relationship is complicated by the involvement of the state and local governments in funding compulsory (and some post-compulsory) education, which results in a division between the recipient and the payment for education. In private, fee-paying schools there is clearly a relationship between payment of fees and receipt of services – but who is receiving the services, the pupil or the parent? The specific relationship of parents to the school and students to the college, both in terms of their being customers in the market, and in terms of their having mutual accountability either as stakeholders or as partners, is one that requires careful consideration to ensure that both the provision and the marketing of that provision are managed effectively and efficiently.

In the case of private education during this compulsory phase, the parents of the pupils are usually responsible for the payment of fees. Given this relationship, it might be the schools will be more responsive to the aspirations of the parents than the educational needs of the pupils. In further education, in situations where course fees are not met by the state, it is likely the cost of the course will be borne by either the student or the employer of the student. In both cases, enrolment will be a positive decision for a specific educational purpose rather than because legislation dictates attendance. In all cases where there is a definite and personal exchange of funds for services, the relationship between the school or college and the individual or corporate employer becomes, potentially, much more intense and demanding. The contract of expectations and services becomes much more explicit. By accepting payment for services, the consumers of those services demand that stated aims and expectations are met.

❑ Customers – a quality definition

The concept of total quality management defines the customers in such a way they are totally involved in the operation of the school or college:

> The principle of focusing on the customer requires that the customer is consulted and involved in designing the process for delivering the product or service, and that suppliers and customers should be regarded as equal partners (FEU, 1991, p. 7).

> Customers are fully integrated into the organisation. This means that possible customer response is the baseline criterion in every decision-making process and that customers are physically incorporated into activities. It is better to involve at the outset than to decide, consult and then have to change (West-Burnham, 1992b, p. 38).

However, by the end of the 1990s, there was evidence UK schools had not moved far in this direction, particularly where the core activities of teaching and learning were involved:

> Basic questions of what constitutes quality education and the values and criteria by which this is judged tend to be a closely guarded area still, from which generally parents, pupils and the wider community are gently deflected. There is not so much debate and openness but dictat and closure; quality remains predominantly a matter for professional and political judgment (Woods *et al.*, 1998, p. 188).

Schools and colleges may respond to pressure from political 'stakeholders' in terms of operating through an agreed curriculum and conforming to externally imposed inspection regimes. However, the final quotation above suggests that the culture of total quality management, where 'customers are fully integrated into the organisation', may not be compatible with what teachers and managers in schools regard as professionalism. The situation may differ in colleges, where vocational provision may be responsive to professional stakeholder groups in terms of what is to be taught, in what ways and how it is to be assessed, and to commercial clients in terms of what is needed for their employees.

❑ The market ethic – parents and students as customers

> The concept of marketing is for most educationalists an imported, even alien concept (Foskett, 1999, p. 34).

Education is one of the most important and life-shaping investments an individual can make in him or herself. As it begins at a relatively early age, the responsibility schools and colleges accept in being providers of education is enormous. Where informed decisions concerning education are made, they tend to take much more into account than pure cost. Parents and students do not just become consumers of education, they immerse themselves into a community – of which the customer relationship is just one.

In the previous chapter we considered the school or college as an open organisation, influenced by perceptions of the information received from an environment which could be complex and uncertain. We have also seen that the school or college is an open organisation that can be dependent on its environment in terms of the availability of resources to support it. The role of the parent in choosing the school, and of the student or employer in choosing the college, is important both in feeding information to the institution about the level of demand for places, and in providing real financial resources to the institution.

Open enrolment, in theory, gives the power of choice of state school to parents. The importance of that choice has led to recognition of the need for marketing. Colleges of further education have been aware of the implications of the market for longer. As early as 1984, the Further Education Unit (FEU) commissioned research on the feasibility of the use of marketing in further education (FEU, 1985).

For parents, open enrolment may not be as entirely open as it seems. In the past, British state schools operated a system of 'catchment areas': pupils went to the school serving the geographical area in which they lived. There was always some degree of flexibility, but systems were set up to discourage choice to allow for managed enrolment of pupils. Now that a system of open enrolment, much more like the non-compulsory sector, has been established, questions have begun to be asked about choice. Who chooses whom?

> In so-called 'free-choice' authorities, just as in catchment system authorities, LEAs had their own ways of constraining parental choice, for example the timetabling of admission procedures with narrow deadlines for parental response; the LEA's policy with regard to transporting pupils (a vital consideration in rural areas); and the LEA's rigidity with regard to 'intended intakes' for individual schools (Johnson, 1990, p. 83).

With limitations on the student numbers schools and colleges can enrol (on grounds of physical space) the more popular ones are able to choose whom to admit. Since fees are set, decisions have to be made about how to regulate numbers – the entrance criteria. Given that schools and colleges are judged on how good they are by the quality of the educational output (final examination grades), there must be a significant temptation to opt to enrol those who are likely to achieve the highest grades.

Students will play a similar role to that of parents in choosing a college and sometimes in choosing a school. Some studies of admissions have shown that potential secondary school pupils are often involved in decision-making (Thomas and Dennison, 1991; Walford, 1991; West *et al.*, 1991). It is difficult to be sure of the extent to which pupils influence the choice of secondary school, but this issue raises questions about the targeting of marketing strategies: 'If children have the biggest say, we should redefine the issue as one of pupil choice (with parental influence). The implication for secondary schools is that their marketing strategies should be directed to pupils and their primary school' (Johnson, 1990, pp. 99–100).

The extent to which the choice of school or college is the student's alone or the extent to which he or she participates in a decision shared with parent or employer will depend mainly on the age, level of independence and work status of the student. The level of participation of the student in the decision-making is a factor that will affect the nature of the marketing of the institution.

Activity

- On what basis do students and children 'choose' to come to your school or college?
- Who chooses?
- What do you know about how they choose?
- What do you do to influence them?
- Do you regard these 'influencing activities' as marketing?

❑ Our comments

Unless someone in your school or college has responsibility for investigating these questions, it is likely you will have only an intuitive knowledge of the answers. If choice exists for your students and children, it would be worth while to investigate why they choose to come in order to understand better your relationship with them.

❑ Exit, voice and loyalty

The concepts of 'exit', 'voice' and 'loyalty' epitomise the challenges faced by schools and colleges in their management of relationships with parents and students.

Open enrolment means parents and students are free to *exit* as long as there is an alternative available in the market-place. The relative ease of potential exit may allow *voice* to operate more effectively, giving parents confidence as consumers. An individual parent may feel more at ease in making a complaint. Alternatively, the ability to exit may deprive a school or college of the knowledge to be gained from the voiced complaints.

One example of parents using their freedom to choose was quoted by a headteacher of a small, rural primary school:

> Location was an important factor . . . but the general feeling was that if they had not been happy with the school, they would have few qualms about moving their children away. 'Now that I have a car I would not hesitate to remove them if necessary' . . . Parents are prepared to spend a lot of time 'interviewing' schools and their staff in order to choose the right school. They are also very child-centred and child-specific in their choices, basing their decisions on the needs of the child, especially the eldest, younger siblings are usually expected to follow (Worrall, 1994).

This last comment is in line with the 'bandwagon' effect observed by Adler *et al.* (1989). This study of parental choice in Scotland indicated that, once an elder child is enrolled at a school, it is likely the younger siblings will also attend the school, the choice of school in effect being made once per family.

The challenge to schools and colleges is to develop *loyalty* from their customers. The definition of marketing that places the needs of the customer as central would suggest that the school or college could harness voice as 'market research' and, in so doing, work to ensure the loyalty of the customer: 'if you are reluctant to leave an organisation or institution because of your sense of attachment to it, you may feel more inclined to try to intervene, and get the organization to change its ways and improve its performance' (Johnson, 1988, p. 72).

There is another type of loyalty that is involuntary and that depends on the difficulty of leaving the institution. This type of loyalty is now less likely to exist but, where it does exist, may be linked to levels of affluence. For one primary school in a rural area: 'The school has always attracted a particular kind of parent, often with two cars. They have to be affluent. For families some distance away it is often: no car, no parental choice' (quoted in Bush *et al.*, 1993, p. 97).

The logic of the market-place may make schools and colleges seek the more proactive form of loyalty from their customers.

❑ The repercussions of parental choice

Activity

Many schools and colleges have developed some assessment of client satisfaction.

- What are your perceptions of the strengths and weaknesses of your school or college?
- What do you think the perceptions of other groups within your establishment (parents, students, non-teaching staff, etc.) to the strengths and weaknesses would be?
- What do you think they are saying about the school or college?
- What do you want them to be saying?
- What changes do you envisage are necessary?

Devise and use a brief questionnaire to discover the perceptions of a class or tutor group. Do the findings show you anything you didn't suspect about perceptions of the school or college? If so, what changes in policy might be needed?

The PASCI project, reported in Woods *et al.* (1998), explores the interaction between parental choice for secondary school enrolment and school decision-making processes in a competitive market situation. Managers are now more inclined to seek and act on the views of the core client base to ensure continued patronage.

Reading

Please read David Middlewood's chapter 'Managing relationships between schools and parents', Chapter 8 in Lumby, J. and Foskett, N. (eds.) *Managing External Relations in Schools and Colleges*, which explores the nature of this partnership between home and school/college.

❑ Working towards partnership?

Partnership carries the idea of 'mutual accountability' (Sallis, 1988, p. 178), that there is a contract with obligations on the part of parent and teacher. This notion of partnership lies within a consumerist model, but does not stress the role of the market. Cardno (1998) identifies three reasons for involving 'partners' in the decision-making processes within schools and colleges: jurisdiction, relevance and expertise.

❑ Our comments

The extent to which the partnership is an equal one is clearly dependent upon many factors, in particular the cultural differences between home and school and the extent to which the school encourages and values involvement. The summary of the differing levels of partnership are concisely contained within Figure 8.3 (p. 123), with an equally useful summary of indicators of effective partnerships in Figure 8.4 (p. 126).

The ultimate authority of the teacher professional has mellowed into a realisation that the responsibility of educating the young is a shared task:

> In a busy world where pressures upon time are enormous, be it the urgent call of a business commitment or the lure of the golf course, there is a need to remind all parents of their responsibilities in the education of their children. Clearly, however, the constraints to partnership cannot be overcome by parents alone, no matter how great their commitment to it. When I left my first child in the reception class of the primary school, I offered to help in any way I could. The quick reply was 'Are you a teacher?' – the inference being that as a simple parent I had nothing to offer (Naybour, 1989, p. 111).

There is obviously a need for both teachers and parents to have the will to work towards partnership. In the case of colleges of further or higher education, and in the upper years of secondary schooling, consideration should also be given to the role of the student in the partnership.

A model of a 12-point programme of partnership devised by MacBeath is referred to in Coleman (1994, p. 373) and some further points illustrating his idea of partnership are given below:

- A termly class meeting to ensure parents understand the curriculum and the part they might play in it.
- The parents' association to be concerned with education and parent–teacher links, not with fund raising.
- Teachers have an accountability, which means they may check on parents with regard to children's welfare.

Macbeth (1993, p. 196) thus points out that:

- parents should to some degree be accountable to teachers, as teachers are to them.

MacBeath *et al.* (1996, p. 122) also identify a list of indicators of effective home–school liaison, complete with the forms of evidence, both qualitative and quantitative, that can be gathered in support of them.

In the context of responsiveness to parental concerns, Robinson and Timperley (1996, p. 67) propose that 'a working concept of responsiveness must recognise that staff and parents have limited time and energy for mutual consultation and, therefore, that consultative effort must be proportional to the issues at stake'.

As a result of this, they offer a definition: 'A school is responsive to the extent that it is open to learning about parental concerns, willing to debate the validity and educational implications of those concerns and able to act on those agreed to be warranted and within its sphere of influence' (*ibid.*).

It is within these constraints that a programme such as that proposed by MacBeath might be devised.

❑ Conclusions

The stakeholder models of customer and partner can be seen as a continuum of involvement, with the customer at a distance from the organisation and the partner as an internal influence. However, looking from a perspective of total quality management, the concepts of customer and partner are very close. Moreover, many institutions have strengthened their partnerships through developing community relations as a means of ensuring effective ambassadors within their community.

Competition and collaboration among educational establishments

❑ The educational market-place

Generally, and particularly in the UK state education system, there has been a tradition of collaboration between schools and colleges but the combined effects of open enrolment, publication of external inspection and examination results, and bidding for funding had a tangible influence in the final two decades of the twentieth century. Bell (1999) comments on the impact of educational legislation in England, culminating in the Education Reform Act (DES, 1988): 'Competition becomes the motive force for policy implementation and through it improvement in the nature and quality of the service will be brought about' (Bell, 1999, p. 61).

The competitive approach to educational improvement is reinforced through funding systems. Initially it was envisaged that by ensuring funding follows the student (the school or college that can attract the greater number of students will also attract the greater funding), more popular schools and colleges would thrive and the less popular ones would be forced to either improve or close. Although this has happened, the analysis is not quite so simple. Due to their geographical locations, some 'failing schools' have been forced to close and then been given a 'fresh start' with new staff and leadership in the same buildings. In other cases there have been significant increases in transport costs (and the accompanying pollution) as students travel further to their places of education.

In the UK, for example, a further by-product has been the increase in the number of permanent exclusions. Schools and colleges that have benefited from open enrolment by taking on more students, to a point where they are able to choose which students they are willing to enrol, have been rejecting students who disrupt or are likely to perform below an acceptable academic level. The relative position of, for example, four secondary schools in a town, may become entrenched where, due to enrolment procedures, the student intake becomes clearly differentiated. Additionally, there has also been a move towards inclusive education for special educational needs students (who tend to require more than average resources). These students tend to find themselves placed in 'mainstream' schools in increasingly high concentrations, not always with the additional resources they require. These schools then tend to have the dual problems of having academic levels well below the national average and being under-funded for the educational needs they have to meet. More recently an emphasis on the educational 'value added' and additional and specific resourcing for designated special needs students has helped to alleviate some of these inequalities, especially when pursued alongside a vigorous 'anti-exclusion' policy where schools are financially penalised for excluding students.

It would appear from this perspective that educational competition is widening, rather than closing, gaps in the relative performance of educational establishments. To some extent, this has been the result of the policy – based on the self-interest of the school – to achieve national recognition through exam results, which sometimes outweighs its duty to serve the whole client community. However, it is notable that where schools and colleges actively market to increase their enrolment it is, almost exclusively, approached very professionally. There is an emphasis on the strengths of the institution rather than the perceived weaknesses of potential competitors. Foskett and Hemsley-Brown (in Lumby and Foskett, 1999, p. 220) offer a diagrammatic representation of the potential competitive continuum, as far as self-publicity is concerned, from the informative (true and ethical) to the deceptive (untrue and unethical).

In overall terms, for competition to be acknowledged as a positive influence on educational achievements, there must be benefits for all, not just those students and those schools or colleges that have managed to attract extra or more able students as a result of their market position. Research by Levačić (Levačić *et al.*, 1998) suggests that in areas where competition among schools for students was greatest, there was a slight fall in overall academic standards as compared with schools in areas with little or no apparent competition. The conclusion to be drawn from the findings was that 'Improvement was worse in areas of high competition. There was no evidence to confirm the claim that competition improves schools' (Levačić, cited in Doe, 1998, p. 1).

There are claims by Davies and Ellison (1999) that there are positive benefits to schools and colleges from the challenge of competition. From a strategic development perspective it encourages the organisation to assess its strategic position within the educational landscape, identifying strengths and weaknesses and the particular niche it occupies relative to other schools and colleges. From this the senior management will be in a better position to identify the relationships they need to focus on and the particular nature of these relationships.

❏ Inter-school or college relations

Where competition does exist between educational organisations, it would appear to be restricted to periods during the year where choices are being made for the progression from one phase of education to another. At these points there is a distinct 'client' or even 'customer' relationship with the student or parent as a result of the competitive practices.

The nature of relationships with other educational organisations can be even more complex. Schools or colleges may find themselves in direct competition with each other to enrol particular groups of students (usually the more able), which encourages them to focus on particular marketing strategies or target groups. Where there is no direct competition for students due either to location or target student groups (e.g. single-gender schools or specific vocational colleges such as agriculture or engineering), there is a greater opportunity for sustained and constructive collaboration to exist, at least over student enrolment.

Educational organisations operating in different phases (e.g. primary/secondary or further/higher) have significant incentives to collaborate, particularly from the perspective of the senior partner. Where there is the potential for vertical integration (e.g. from primary to secondary or secondary to further), through a careful and constructive management of the relationship, student choice may well be influenced. Secondary schools, as a means of making the transition to their school more straightforward than to potential alternatives, have been encouraged to develop special relationships with the primary schools that 'feed' students into them. This relationship may take on a number of forms. For example:

- Use of facilities (sports fields or arenas – swimming pool, specialist equipment – laboratories or computers, theatres, etc.).
- Use of staff (to teach specialist subjects not normally available (e.g. a foreign language), to provide specialist support or training for teaching staff).
- Access to training (to attend training sessions that would otherwise be unavailable).
- For cultural collaboration (schools which share the same cultural or religious identity, e.g. Roman Catholic primary and secondary schools).

Activity

Consider an existing relationship between your school or college and another educational organisation operating in a different age phase:

- What is the nature of the relationship?
- What are the benefits to your school or college?
- How do they benefit?
- Who manages this relationship?
- How might the relationship be enhanced?

Clearly, the incentive for the secondary school working with a primary school is to encourage students to choose the secondary school as their destination on transition. Although this is obviously a marketing ploy to attract student enrolment, the approach also has the potential to ease the student's progression from one phase to the next through the development of personal relationships, familiarity with systems and structures, and a common culture.

❑ Collaboration within phase

While cross-phase collaboration can be perceived and explained in terms of a marketing relationship, the relationship between educational organisations operating in the same phase cannot. Schools and colleges operating in the same phase, in the same locality, are effectively in competition with each other for students in an educational environment based upon open enrolment, and this would appear to militate against collaborating. But collaboration does take place. It might be argued that the professional tradition of collegiality outweighs the competitive forces.

 Reading

Please read the chapter by Margaret Preedy, 'Collaboration between schools', Chapter 10 in Lumby, J. and Foskett, N. (eds.) *Managing External Relations in Schools and Colleges*, which explores the case for collaboration between schools/colleges for the benefit of both individual students and the school/college as a whole.

❑ Our comments

The key issues (listed on p. 158) offer a starting point for evaluating the strengths and weaknesses of a collaboration. They may even offer a possible means of assessing the educational environment to determine the desirability of initiating a collaborative arrangement and identifying the most appropriate partner(s). The most frequent reason for entering into such an arrangement is for economies of scale:

- Small schools or even small education authorities (groups of many schools) join together in purchasing consortia to extract larger discounts from suppliers.
- Curriculum provision – individually, secondary schools in a particular locality may not be big enough to make advanced-level courses financially viable but, together, acting as a consortium, they have sufficient numbers among them, with each school offering a different range of specialist subjects.
- Colleges offering different or complementary subject specialisms (e.g. a catering college and an agricultural college) at the same level may seek collaboration to share certain essential central services (e.g. computing or library facilities, personnel services).

❑ Collaboration for professional development

In England, during the academic year 1998/99, the Beacon Schools Initiative was launched based upon positive responses to a similar initiative developed previously in the USA. Expertise, identified in particular schools through external inspections, was to be made available to other schools and employed to assist the development of these areas. This initiative, based upon peer teaching, encourages the development of collegial partnerships between schools. Research by Burton (2000, p. 163, emphasis added) suggests a strength of this relationship is based around the Beacon school recognising 'The importance of treating the "customers" (*the school that the Beacon is working in partnership with*) as professionals, who are able to offer expertise in their own right'.

Clearly there is a suggestion of a 'client' relationship between the Beacon school and its partner(s) and this is consistent with the service (professional training) being provided. What is significant is that it is in direct contradiction with the competitive market model of the relationship between schools previously fostered by British government policy. The support and guidance offered by one professional to another are a clear indication a more collegial relationship is possible.

Previously such 'client relationships' have been the domain of state or locally appointed professional experts (educational advisers or advisory teachers), educational consultants or academic departments of universities and colleges with a specific responsibility for teacher training. Individuals in these posts can be perceived by teaching professionals as having been appointed because of particular skills and expertise and so respected because of their positions. Where support and training are supplied by a fellow teacher, the relationship is more dependent upon professional competence and earned respect rather than reverence for the post.

From another perspective a school or college may have a relationship with another educational establishment as a provider of professional development rather than a client. Students of other establishments, such as teacher training colleges or university education departments, may be given professional placements in school or colleges. The relationship here is often complex due to the involvement of different regulatory bodies and the quality criteria they dictate. A student teacher on a professional placement in a school may be required to meet quality standards set by the school, the school inspection service, the student's institution and the body that assures the quality in that institution – clearly a series of relationships that have to be carefully managed to appease the priorities of all concerned parties. The management of individual relationships in such circumstances is explored in Section D of Bush and Middlewood (1997) *Managing People in Education*.

Managing relations with the local community

One of the key problems of managing relationships with the local community is defining who or what the 'local community' actually is. A case study produced by the Association of Metropolitan Authorities (cited by Cordingly, 1996, p. 22) explored the potential different stakeholder groups. It is important to identify just who is perceived to be a member of this community and to determine how far this concept of 'local' actually extends. The extent of the influence of the school or college will vary according to the elements within the community being discussed. It will also depend upon the extent to which the school or college wishes to be perceived as an integral part of the community. Cairns (1998) suggests there is much to be gained by sharing and communicating values, while Plank (1997) examines the overtly political nature of such relationships.

The means by which the institution and the particular community group communicate will also vary considerably. Clearly it is also quite possible for individuals and groups to belong to a number of different community groupings. If we take the example of a small shop located near to a school, it could be perceived as a neighbour, a local business, a potential employer of students: the owners may even be the parents of students! Each relationship will need to be acknowledged and managed effectively for positive and constructive links to be maintained. More formal links between the school or college and the community may be established and maintained through membership of a governing body or school board. The formal and legal framework for this particular relationship is addressed in Chapter 7.

The size of the community to be addressed by the school or college is, to a large extent, determined by the geographical range of the student intake. A small village primary will relate strongly to the village it serves; likewise, a college to the town that provides its student catchment. It is more often the case that a school or college does not have a monopoly over all the potential students living nearby. By personal choice or because of the education offered, students will not always attend their nearest educational establishment: in addition, colleges may operate training at locations outside the town where the college is situated, and their distance learners could be located anywhere in the world. For schools and colleges this means they have overlapping communities; for the communities there may be a degree of ambiguity as to where their allegiances (if any) lie (Connor, 1997). This issue is one addressed by Chitty (1997) as an example of the changing nature of schools as a focus for social integration. A typical problem might be, for example, that the reputation of a secondary school is being tarnished locally by the behaviour of a group of students on the way home from school – the key element being that, although the students live locally, they actually attend a different school. The school must communicate with the community group affected to overcome the misdirected concerns.

Activity

A key task of management is to identify the different sections of the community and to determine the form of relationship. The next step is to consider communication – the purpose and form of any communication – and who will take responsibility for the process.

For your own school or college, begin to list some of the issues, using Table 6.1 as a guide.

Table 6.1 Relationships with stakeholders

Community group	Potential relationship	Impact on reputation	Forms of communication	Management responsibility
For example, neighbouring households	Possible parents/students, use of facilities	Traffic congestion, litter, student behaviour, property values	Word of mouth, local media, posters, flyers through letter boxes, incoming telephone calls	Office manager and receptionist, deputy principal who lives locally

Although the headings used above may give the impression that if the group does not have an impact on the reputation of the organisation then the relationship is unimportant, this is not the intention. It may be used, however, as a means of prioritising effort. For example, when deciding which local shops to begin a dialogue with concerning issues of mutual interest which affect the way the school or college is perceived, it may be that an analysis similar to the one above will identify a local snack shop and an estate agent as being the most influential. The snack shop would be identified because it is a potential source of refuse which would annoy other members of the community, and the estate agent because their comments to potential house buyers may have a significant influence on the choice of schooling and, hence, be a key influence on the reputation of the school.

❑ Core communities

In many educational systems, the school is seen as being at the heart of the community, carrying with it the values and aspirations of that community. In Britain this is often reflected in the religious affiliations of the school (Covrig, 1997; Kucukcan, 1998; Morris, 1998; Saqeb, 1998); the needs of particular ethnic groups (Kahin, 1998); or sporting links (O'Neill, 1998). This allows the school or college to 'tap in' to particular sectors of the community for specific support and specialist resources to enhance learning and teaching.

In other systems education is often perceived as being a binding force. Education can be used by newly established states, such as Israel, to instil a sense of national community (Nadirbekyzy and DeYoung, 1997), or to recognise particular needs within the community (Guimaraes, 1996; Tshireletso, 1997). It is clear that schools are being employed both to reflect and direct the development of communities. In Britain this can take the form of initiatives with clear and mutually beneficial goals for both school and community partners, such as attempts to discourage teenage smoking (Whitear *et al.*, 1997) or community education programmes (Turner, 1997).

Some colleges, for example, may be closely affiliated to particular employment sectors or to particular employers. Private schools may have particularly close financial ties with specific benefactors, companies or sections of society. The nature and strength of these relationships will clearly be of crucial importance for the continued success of the institution. The resources and energy that the institution invests in maintaining and developing these partnerships will be a major influence on the management, organisation, ethos and culture that exists.

Activity

Many schools and colleges have either clearly identified or implicit core communities with whom they have been able to establish and develop particularly close relationships. For your school or college, attempt to identify and analyse the impact of your core communities:

- Who are they? (How are they a distinctive and identifiable group?)
- What is their influence within your school or college?
- To what extent is your institution adapted to servicing this core community?

❑ Business links

Clearly the institution is likely to have a number of relationships with businesses as a consumer of products and services, but such relationships can often be developed further to the benefit of both the school or college and the company concerned. Currently, throughout much of western Europe, North America and Australasia there is an increasing tendency for schools to enter into commercial agreements with companies in order to gain particular goods or services at reduced rates or to receive further direct funding (see Anderson, 2000b). Where businesses directly sponsor educational establishments the nature of the relationship changes significantly. Often this relationship will be subject to a contractual agreement that places particular obligations on the school. Where a multinational company offers financial support to a school in return for providing an education to the children of expatriate workers, there may be certain curriculum expectations or conditions that have to be met. A college may enter into an agreement for the provision of cold drinks dispensers which effectively ties the college into tacitly promoting one producer over another. The moral position of such relationships must meet with the approval of other stakeholder groups.

The vocational elements of education can be cultured and enhanced through the development of closer ties with local employers. Clearly where college-based vocational courses are offered these will often be either as a partnership or in a client role, fulfilling the industry's training requirements. Davies (1999, p. 138) comments that 'virtually all . . . FE-sector institutions in the UK identify the corporate market of employers as one of the main segments for which they aim to cater'. The other main segments are young people and adults, some of whose needs will also focus on the requirements of local and national employers. Courses designed for the customer – on college premises, work premises or via electronic links – are a key strategy in managing this relationship; another is to collaborate with client employers as to how best to meet the national training requirements for their business. Further strategies are explored in the reading below.

 Reading

Please read the chapter by Peter Davies, 'Colleges and customers', Chapter 9 in Lumby, J. and Foskett, N. (eds.) *Managing External Relations in Schools and Colleges*, for a full examination of the relationship between colleges and their customer base.

Although the mix of academic and practical curricula offered in compulsory education is not, in most countries, designed purely to prepare children for their role within employment, often the school learning can be given greater import through appropriate examples of application. Through business partnerships, students and teachers can gain valuable insights into the use to which academic learning can be put, and industry can gain a greater understanding of the educational processes.

 Reading

Please read the chapter by Marianne Coleman, 'Working with employers and business', Chapter 11 in Lumby, J. and Foskett, N. (eds.) *Managing External Relations in Schools and Colleges*, which explores the mutual benefits to be derived from such partnerships.

❏ Our comments

For both readings, the rationale of business-education partnerships is the relationship between learning and earning power (DfEE, cited in Lumby and Foskett, 1999, p. 165). This key driving force is active on many different levels – for the individual student, individual employers, business sectors and ultimately the nation as a whole. Education is seen as a long-term investment in the human capital of the nation, and this can be made more effective by ensuring at the basic interface level that the necessary skills and knowledge for continued prosperity are nurtured through the positive development of such relationships.

Many schools and colleges have either explicit or implicit relationships with commercial concerns. Try to list some for your institution, considering the positive and negative aspects of the relationship. Suggest how they might be enhanced for the benefit of all parties concerned. Use Table 6.2 as a guide.

Table 6.2 Relationships with commercial concerns

Commercial partner	Form of Relationship	Benefits to us	Benefits to them	Potential developments
For example, contract catering services	Client	Provision of student meals	Employment, profits	Links with 'healthy eating' campaign, source of vocational experience for HE students, potential source of practical application of mathematics, design, etc, (curriculum enhancement)

Education and the state

The nature of the relationship between the state and education institutions is a product of the education system and the extent to which there is state funding of education. Privately funded education of students of a compulsory education age will normally have to meet certain standards and requirements (educational entitlement, health and safety) for the institutions to be recognised as schools. Beyond that the state may, or may not, have a role, so the relationship may be a loose and distant one. Where a college or school receives public funding they are accountable for the use to which that funding is put. Where funding is devolved to the school level, such as in the UK, Australia, New Zealand, Canada, the USA and Hong Kong, among other countries (see Caldwell and Spinks, 1998, pp. 6–10 for further details), there are often certain checks and administrative requirements put in place to ensure appropriate procedures are followed and educational provision of a defined quality is assured. These provisions may include:

- a statutory national curriculum;
- national standardised and regular testing of students (results to be published);
- a national system of regular whole-school inspection to be carried out according to strict parameters; and
- a requirement to produce a budget and audited accounts.

This clearly defines the relationship in terms of accountability. The implications for management of such a relationship are that the values, direction and educational content and approach will need to meet the quality thresholds as prescribed before any other priorities can be considered.

 Reading

If you have not done so already, please read either the chapter by Jane Hemsley-Brown 'The state and colleges', or the chapter by Keith Foreman 'Schools and the state', Chapter 6 and Chapter 5 in Lumby, J. and Foskett, N. (eds.) *Managing External Relations in Schools and Colleges*. These chapters explore the nature of this relationship from the perspective of compulsory and post-compulsory education.

❏ Our comments

In both cases there is a pattern of greater 'freedoms' within clearly defined parameters. While market rhetoric is employed there is also a 'creeping centralism' to limit choice and reduce individuality at the core of educational activity.

Currently, there is a significant emphasis within state-funded education in England for education to focus on the production of 'evidence'. As most state-defined and controlled targets are evidence based, much of the relationship revolves around the presentation of the evidence. It is possible for managers to lose sight of the aspirations of other stakeholders and focus on the demands of one key group (the state) to the possible exclusion of others.

❏ Conclusions

Stakeholders are a diverse collection of groups, each with their particular expectations and priorities within education. It is the role of educational managers to identify these groups and communicate effectively with them. The strategic manager is able to reach out to the stakeholders, articulate their educational demands and prioritise them appropriately to provide direction and leadership.

❏ Building on key learning points

- This chapter has explored the potential nature of relationships with different stakeholder groups and how these are closely linked to the context the school or college finds itself in. Each group will have a different motivation or purpose for developing a relationship and it is necessary for the school or college to be sensitive to this and to respond appropriately.
- The different ways these relationships may be defined provide an indication as to how these relationships can be effectively responded to and therefore managed. The impact particular groups may have on the institution will vary and lead to a prioritising of response in terms of perceived importance. It is also likely that an institution will respond with different, though hopefully complementary, messages to different groups.
- For a school or college successfully to provide for its client base it is necessary for effective channels of communication to be established and maintained. This level of responsiveness will enable the school or college to develop and maintain a sustainable reputation where stakeholders are made aware of and share values and aspirations.

---

7. Working with governing bodies

This chapter considers:

- the nature of 'governance';
- what is a governing body?
- models of governing bodies;
- the membership of a governing body;
- roles and responsibilities of governing bodies;
- the role of FE college governors – the effect of incorporation;
- governor training; and
- conclusions: issues for management.

The nature of 'governance'

The previous chapters have considered the theoretical perspectives of external relations as well as specific examples of ways in which the school or college may manage links with various stakeholders. The governing body (sometimes known as the school board, board of trustees or school managers) provides a more formal forum for the views of these stakeholders to be represented and their views taken into account. There are models of self-governance, such as those of England and Wales (Pierson, 1998) and Australia (Gamage, 1996), where the process of decentralisation has transferred responsibilities to the governing body rather than the headteacher or principal. The link between the governing body and the educational institution is unique in that it spans the boundary between the educationalists within the school or college and its community. From the perspective of the manager the relationship between the staff and the governors is crucial, largely because of the power vested in the governing body, although the amateur status of its members is also a significant factor. Moreover, the line between governing and managing is fragile and the relative ambiguity of the position and perspective of governors can be a source of stress for educational managers. Thus, the ability to work with the governors to be responsive to stakeholders is a vital skill for effective school and college managers. In this chapter we consider these issues in more detail in order to explore the context for, and scope and range of, this management relationship.

From the experience of over 20 years of school boards of governors with decentralised decision-making powers, Maha (1997), in the context of Papua New Guinea, reports on research into the roles and functions of the boards and their strengths and weaknesses. He identifies five factors that, he argues, have the potential to influence the success or failure of school boards at the individual school level. These are as follows:

1. Legislation allows for individual school needs to be catered for in terms of community participation.
2. Care is taken in appointing or electing both members and the chairperson so as to ensure appropriate participation.
3. There is a clear understanding between the principal and the board members about the roles and functions played by the board.
4. Boards have full autonomy in relation to curricular and personnel matters as well as in respect of administrative functions in order that they can ensure the main technology of schools (learning and teaching) is relevant to local needs and to increased accountability.
5. Training is provided for members and principals that focuses on the demarcation between the principal and the board as well as decision-making and implementation.

With these points in mind, we approach the examination of the structure of governance.

What is a governing body?

In many respects the governing body of a school or college is similar in concept to the board of directors of a public company (Patel, 2000). Shareholders nominate and elect representatives, often with special talents of benefit to the long-term success of the company, to protect stakeholder interests and to oversee the actions of those employed to manage on a day-to-day basis. In the case of schools and colleges, a group of people are elected, nominated or co-opted to serve as a corporate body, as a single entity, in overseeing the functions of a school or college. Additionally, in the case of state-funded organisations, they may be held accountable for the use of public monies. For this reason, the governing body has a key role to play in terms of its contribution to the strategic direction and management of the school or college.

Unlike their counterparts in the commercial world, the members of a governing body do not generally receive payment for their work although they may receive reimbursement for expenses incurred as a result of it. Additionally, in some circumstances, being a school governor may be considered to be 'part of the job' or even an honour. For example, a school district officer or adviser may be required as part of his or her role to be a school or college governor and a teacher may regard the position of 'teacher-governor' within his or her school as prestigious.

Models of governing bodies

Writing some years before self-management of schools and colleges had become established in the UK, Kogan *et al.* (1984) identified four models for governing bodies, each based on different purposes. The models suggested are:

1. the accountable governing body;
2. the advisory governing body;
3. the supportive governing body; and
4. the mediating governing body.

For the *accountable* governing body, the purpose centres on ensuring the organisation is operating according to the policies and prescriptions of the public authority to which it is responsible. The *advisory* governing body requires that it be informed of what the organisation is doing and acts as a 'sounding board' of the local community, playing a largely 'external role'. In contrast, the *supportive* governing body supports the organisation in its relationship with external agencies and, to that extent, represents a more 'internal' role for the governors. The *mediating* governing body has wider horizons and is concerned with the local educational system, ensuring the school or college fits into the broader pattern. Thus governors may 'serve as delegates for particular interests' (Packwood, 1989, p. 170).

Kogan *et al.* (1984, p. 146) differentiate the models under headings relating to the 'inputs that are necessary for the governing body to achieve its purpose', such as the level of information available to the governors. They also consider the image of the board of governors, its style of working and the nature and level of the demands of work. Based on their own research at that time, these writers concluded that governors' more usual role was as advisers and supporters.

Following on from the work of Kogan and his colleagues at the start of the next decade, Baginsky *et al.*'s (1991) research among governors of English and Welsh LEA schools points to governors regarding themselves most frequently as a board of directors. Governors subscribing to this view referred to the governing body as the policy-maker, the decision-maker and the controller of the school. Their comments included:

> We are in overall control – we are the body that makes decisions and determines policy. We have to know what is practicable, available and above all desirable.

> We are there to take the decisions which dictate the way the school goes.

In order of priority the other ways in which they saw the governing body operating was as a support, a consultant and a helper. As Baginsky *et al.* (*ibid.*) point out their first choice – board of directors – aligns with Kogan's accountable model while the next two compare appropriately with his supportive and advisory models.

Thody (1992) provides a similar typology for the role or roles of individual governors. It involves three players:

1. the director
2. the consultant
3. the representative.

She suggests that governors have a choice as to which role or roles they want to adopt in fulfilling their responsibility to the school, and includes a list of factors that may be influential in determining that choice.

Whilst the models may not be expected to fit any one governing body or individual governor exactly, they may usefully be employed to differentiate the variety of purposes of governing bodies and their members in operation, and the predominant disposition of the governors with regard to the boundaries of the school.

❑ Pressures on governing bodies

Research undertaken by Pascal in the early 1980s clearly identified a range of conflicting pressures on school governing bodies, supporting Packwood's (1989, p. 156) contention that 'it is hardly surprising that members of a governing body differ widely in the way they see their role . . . Much, then, depends on what is seen as important at any one time, who sees it as important, and the strength of particular interest within the governing body'.

Pascal (1989) identifies four dichotomies:

1. elitism versus pluralism;
2. centralisation versus devolution;
3. professionals versus laity; and
4. support versus accountability.

The first two refer to conflicting forces at work on a national level.

❑ *Elitism versus pluralism*

The move towards democratisation in education can be seen on the one hand to be a facade masking the continuation of power in the hands of an elite educational establishment and on the other to be a sharing of power between pluralist groups. The evidence from research indicates that the conflicting interpretations may be synthesised in a ' "neo-pluralist" perspective which allows for the domination of one interest but where significant power is distributed between a pluralism of other interests' (Pascal, 1989, p. 86).

❑ *Centralisation versus devolution*

Centralisation and decentralisation are intrinsically linked through the swings that are observed from one to the other and back (Brown, 1990, p. 37). Furthermore, changes between them are seldom total (Lundgren and Mattsson, 1996, p. 141). Caldwell (1993), in discussing the shifting pattern of school governance internationally, highlights the current trend to centralise in terms of goal setting, establishing priorities and frameworks for accountability and to decentralise authority and responsibility for key functions to school level, thereby laying the overall responsibility in the hands of the governing body. He writes about a 'centralisation – decentralisation continuum' and suggests the shifts in either direction which are occurring simultaneously or in rapid succession are responsible for 'much uncertainty' (*ibid.*, p. 159) – a view that is supported by Angus (1993, p. 15):

> The centralisation/decentralisation dichotomy is exemplified in the UK by the 1988 ERA which introduced the National Curriculum, standardised assessment, LMS and GM status into schools in England and Wales. As a result of this single piece of legislation, curriculum and assessment were centralised while practice and management responsibility for human and physical resources were decentralised. Although the Conservative Government responsible for ERA promoted the legislation on the basis of autonomy, choice and diversity, in other words, decentralisation, the Act did, in fact, centralise many significant powers to the Secretary of State for Education. With respect to ERA, Whitty (1990) takes a particular ideological view and argues that 'the rhetoric of decentralization is a cover for centralization' (p. 22) while other writers (for example, Thomas, 1993; Levačić, 1995) also comment on the polarisation of aspects of education policy and practice within the reforms introduced through this Act.

As Earley and Creese (1999, p. 101) point out, the paradox is not confined to England and Wales. Similarly, changes took place in Sweden and New Zealand during the same period.

The third and fourth dichotomies apply at the level of the individual governing body.

❑ *Professionals versus laity*

Governing bodies must reconcile the demands of professional and lay interests at two levels:

1. In the body itself, where the research showed lay governors see their role as school-based, monitoring, providing an alternative opinion, linking school and community and supporting. Professionals, however, tended to have a broader view of their role as part of a wider system of education. Since lay governors relied on professionals for information, the professionals then tended to dominate.
2. Between the governing body as a whole and the school it governs. It is difficult for part-time amateurs to govern full-time professionals and this dichotomy could lead to conflict.

Confusion over the role of governors since 1980s in the UK is evident from both the popular press and from the academic literature (for example, Golby, 1992; Gregory, 1994; Pierson, 1998). *The Times Educational Supplement* (TES) includes a weekly column in which Joan Sallis, an acknowledged expert on governor matters, answers questions from concerned governors. She highlights the issue in her comment: 'most governors who write to me say, in different ways, that they are confused about their role, whether they are in effect supporters, inspectors, ambassadors or go-betweens' (Sallis, 1991, p. 217). Such confusion can, and has, led to conflict between headteachers and their governors. This was particularly evident in GM schools, especially in the early days of the policy (see Feintuck, 1994, pp. 78–80, for details of the dispute at Stratford school in the London Borough of Newham). Furthermore, in response to such disputes, the Grant Maintained Schools Foundation published (in association with Longman) a guide, *The Roles of Governors and Heads in Grant Maintained Schools* (1992), which specifically addressed the issue of governing versus managing.

In UK FE colleges too, before incorporation, there was evidence of the divide between the professionals and the laity:

There have been complaints about the use of educational jargon and reluctance among some college managers to change old ways of working. Some governors feel isolated. Employment interest governors may be discouraged by political in-fighting particularly between LEA elected members. Staff governors may feel uncertainty about their role. Governors may lack information on what is happening in their college and often rely too heavily on the interpretation of the college principal and the chair. Some governors may be frustrated because they are excluded from participation in key governing body committees. Some even complain that their college principalship has often already decided matters and reduced governors almost to a rubber stamping role (Graystone, 1991, p. 573).

❑ *Support versus accountability*

The dichotomy of support versus accountability is similar to the model identified by Kogan (1984). The governing body is expected to take the 'internal' role of supporting the school in the community and also to exercise the accountability of an 'external' role. The expectation is that governors will be both supportive to the institution and hold it to account:

It appears that little thought has been given to the underlying requirements of the various tasks expected of governing bodies. Expecting one body to act as supporters and evaluators at one and the same time, with little guidance as to how to resolve the conflicts inherent in pursuing these functions, is rather a lot to demand (Pascal, 1989, p. 90).

Activity

In the UK the minutes of the open sessions of governors' meetings are now available on request. If your circumstances allow, obtain copies of recent minutes and consider what these show of the nature of your governing body in terms of Packwood's four models:

1. the accountable governing body;
2. the advisory governing body;
3. the supportive governing body; and
4. the mediating governing body.

How far do you think the minutes might not reveal the true nature of the governing body at work?

❑ **Our comments**

The analysis of the minutes may tell you more about the minute taker than the meeting, but it is likely you will see whether the governors are approving policies, developing them according to their own ideas, adding weight to the school in 'battles' or intervening between the school and the external environment. You might also get some idea of whom the powerful voices belong to, where the power groups lie and the processes by which intervention is managed. You might also see some evidence of governor involvement in a much more active way than was formerly so and gain some idea of the relationship between governors and the executive of the school or college.

The membership of a governing body

The actual size and composition of the governing body of a publicly funded school or college are usually laid down in legislation and are dependent on the size and type of school or college. For example, in publicly funded schools in South Africa, parents must be in the majority group of governors with voting rights, and learners (pupils) are also represented. In addition, South African school governing bodies comprise educators (teachers), members of staff at the school who are not educators, the principal and co-opted members (who do not have voting rights). There are generally 9 full members of a governing body of a primary school and 13 governors on that of a secondary school, with up to 5 additional co-optees. In contrast, from 1 August 1999, business members have made up the largest single group on the governing body of further education colleges in the UK. These boards comprise between 12 and 20 members who include staff, students and co-opted members, the principal and others nominated by local community bodies or the local authority (Shattock, 2000, p. 91).

Similarly, the length of service of any governor is specified in law. The headteacher or principal of a school or college is usually an ex-officio member; that is, he or she is on the board by virtue of his or her position in the school. This is the case in South Africa, but in the UK, school heads can be either an ex-officio member or they may opt to be a governor with full voting rights. Members of the school or college's senior management team are also often invited to attend governing body meetings in order to provide professional input, although they are generally not formally co-opted on to it.

What is important here is that, unlike other formally defined stakeholder groups, the governing body of a school or college is there to offer representation for other, defined, stakeholder groups among its members – for example: parents, teachers/lecturers, other employees of the school/college, business and industry representatives and those representing, or appointed by, local government. Bush *et al.* (1998, p. 186) note that in China this 'Committee for School Management' will also include the secretary of the school branch of the Communist Party. Publicly funded schools and colleges in the UK which are 'aided' or 'controlled' by particular religious denominations or groups will have appointees on their governing bodies – for example, the local priest in the case of a Catholic school. Thus, the governing body of a school or college can be considered to be 'on the boundary' and 'can act as a bridge between the school (or college) and the community' (Earley and Creese, 1999, p. 98).

Schools in the UK are generally becoming more systematic in their appointment of governors to reflect the specialist needs of the school and the sometimes diverse communities they service:

> We identified areas we felt we should like filled by professional ability, eg accountant, solicitor, builder, medical. We approached parents in those capacities, also one from local business and one from higher education.

> The first governors were selected because of their interest in the school, their different types of expertise and to ensure that all the local villages were represented (Bush *et al.*, 1993, p. 181).

The extent to which these bodies reflect a true representation of the community they serve is variable. Hall (1999), in a survey of the principals of the 25 technical colleges in the South African province of Kwazulu Natal, found significant racial imbalance among council members, particularly in state-aided colleges. He comments that these councils are 'neither representative of the students attending the colleges nor are they representative of the communities that the colleges are serving' (*ibid.*, p. 143). Bisschoff (2000), in the context of school governance in South Africa, reports on the findings from a structured questionnaire survey carried out among governors. Of the groups represented on governing bodies, principals are strongly in favour of co-operative governance and the presence of non-educators (cleaners, clerks and gardeners) on governing bodies is generally supported. Both the principals and the learners (pupils) are concerned about the influence of educator unions on school governance.

In schools and colleges not funded by the state, the membership, or even the existence, of a comparable body will vary for each unique situation. In many cases a board will be formed by those with particular and significant financial interests in the school or college. An international school, which relies on the enrolment of children of expatriate workers of a particular company, may well invite that company to appoint a representative to sit upon its governing body. Suffice to note that due to the unique nature of many private educational institutions, it is not possible to generalise further on the membership of their governance.

The implication of the very significant 'position' governors occupy, together with the general movement towards self-managing maintained schools and colleges in many parts of the world, which has enhanced the role and responsibilities of governors in many countries, is that the way in which school or college managers interact with their governing body is crucial to ensure success.

Activity

Find out about the governors in your school or college. In particular, ask:

- How many governors are there?
- How many different stakeholder groups do they represent?
- How many governors are there in each group?
- Is the length of office the same for each group?
- What specialist skills or knowledge do they bring?
- Are there interesting or special circumstances associated with any of the governors?
- How easy is it to recruit governors?

❑ Our comments

In the UK, changes as a result of the Schools Standards and Framework Act require parent governors to be the largest group on school governing bodies. Similarly, in South Africa and New Zealand, parents are in the majority on school governing bodies, and there is considerable imbalance in the composition of the governing councils of South African technical colleges. It is also evident that individuals take on the task of school or college governance for a wide variety of reasons, and that they approach the task from different perspectives. Later in this chapter we consider some of the issues about participation in governorship.

Roles and responsibilities of governing bodies

As stated above, the governing body of a school or college has responsibilities vested in it as a whole (for example, to oversee the functions of the organisation and to be held accountable for the use of its monies). In circumstances where there is a specified curriculum, governors may be responsible for ensuring it is delivered in such a way as to ensure appropriate balance and breadth. The governing body may be responsible for the oversight of the admissions arrangements of a school, including the appeals procedure. In the case of private, or independent, schools that are recognised charities, the governors, or trustees, corporately may have legal responsibilities in respect of the school's charitable status.

Hall (1999) found, in the context of FE college councils in South Africa, that they were assuming varying degrees of responsibility for the appointment of staff, the disciplining of staff, the disciplining of students and the control of college finances. Responsibility for academic matters is lodged in the academic boards or senates.

Bisschoff (2000, p. 13), also in the context of South Africa, but this time schools, highlights the importance of the involvement of the community and the role that governors have as 'messengers'. In conclusion, he comments (*ibid.*): 'the key to the successful execution of the governor's duties are to learn about the school's strengths, weaknesses and opportunities that exist so that they can effectively cope with the threats facing the schools'.

However, with governing bodies in the UK operating in a market environment, they tended to display the pressures of competition and marketing:

> the governing bodies of secondary schools seemed to be more preoccupied with keeping their pupil numbers high and were also much exercised by the issue of parents comparing the exam results of different schools. Such governing bodies were not particularly disposed towards favourable relationships with similar schools in their area, whom they regarded as being their competitors, even though some individual governors were either also governors at 'rival' schools or had children attending them (Deem, 1994, p. 114).

Nkata and Thody (1996) list the responsibilities of school governors in England and Uganda as:

* school policies;
* formulation and supervision of school budgets; and
* student and staff disciplinary procedures.

Ugandan school governors also oversee educational performance and school infrastructure expansion, and English governors hold responsibility for staff appointments and student admission policy.

Creese and Earley (1999) report on their research into improving schools and governing bodies in England. In turn, they consider the role of the governors in:

* the curriculum and teaching and learning;
* strategic planning;
* target-setting and school improvement planning;
* review, evaluation and monitoring;
* Ofsted inspections;
* parents, pupils and the community;
* accountability; and
* school improvement.

They exemplify some of these areas with the following practical examples of the way in which governors can be involved:

Raising standards
* Governor involvement in monitoring exercises/target-setting.

Enhancing quality
* Governors planning improvements to a school playground.
* Governors undertaking pupil-tracking exercises (including a child in a wheelchair).
* A governor assisting with music teaching in a junior school.
* Governor involvement in faculty/department reviews and evaluations.

Increasing efficiency
* Governors contributing ideas for energy conservation.

Achieving greater success in promoting pupils' spiritual, moral, social and cultural development
* Governors attending school council meetings.
* A Governors' Pupil Services (Welfare) Group meeting pupils and parents.

Increasing the school's capacity to manage change
* Governors using business experience to improve the school's development-planning process (*ibid.*, p. 15).

Finally, according to the governors they interviewed, the factors that make efficient and effective governing bodies include:

- good teamwork and co-operation among the governors;
- an effective committee structure;
- the expertise of the headteacher and his or her attitude towards the governing body;
- a good relationship with the staff; and
- a strong commitment to the school and the absence of party politics.

Well chaired meetings and a knowledgeable clerk to the governors were among the other factors mentioned (*ibid.*, pp. 21–22). This leads us to the importance of defining the structure of the governing body.

❑ Structure of governing bodies

In order to fulfil their responsibilities, governors need to have an understanding of the school or college and its particular circumstances and to contribute to its strategic development. The main way in which a governing body usually operates is through a committee structure. Generally, a chairperson is elected for a specified period, together with a deputy. Regular meetings of the governing body are held at which various types of business are discussed (for example, financial, staffing, curriculum, pupil/student matters and site and premises). In the UK, in both schools and colleges, it is usual for there to be subcommittees of the main governing body, each with its own chairperson, which focus on one type of business as listed above. (The precise nature of business considered and title of the subcommittee may vary from institution to institution.) Subcommittees have their own cycle of meetings and report back to meetings of the full governing body.

Governors are generally involved in the selection of staff and will therefore be involved in selection interviews and other similar activities. They may also sit on other committees associated with the school or college or the local area (for example, appeals committees relating to pupil admissions and local organisation committees relating to local planning). Depending on the nature of their appointment or election, and the group of stakeholders they represent, governors may be required or expected to report back to their own group or be available to consult with other members who are not governors. For example, parents may seek support from parent governors in respect of an issue upon which they have views. Similarly, teacher/lecturer governors have to be prepared to represent their colleagues' views and to report back those of the governing body objectively.

Governors also play a key role in supporting the staff, students and pupils. For example, they are usually expected to attend events such as productions and concerts, prize givings and sports days. Hardcastle (2000, p. 33) also argues that governors have a major role to play in improving staff self-esteem, particularly by promoting the school or college within the community and to parents, as a way of relieving and/or managing staff stress. Research undertaken among headteachers in Leicestershire, England, suggests that governors are themselves a major source of stress to many headteachers, and Hardcastle (*ibid.*) offers suggestions as to how governors 'can . . . become part of the solution rather than the problem'. These include monitoring staff absence and workloads and pressing local/district authorities for appropriate support and resources.

❑ *The role of the individual governor*

School and college governing bodies sometimes organise themselves so that individual members are linked to specific areas of the school or college or the curriculum. In such cases, governors may spend time in these areas of the school or college gaining an in-depth understanding of the work and contributing in a variety of ways. Furthermore, governors may use their own expertise to contribute to the school or college on a regular basis or as part of a specific project. For example, a governor with an accounting background may make monthly audits of the accounts, and an architect governor may play a key role in a building project. In some circumstances, governors play a key role in fund-raising for the school or college (see Chapter 3 in the reader *Managing Finance and Resources in Education* for a discussion of entrepreneurial activities in education).

Despite the reduction of the role of LEAs in England, there is still a sense in which governors of community schools may act as an intermediary between the school and the LEA. The appointment of representatives from the LEA may even make governing bodies seem 'an extension of the political system, determining that professionals follow the wishes of the public' (Packwood, 1989, p. 155). This role may appear similar to the example from China presented above.

However, the role of the 'political' governor simply toeing the party line is probably less relevant today. Research into the work of ten governing bodies undertaken between 1988 and 1992 showed that 'many of our governors were extremely critical of their LEAs; no category of governor was exempt from this and LEA nominated governors were amongst the most critical' (Deem, 1994, p. 110).

The move towards making schools responsive to the market and allowing parents a greater say in how schools are governed means parent governors are seen as having a more substantial role to play on the governing bodies of schools since the Education Act 1986:

> Parent governors are not elected specifically to represent the views of other parents, yet there is a strong case for clarification and extension of their role, for four reasons. First, in the future schools will need to liaise far more closely with parents than they have before. Second, the legislative framework now exists whereby parents have greater representation on governing bodies than before and it may be appropriate to raise their status. Third, with training, parent governors could provide useful support in tasks that school management teams could reasonably delegate, for example, the review of the prospectus or consultation with parents . . . Fourth, parent governors need ownership if they are to develop as useful helpers. They are there to provide a parental perspective and, as such, have a vitally important role to play in many aspects of the development of a school (Hanford, 1992, p. 114).

It is worthy of note that Robinson and Timperley (1996), reflecting on issues of responsiveness to local school communities in New Zealand that were to be addressed by members of 'boards of trustees', found problems. These elected or appointed individuals frequently had very limited access to their constituents and even where they did, they often lacked the necessary skills to disseminate and collect views.

Of course, there is a different, but just as difficult, situation in respect of teacher governors. It cannot be taken for granted that professionals present a united front, and there is confusion about whether they are representatives or delegates and the related issues of whose views they put forward. Kogan *et al.* (1984) found that teacher governors sometimes used governing body meetings to confront headteachers with opposition to certain developments in school life, although it should be noted this research took place during a period of considerable teacher militancy.

The role of teacher- or lecturer-governors can be an ambiguous one. Based on the examination of ten governing bodies and their schools in two local education authorities, Deem *et al.* (1995) offer an interesting analysis of the role of the teacher governor in relation both to the headteacher and to the wider governing body. Deem and her colleagues found that because of headteacher 'power of patronage', individual teacher governors tended to tread warily in order not to engage in direct confrontation with heads in governing body meetings. Damage limitation strategies might have been adopted to avoid this situation:

> In several schools the headteacher would meet with the teacher governor(s) prior to the governing body meeting in order to be briefed on the line the teacher governor(s) would take in the meeting. In two such schools, it was clear that the purpose of this meeting was to reach a consensus prior to the meeting so a united 'professional' front could be presented. As a teacher governor in one of these schools expressed it: 'It is not necessarily a clever idea for staff to be seen to be anything except reasonably along the same lines' (*ibid.*, p. 127).

Where decision-making of the wider governing body was concerned, the research team observed that some teacher governors found it difficult to establish a meaningful role. Some were acutely conscious of their 'employee' status in relation to the governing body (*ibid.*, p. 126); others felt silenced by irreconcilable differences between lay and professional perspectives (*ibid.*, p. 86).

However, as Deem *et al.* (*ibid.*, p. 131) conclude, governing body reforms have not reduced professional influence to a minimum: 'Teacher governors may be marginalized by other governors in a number of contexts since other governors are – nominally at least – their employers; however, unlike lay governors, teachers work in the school and influence what happens on a daily basis.'

❑ *The chair of governors*

In any sizeable committee the role of the chair is an important one. The governor elected to the chair of a school or college governing body holds a time-consuming and influential role. There are certain restrictions on the category of governor eligible to take the chair. In both English schools and colleges the chair and vice-chair must be chosen from governors who are not employed or studying at the institution (Statutory Instruments, 1999, no. 2163, s. 29 (2); FEFC, 1995, s. 87).

The *Guide of Good Governance* (DfEE, 1996, p. 10) for schools in England lists the chair's functions as including:

- Ensuring that the business of the governing body is conducted properly, in accordance with the legal requirements;
- Ensuring that meetings are run efficiently, focusing on priorities and making best use of the time available;
- Ensuring that all members have equal opportunities to participate fully in discussion and decision-making;
- Encouraging all members of the governing body to work as a team; liaising with the headteacher;
- Acting in cases which may properly be deemed 'urgent'; making public statements on behalf of the governing body where delegated to do so.

This list gives prominence to the 'meetings' aspects of the chair's role. For English further education colleges, the *Guide for College Governors* (FEFC, 1994) seems to take 'meetings skills' for granted, although attention is drawn to the duty of the clerk to advise the chair of procedure. More emphasis is placed on the need for a constructive working relationship between the chair of the governing body and the college principal. This relationship is seen as a 'critical element in the effectiveness of a college' (FEFC, 1994, *ibid.*, s. 5.12).

Research on what makes an effective school governor, carried out by Esp and Saran (1995), was designed on the basis that the chair and headteacher are key players in school governing bodies and that their role was central to the implementation of the many changes required by legislation in the 1980s and 1990s. From their research, they found that a number of common themes emerged when chairs and heads talked about their joint roles. These included having a shared vision, the chair being a critical friend to the headteacher and the fragility of good relationships. For example, one chair said that 'schools need their own character. We have tried to define it' (*ibid.*, p. 74). While the head of a primary school, whose chair was an additional member of the Education Committee and had great status in the county, suggested 'the chair is my best ally and fiercest critic' (*ibid.*, p. 73). In contrast, Esp and Saran report another headteacher as reporting on her relationship with a long-serving chair with a strong personality and tendency to intervene as

I am prepared to accept the situation that I am not fully in control. Colleagues wonder how I manage. He wears me out . . . keeps me on my toes . . . I don't want to spoil a good relationship . . . I don't see who can succeed the chair. I feel he respects me (*ibid.*, p. 72).

◎ **Reading and** Activity

Please read pages 98–103 of Peter Earley and Michael Creese's chapter, 'Working with governors', Chapter 7 in Lumby, J. and Foskett, N. (eds.) *Managing External Relations in Schools and Colleges.*

As you read this section compare and contrast their views with what you know about the situation in your own school or college (regardless of whether you work in a UK-based school or college). If your institution has a governing body, find out the parameters under which it operates.

What roles do they perform and what is their relationship with the stakeholders?

❑ Participation

Another feature of the reform of the governance of schools in England and Wales since 1980 is the increased parental and community representation on governing bodies, a move shadowed by New Zealand later in the decade with the establishment of parent-dominated 'Boards of Trustees'. This change is significant because it raises questions in connection with the availability and motivation of these lay governors.

Brehony (1992) asks 'Who are the governors?' and reports on his own and NFER studies (Keys and Fernandez, 1990) into how representative governing bodies are of the population as a whole, and of the parents of the school. Earley and Creese (1999) also raise the issue of the extent to which governing bodies represent their communities in terms of race and gender, echoing Hall (1999), who found significant racial imbalances in the membership of South African FE colleges' councils. Evidence varies with respect to representation by gender but, in all three studies considered, black and Asian governors in England were under-represented. Indeed, this situation was highlighted much more recently by Hinds (2000), who reports that 'the Government wants more people from ethnic minorities on governing bodies'. Additionally, the data from the studies mentioned above indicate the majority of governors are from professional and managerial or executive backgrounds. However, again much more recently, Marriott (2000, p. 29) discusses the tension between the need for governors to be 'a body of local people representing the public interest in the school's affairs' and the growing pressure for expertise (Ofsted, 2000). The trend, it seems, is towards 'specialist governors' linked to an area of the curriculum. But, as Marriott (*ibid.*) points out, 'as governors become quasi-professional, there is a greater possibility of territorial conflict with real professionals'.

Brehony (1992), in the context of English schools, suggests, however, that the pertinent issue is about the participation – at meetings – of different groups of governors rather than resignations or vacancies. Like Brigley (1990) before, Brehony found parent governors quieter than other governors. He also reports structural divisions excluding certain categories from the debate (for example, women and working-class governors on secondary school governing bodies and black governors where they were in the minority). It seems that while the non-participant governors have the formal opportunity to participate, they do not do so. As Brehony (1992, p. 210) comments: 'in some cases, this might be explained by the fact that on numerous occasions contributions by women and black governors have been at best ignored and at worst interrupted'.

Turning to the reasons for governorship, Deem *et al.* (1995) identified three types among their sample. For some, being a school governor was not their only experience of voluntary activity in the community. Often but not invariably, people in this group had been elected local politicians or active members of a political party. For others, being a parent, especially a mother, was the springboard to governorship. Finally, a group of more recently recruited governors came from business and industry and perceived themselves 'lending their expertise to schools previously innocent of the world beyond the public sector' (*ibid.*, p. 3).

From their research into participation in voluntary activities, Lynn and Davis Smith (1991, p. 82) found that a large number of their sample became involved because the activity was connected with a personal need or interest or one connected with their family or friends. Although Brehony (1992, p. 211) did observe some instances of private interests – for example issues concerning a governor's child – being pursued through the governing body meetings, he adds that such instances are relatively rare. He also reports that some of the chairpersons in his sample mentioned private interest as their main reason for their initial involvement. However, Brehony (*ibid.*) found the main reason for the involvement of the governors in his sample was that they had been asked to become one. Interestingly, Lynn and Davis Smith (1991, p. 81) found the same main reason among their volunteers.

The matter of what is the motivation for lay participation in the governance of schools requires consideration of the nature of citizenship in a democratic society (Deem *et al.*, 1995, p. 21). Deem *et al.* (*ibid.*) identify the key issues in relation to active citizenship and the governance of schools and explore them in detail in their book. In developing their argument, they quote Barker (1994, p. 19), who contends that 'the politics of citizenship have replaced the politics of social and economic policy. How things get done, and the way in which people take part in their own government, have become as important as the distribution of wealth and opportunity.' Deem *et al.* suggest that this description aptly applies to education in the 1990s (Deem *et al.*, 1994) and go on to question whether 'school governors are . . . acting as empowered citizens in the community or whether they are merely state volunteers' (Deem *et al.*, 1995, p. 157). The conclusion they reach from their own research and that of others is that 'the exercise of truly democratic citizenship is [not] high on the political agenda in contemporary societies' (*ibid.*, p. 170).

❏ Lay governance

In addition to issues about the availability and involvement of lay governors, we also consider the nature of the lay governance, particularly in respect of lay–professional relationships.

Prior to the 1980s' reforms of English and Welsh governing bodies and the 1988 ERA, lack of control over resources meant governing body influence and power were largely lodged in the political contacts of governors (Kogan, 1984; Golby and Brigley, 1989). The changes in composition, powers and responsibilities introduced during the 1980s were, in part, designed to depoliticise governing bodies (Field, 1993, p. 166; Deem *et al.*, 1995, p. 64). However, these writers suggest that their own research shows the reality has been that governing bodies may have been depoliticised from party politics but with so many different interests being presented, governing bodies are 'intensely political' (Deem *et al.*, 1995, p. 64).

A partial explanation for this may lie in the fact that, in the main, school and college governors are not educational professionals. This, in turn, means that, often, the knowledge and understanding they draw on in governing are varied and sometimes lacking in detail. This view is borne out by early research on school governing bodies. Lay governors find many aspects of educational practice difficult to understand or do not have the confidence to involve themselves in professional matters (Bacon, 1978; Kogan, 1984; Golby and Brigley, 1989).

Furthermore, these findings are confirmed by more recent investigations and writings. Field (1993, p. 168) reports governors she interviewed referring to themselves as 'a bunch of amateurs' and 'lacking in expertise'. She highlights the governors' worries about the relationship between lay and professional issues as being 'concerned with potential problems' and sums up their general attitude by quoting the vice-chair: 'The professionals run the school and the governors bring their outside experience to bear on the partnership. The Head and SMT know what they are doing. It is not the task of the governors to challenge that' (*ibid.*).

Booth and Hill (1996) raise questions about the accountability of governors and ask the question 'are governors ungovernable?' These writers also describe the governing body as 'made up of amateurs' and 'sandwiched between the professionals – the headteacher and the local authority'. This arrangement, they suggest, provides 'plenty of room for conflict'.

Deem *et al.* (1995) consider governor knowledge, both generally and about education. With regard to the latter, they comment on the 'observed, predictable, asymmetry between professional and lay governors in terms of the amount of expert or technical knowledge of education that each possesses . . . [which] extends beyond knowledge of a particular school to knowledge of the teaching and learning process' (*ibid.*, p. 77). Indeed, Deem *et al.* (*ibid.*) go on to suggest that, in addition to lack of knowledge about education, governors' values about education may be at odds with those of the professionals. Although these writers do not suggest this, in itself, is a 'bad' thing, they assert that it is 'productive . . . of conflict' (*ibid.*).

Before we leave the question of the lay/professional interface, it is worth noting that another form of interface may be observed in the governance of certain schools. In voluntary schools the interface on the governing body between the laity and the ordained clergy may be an important feature (Arthur, 1993). Voluntary schools are a significant subsector of the UK educational system (Johnson, 1990, p. 36). There are several research enquiries that provide case studies of governing bodies of voluntary schools (Kogan *et al.*, 1984; Baginsky *et al.*, 1991; Earley, 1994).

Activity

The relationship between governors and the management of a school or college has been summed up by Wirt (1981) as a five-stage development between 'laity' and professionals in education:

1. Quiescence where professionals dominate and laity support.
2. Issues where laity begin to question.
3. Turbulence where conflict arises over control.
4. Resolution where conflict is investigated.
5. Closure where the role of the professionals has been redefined.

In the UK the minutes of the open sessions of governors' meetings are now available on request. If your circumstances allow, obtain copies of recent minutes and suggest which stage has been reached in relation to:

- the curriculum
- personnel management
- site management.

❏ Our comments

It is likely that in matters of curriculum which governors frequently say are 'professional', the discussion will only have reached Wirt's stage 2, but in matters of personnel management, according to the degree of control they have wrested from the school or college, a small group may well have reached a higher level. Indeed, within the grant-maintained (now Foundation) sector (Bush *et al.*, 1993), professional roles have been redefined in new policies. It is generally believed all governors consider they have reached stage 4 or 5 regarding site management but may well revert to level 2 when any new issue arises. This was seen in many colleges following incorporation (see below), as the reality of responsibility became apparent to the governors. It is likely the sequential pattern will be seen at work in different ways as the role of the governors is redefined following legislation.

⊚ Reading and Activity

Now read the section on practical examples of involvement, pages 104–107 of the chapter by Peter Earley and Michael Creese, Chapter 7 in Lumby, J. and Foskett, N. (eds.) *Managing External Relations in Schools and Colleges.*

Again, compare and contrast with your own situation.

❏ Tensions between governance and management

The tensions between governance and management of schools, particularly those that formerly had GM status in the UK, have already been highlighted. The publication *Guidance on Good Governance* (DfEE, 1996) includes a number of 'good practice' examples of the division of responsibilities between the governing body and the headteacher on such matters as curriculum, staffing, finance and budget. However, the dividing line between policy-making and operation is not always clear cut and it may not be in the interests of either governors or headteachers and principals to try to make it so (Baginsky *et al.*, 1991, p. 81).

From their research in the early 1990s, Shearn *et al.* (1995) identify various categories of working relationship between headteachers and governors. In one category the head took the major role, either with governors' approval, or by default, or by outmanoeuvring governors. In a second group both parties had a more defined role – responsibility either being shared between the head and the chair of governors on an implicitly agreed basis, or between head and governors in a nurturing relationship, or between head and governors with the latter emphasising a monitoring role. A third group, however, were categorised by varying degrees of conflict, with areas of responsibility contested between head and governors.

❏ Disputed responsibilities

As early as 1985 the national press in the UK was giving coverage to a number of examples of turbulence in school and governing body life (The Open University, 1988, p. 30). Governors who had hitherto kept a low profile in their interactions with the school, the LEA or the diocesan board suddenly found themselves interviewed by the national press. From time to time individuals, or local groups, continue to emerge and attract considerable media attention.

One of the most public and vociferous disputes occurred at Stratford School in Newham, East London, in 1992. Among others, Bush *et al.* (1993) and Feintuck (1994) describe the situation where the opportunity for the school to become self-governing through the GM policy initiative was used by some of the local community to attempt to influence the overarching culture of the school in favour of the priorities of Asian parents, despite the ethnic diversity of the local area. The newly appointed headteacher found herself enmeshed in a high-profile dispute which required the Secretary of State to intervene and use his powers to appoint additional governors. The situation was eventually resolved when the chair of governors resigned and the balance of power on the governing body changed with the selection of new parent governors. However, the Stratford debacle did raise a central issue in relation to GM schools as to who was running them. While various blames were laid it was clear there was no simple answer. From the perspective of the governors it seemed there was a paradox between the rights afforded to parents and the local community through GM status and what happened at Stratford School. As one governor who positioned himself against the headteacher commented about the NAHT, the headteacher association acting on behalf of the headteacher of Stratford School, 'the NAHT wants the head to become supreme in the school . . . that makes a mockery of the legislation and the rights of parents' (*TES*, 22 May 1992). Similarly, the Asian chair of governors who resigned also pointed towards 'what he sees as the hypocrisy of ministers in promoting parent power and status of governors, then interfering when they do not like what a group of Asian governors is doing' (*Independent*, 6 February 1992).

Brigley (1994) chronicles a less public but fiercely contested dispute between governors and parents and suggests that one long-term effect of devolution of powers through local management of schools is to lower the point of political engagement: 'Governors may find increasingly that they are in the front-line, fielding the kind of complaints which the LEAs used to receive from them, and feeling singularly ill-equipped to do so' (*ibid.*, p. 78). Some conflicts eventually generate formal enquiry, whether by the LEA (for example, the report by Nottinghamshire County Council inspectors on Manton Junior School, 1997) or through emergency inspection by Ofsted (for example, the inspection of Ridings School in Halifax, Ofsted reference 82/96/SZ).

❑ **Partnership**

Continued concern about the role ambiguity of governors in schools in England and Wales, together with the heavy workload expected of unpaid governors and the consequent burden they place upon headteachers, has prompted the government to set up a taskforce on red tape. In April 2000 the leader of this Better Regulation Task Team identified practical ways of freeing up governing bodies so they can focus on their primary objectives (Patel, 2000, p. 27). Patel suggests the responsibilities of governors should be simplified to allow governors to concentrate on the overall performance of the school rather than its day-to-day management and that the role of governing bodies needs to be realistic and clear. Patel (*ibid.*, p. 27) indicates the task team's preference: 'We like the model of a private company's board of non-executive directors, which approves the appointment of the chief executive, monitors his or her progress, endorses the firm's broad strategies and policies but does not get involved in its day-to-day operation.'

Responding to Patel, Westcott (2000, p. 26) argues that accountability should not be neglected at the expense of effectiveness and cites a recent DfEE publication, *Schools Plus: Building Learning Communities*, which reaffirms the wider role of the school as a community resource and its leader as a community champion. She explains that the shortcomings in approaches in further education that encouraged FE leaders and governors to act in an individualised manner have now been recognised and 'structures which support collaboration and coordination are replacing those requiring isolation and competition' (Westcott, 2000, p. 26). She goes on to state:

> We are trying to recreate the FE governing body as a place where decisions are made on educational grounds in the context of local needs and the strengths of the various providers serving it – not enterprises which, in some cases, have expanded so far beyond their own quality assurance *cordon* that governors are not quite sure what they are doing, or why (*ibid.*).

New regulations – the Education (School Government) (Terms of Reference) (England) Regulations 2000 – came into effect on 1 September 2000. The regulations are not intended to give governing bodies new duties but clarify how they should approach existing duties in a mainly strategic way and act as a 'critical friend' to the headteacher. However, it seems the issue is far from resolved because, at the time of writing, heads were already predicting the role of governors as a 'critical friend' could well be a recipe for confrontation (Thornton, 2000, p. 27).

 Reading

Please now read the remaining part – pages 107–108 – of Peter Earley and Michael Creese's chapter 'Working with governors', Chapter 7 in Lumby, J. and Foskett, N. (eds.) *Managing External Relations in Schools and Colleges*.

❑ **Our comments**

There is no doubt that the model of partnership proposed by AGIT is attractive for all parties. It addresses the dual role of the governors in terms of school effectiveness and accountability. However, whether it provides a resolution to the current concern among headteachers in England and Wales that governors contribute to their stress has yet to be seen. Likewise, its transferability to other systems and cultures is unclear.

The role of FE college governors – the effect of incorporation

The incorporation of the English FE colleges in 1993 as self-managing organisations brought with it an increase in the powers and responsibilities of the governors:

> Further education corporations are given wide ranging powers relating to the provision of further and higher education and the supply of goods and services. They may acquire and dispose of land and property, enter into contracts, borrow and invest money, accept gifts, and provide scholarships, grants and prizes (Brooks, 1993, p. 226).

Shattock (2000) highlights the fact that this was perceived as 'risky' because the colleges were not experienced in self-management and the tradition in schools of interested and committed governors had not been translated into further education colleges. Apart from a few exceptional cases, these concerns have proved unfounded.

Gleeson and Shain (1999), focusing on research carried out six years after incorporation, consider issues of concern in governing corporate colleges. They report on the emphasis on funding and managerial matters in corporate management proceedings at the expense of education issues, and comment: 'Whilst ostensibly the policy rationale for packing FE governing bodies with representatives from industry and business was to provide a clearer business steer for FE, it has succeeded more in terms of the way colleges are managed than in relation to their pedagogic functions' (*ibid.*, p. 550).

Like Hall (1999), commenting upon South African FE governors, Gleeson and Shain (1999, p. 551) draw attention to the unrepresentativeness of English FE governing bodies and on the 'centring of masculinist power within them'. In terms of the latter, they refer to what they call a 'special relationship' between principals (chief executives) and their chairs of governors. Their research findings highlight the importance of the strategic relationship between chairs and principals as well as the 'fragile nature of accountability through which governance and managerialism find expression in the FE sector' (*ibid.*, pp. 553–54). The point is that much hangs on the relationship between these two key players because it is, by the very nature of their roles, intense and often isolated from the main governing and staff body as well as being '*framed* in a formulaic fashion in which "bottom line" funding and managerial priorities take precedence over teaching, learning and professional concerns' (*ibid.*, p. 554).

Furthermore, Shattock (2000) describes the constitutional changes that have been implemented since 1 August 1999. He points out that these reflect 'an unease in the sector itself over the ideological bias of the previous . . . arrangements and the extent to which they were, in practice, effective' (*ibid.*, p. 91) and have been introduced in response to various breakdowns and examples of malpractice. (See *ibid.*, pp. 89–101 for such examples.) The changes include a shift away from the 'business-led, free market approach, back towards a more local, community-based membership' (*ibid.*, p. 92) of the governing body as well as improving audit arrangements. The approach to the latter is summarised through the publication by FEFC in 1998 of *Audit Code of Practice*, which emphasises the need for a 'rigorous framework of audit and internal controls' to assist governors to maintain the 'high standards of conduct' necessary to meet their public responsibilities.

Shattock (2000, pp. 100–101) summarises the situation:

> The FEFC's approach to improving governance and to curbing impropriety has been to try to institutionalise transparency and openness, and to impose on professionals – audit firms and clerks to governors – a duty to report on key issues. Such an approach . . . has had the effect of greatly increasing lay governors' awareness of the job they are being asked to do. But too much emphasis on governor training, search committees and giving high scores at inspections for observing the letter rather than the substance of the job will be counter-productive. It will turn off active and committed governors who will find better outlets

for their civic energies if they think they are being patronised by procedural bureaucracy. There is a danger of expecting too much from lay governors. This applies to both the time they can be expected to commit to a college, and to the extent of their understanding of the complex and now highly bureaucratic world of further education, its financial structures, quality frameworks and maze of qualifications.

In conclusion Shattock argues that, in future, the way to improve governance is through the professional input of principals and senior staff, rather than through rules and constitutional change. Governors will want to be involved when they can take pride in their college's performance. He highlights the characteristics of effective FE governing bodies, and includes:

- support for a good principal;
- asking probing questions;
- keeping a firm check on the executive without stifling it; and
- using members' professional experience to suggest new ways of approaching difficult problems.

Finally, Shattock (*ibid.*, p. 101) points out that 'conducting college business according to best practice procedures is important and necessary, but it is not the essential substance of college governance'.

Governor training

The issue of governor training is often difficult. In the main, governors give their time on a voluntary basis. Therefore it is difficult for governments, local authorities or schools or colleges to do more than encourage governors to participate in training. Furthermore, the diversity of governors' backgrounds as well as experience makes decisions about the nature and style of the training problematic. Mahoney (1994, pp. 177–93) describes 'a little learning [as] . . . a dangerous thing' and he documents the development of governor training in the UK during the period 1987/94 at a time when there were significant additional roles and responsibilities bestowed on governors. He concludes that, at that time, the role of governors was only covertly democratic and managerial and that:

> the challenges for the year 2000 and beyond are how to make the illusion of democracy a reality. How can governors be involved as active citizens in the management of schools? How can there be protection and extension of the many varied and excellent governor training initiatives undertaken so far?' (*ibid.*, p. 191).

An example of how this may be addressed is provided by Smith (2000, p. 28), who reports on an initiative in Wales. The recently established Welsh Assembly is keen to improve governor training and has set up a centre specialising in this and governor research at Swansea University's School of Education. The centre has started its work by analysing existing training provision and assessing future needs of governors in Wales, and intends to draw comparisons with practice in England and other countries.

Activity

Find out about governor training in your school or college:

- Who is responsible for governor training?
- How is it organised?
- How are the differences in governors' backgrounds and learning styles catered for?
- Is it compulsory?
- What is the uptake?
- What are the governors' views on it?
- How is it evaluated?

❑ Our comments

The key questions above highlight the areas of difficulty for governor training. There are no easy answers. We suggest that managers need to ensure, as far as possible, that the training offered to their governors is of the highest quality and that the relationship between the school or college and its governors is such that the commitment of the latter ensures full participation in training is normal.

Conclusions: issues for management

Whilst various models of governance can be identified which fulfil different degrees of accountability, the role of governors remains ambiguous, especially in countries where new systems of governance are in place. There may be strong political representation, such as the presence of the Communist Party secretary on governing bodies in China, or strong religious affiliations to be taken into account. There is potential tension between the professional and the lay, between governors and managers, which can be difficult to reconcile:

> Governing bodies are . . . faced with reconciling the demands of professional and lay interests at two levels: first, within the governing body itself . . . and secondly, between the governing body as a whole and the school it governs. There is potential for conflict at both levels, as these two interests have different, and sometimes opposing, aims, purposes and approaches to the issues they jointly face (Pascal, 1989, p. 88).

There may be difficulties in recruiting people to a role that is generally unpaid, yet can carry a significant level of responsibility and further problems associated with governors' availability and motivation to be trained.

It is a tribute to governing bodies around the world that, in this context, people do come forward in the spirit of community involvement and shared expertise to participate in this work. Success will depend on the level of partnership achieved and a clear understanding of respective roles. This is summed up by Sallis (1995, p. 116):

> The key to a working relationship . . . is the sense of collegiality, of shared purpose, that the governing body is able to develop . . . First, governors and staff must share an understanding of their respective roles. Secondly, they must develop the confidence in each other to fulfil those roles in partnership, with the aim of improving the quality of education within the school.

❑ Building on key learning points

- Governors are accountable for the overall effectiveness of the school or college and the use of public monies.
- Governors have a key role to play in terms of the strategic direction and management of a school or college.
- There are various theoretical models of governing bodies given in the literature.
- The composition, roles and responsibilities of governing bodies of maintained schools and colleges are laid down in legislation.
- In many parts of the world the shift towards self-management of schools and colleges has brought with it more responsibility for governing bodies.
- In the UK there have been incidences of tension between school and college managers and governors.
- Partnership is considered the way forward for governing bodies and their school or college.

---

8. Conclusions: a final word on accountability

Throughout this book, the focus has been upon the levels of autonomy schools or colleges possess; this in turn is based upon the degree of self-management the educational system of the country confers upon the institution. The balancing factor upon which autonomy rests is accountability: if an institution is given a level of freedom in which to operate, it is accountable to those who confer that freedom. At a macro level, four dimensions of accountability can be identified:

1. *Political*: in a system that is supported by public funds, the institution is accountable for the best use of those funds.
2. *Market*: it is accountable to its customers, partners and stakeholders.
3. *Professional*: schools and colleges are accountable for maintaining the highest possible standards of teaching and training.
4. *Cultural*: education can be seen as fostering new insights, knowledge and understanding; it can be a force for change in society (after Scott, P. 1989).

The situation of accountability is delegated and dispersed within the school or college to a greater or lesser degree, according to the policies and systems in operation and the leadership styles of the senior managers. For example, if responsibility for managing part of the school budget or for managing a section of the external affairs of the college is delegated, the manager to whom it is delegated is accountable to the whole institution for carrying out that responsibility successfully.

We hope the various chapters of this book have enabled you to understand the level of self-management, and therefore the context of accountability, within which you work. Hopefully, you will have understood that there are many frameworks for analysing the activities of your school or college, with regard to its management of finance, resources and stakeholders. Whilst one particular framework may seem to apply best to one type of institution, none is offered as prescriptive: it is often through considering a situation through a range of perspectives – such as those we have offered on managing stakeholders – that an appropriate way of analysing the management of your own institution may become clear.

The final thought on accountability should rest upon the quality of the learning experience offered to the individual child or student. The school or college does not exist for its own sake, but for the sake of its children and students: the management of the institution's resources, and the effectiveness with which it operates in the educational market-place, can best be judged by their direct and indirect impact upon the learning experience.

Appendix: Self-management in education – vignettes from around the world

The vignettes that follow provide an insight into the ways in which governments around the world have structured their education systems in recent times, with particular emphasis on policy shifts towards self-management. We make no apology for the variation in the detail provided; to some extent this is indicative of the level of development of the concept in that country. It is also a function of the fact that legislation and policies change with time and governments so that producing a definitive 'pen picture' of levels of responsibility and control of financial and resource management in different education systems is not straightforward. However, in reading and considering them, you will develop your own understanding of the situation you are presently working in, as well as your awareness of the way in which it compares with the phenomenon internationally.

Authors who provided material or who offered comments on self-management in their country are acknowledged in the individual vignettes.

Australia

Caldwell and Spinks (1998) describe the steady shift to self-management in Australia over the last 25 years. They highlight Victoria as having the 'most noteworthy manifestation of self-managing schools' (*ibid.*, p. 8). It began in 1983 when school councils (the equivalent of governing bodies) were given the authority to determine the education policy of the school, within guidelines provided by the Minister for Education, and to approve the budget. By the end of 1992, school councils had budgetary control of all items except teaching staff salaries. The following year saw the election of the Liberal–National Party coalition government and the launch of the 'Schools of the Future' (1993) programme. Although the pilot programme was initially intended to include 100 schools, over 700 schools applied and 320 entered its first phase. Successive expansions have meant the vast majority of Victorian schools are now in the programme, nearly all intermediate levels of government have been removed and the state department of education is only one quarter of its original size (Whitty *et al.*, 1998, p. 24).

Under the Schools of the Future framework, each school is governed by a school council of up to 15 members, of which no more than one third can be education system employees. More than 90% of the state education budget is decentralised to schools and the councils have responsibility for recruiting staff. Although there was some curriculum flexibility initially, schools are now required to operate within frameworks for the curriculum and standards and for accountability. The latter provides annual reports to the education department and the community and a triennial review that assures external validation. Coherence is attained by means of a school charter that sets out the distinctive nature of the school and the manner in which it addresses systems and local priorities. The charter has a life of three years and, thus, is linked to the triennial review. The second terms of the Liberal–National Coalition from 1996 brought a consolidation of Schools of the Future, with a modest initiative under the banner of 'Schools of the Third Millennium', in which some schools may seek a higher level of autonomy (Caldwell and Spinks, 1998, p. 8). However, Maslen (1999) reports the abandonment of self-governing schools in 2000 as part of the new Labour government's rationalisation of the previous administration's education policies. The education minister, Mary Delahunty, is reported as telling the state parliament: 'From next year [2000], all schools will enjoy the same funding and employment conditions. We believe all students should have the opportunity to achieve excellence wherever they are' (*ibid.*, p. 5).

Although the reforms are considered by some to have been one of the most advanced approaches to decentralised school management (Odden, 1995, p. 10), Whitty *et al.* (1998, p. 25) point out that they need to be seen against a background of sharp reductions in the level of resourcing from the state. During 1993/94, over 600 schools were closed and there was a 20% reduction in the number of teachers employed as a result. Moreover, they point out that the introduction of the curriculum and standards framework has increased direct state control over the curriculum.

There have been similar developments in other states and territories. In 1987 the publication of the *Better Schools* report heralded the devolution of many administrative responsibilities to schools in Western Australia. Described by Caldwell and Spinks (1998, p. 8) as 'modest developments', the state determined each school's block grant and basic staffing entitlement but schools were given responsibility for teacher selection and non-staff budgets. The report also introduced the 'unit' curriculum and mechanisms for monitoring performance.

In the same year, the Northern Territory government set out its plans in the document, *Towards the 90s*. Although in many ways similar to *Better Schools*, it did retain more functions at the centre. New South Wales implemented its first decentralisation programme with the publication of the Scott report, *Schools Renewal* (Scott, B. 1989). This involved the restructuring of school management to enable self-management as well as deregulating school zones to stimulate competition. New kinds of specialised schools were also introduced and a gradual return to academic selection. Developments in South Australia are described by Ryan (1993). Significant powers have been delegated to school principals alongside the introduction of teacher competences. In Queensland, similarly, the publication of *Focus on Schools* (cited in Whitty *et al.*, 1998, p. 24) in 1990 described the restructuring of its education system. The 'Leading Schools' programme that followed meant that, by 1998, significant steps in the self-management of schools had been achieved. The Tasmanian programme, 'Directions in Education', has produced similar outcomes.

Finally, Whitty *et al.* (1998) point to the large private school sector in Australia and its part in the picture of self-management in that country. Accounting for almost one third of student enrolments, the federal government subsidises all private schools using a sliding scale formula that is linked to their private resources from fees and donations. This subsidy varies from 12% to almost half the average cost of educating a pupil and, in all cases, it is topped up by state government.

Hong Kong

Vincent Chiu Shiu Yim, Senior Lecturer, Hong Kong Institute of Education, Hong Kong.

The 1990s saw important developments in self-management in schools in Hong Kong where only 8% of its approximately 1,200 schools are government schools. The other schools, in the so-called aided sector, are owned by a range of foundations, trusts, churches and private organisations. However, all schools receive substantial funding from government and there are very few truly private schools (Caldwell and Spinks, 1998, p. 10).

Following a review of the public sector, the report *The School Management Initiative: Setting the Framework for Quality in Hong Kong Schools* (Education and Manpower Branch and Education Department, 1991) formed the basis of a major policy initiative within the public sector. Entitled the 'School Management Initiative' (SMI), the programme was run in preparation in 1991/92 with 21 participating schools and in 1992/93 with an additional 13 schools. The following year, 1993/94, SMI was formally started and, by 1997, 290 schools had volunteered to join the scheme, including most government schools. Under SMI, a large proportion of government grant was decentralised to a local level providing schools with the opportunity to involve the community as well as their teachers in decision-making. Additionally, new accountability mechanisms were adopted. Wong *et al.* (1998, p. 67) quote an official aim of the

SMI as 'to encourage more systematic planning and evaluation of programmes of activities in schools and reporting their performance' (Education Department, 1991).

However, with a view to encouraging schools to achieve quality education and to develop their own individuality and characteristics, SMI was replaced in 1997 by school-based management. All public sector schools were now required to submit a school report for the 1998/99 school year as well as establish a constitution for a school management committee. The latter has responsibility for managing the school on behalf of the government and a sponsoring body (which contributes the full cost of furnishing and equipping the premises). In 1999, an advisory committee was set up to develop a framework of governance for school-based management as part of a strategy to enhance transparency and accountability of schools and, in February 2000, the advisory committee published a report on improving schools in which it stated:

> The school management committee (SMC) should set goals and draw up policies in teaching and learning, administration, finance and personnel matters . . . [it] should have a clear constitution to govern its operation and should comprise representatives of the School Sponsoring Bodies, teachers, parents, alumni and other persons appointed by the Director of Education where necessary (Advisory Committee on School-Based Management, 2000, p. 9).

SMCs are also required to have a participatory decision-making mechanism and a staff performance management system in place by the start of the 2001/02 school year.

Israel

Tova Ron, The Centre for Educational Technology, Israel.

Transition towards school self-management in Israel has been very gradual, beginning with the notion of autonomous schools. The original proposal by Yonai (1984), Foor (1985) and Reshef (1985), for school development, was that each school would initiate certain activities to promote its autonomy:

- defining school educational policy and planning its own procedures;
- developing a school-based curriculum;
- conducting procedures of educational assessment;
- integrating the school community into its activities, collaboratively; and
- creating mechanisms of staff development and involvement in decision-making.

At that stage, there was some mention of financial autonomy; however, even the most daring principals rejected it in view of massive budget reductions. On the other hand, local authorities that receive educational budgets and allocate funding to schools were not keen to give up easily this kind of power, and rejected any proposed change.

During the late 1980s and the early 1990s, about a hundred primary schools carried out some autonomous procedures, with academic support from the Experimental Unit for Educational Autonomy, in the School of Education at Tel Aviv University. Meanwhile, defining school policy has become a widespread phenomenon in primary schools, less so in high schools. Principals considered that, while primary schools are academically stress-free, high schools are committed to their students' success in matriculation and are thus not liberated to form any other focus of policy. This may explain why school-based curricula and assessment have been developed in part of the primary school system only.

The notion of self-governance in education, although discussed in Israel since the 1970s, has been practised in a limited format, as indicated, since the mid-1980s (Friedman, 1994). In 1993, the recommendations of a steering committee for self-managed schools were accepted as an official policy of the Israeli Ministry of Education (State of Israel, Ministry of Education, 1993; Friedman and Brama, 1998) and the ministry initiated steps for its realisation. The official announcement declared that, within seven years, all Israeli schools would be self-managed (State of Israel, Ministry of Education, 1993).

The recommendations (*ibid.*) included a draft of the 'seven-year plan' for the transition, including an increase of 70 million Israeli shekels of primary education budget, pooling of all existing educational budgets and school flexibility in conducting their financial procedures.

In order to assist schools and local authorities during the transition, the Ministry of Education formed a training centre for school principals. It also advised local authorities about the process and persuaded them to join it. Principals who function in 'recruited' towns studied in the centre, taking the course of three annual seminars for two years. The main topics in these seminars (adapted from State of Israel, Department of Planning, 1997) are as follows:

1. *Presenting the topic of self-governed schools*: principles and models around the world and within the Israeli experience; opportunities and risks; and attitudes of different participants towards the change.
2. *Forming a learning organisation*: andragogy, learning styles, resources for teaching and learning.
3. *Accountability*: the school as an accountable leading organisation, in relation to its consumers.
4. *Decentralisation, empowerment and dividing authority*: the tension for principals between authority, collaboration and accountability; patterns of collaborative management.
5. *School-based curriculum*: forming an organisational ethos at the school; the hidden agenda within the school curriculum; principles and practice of planning a curriculum.
6. *How to use consultation*: defining the need to consult; choosing a consultant and deciding about his or her roles; and consumers – the main role of the principal.

One of the first municipalities to join the enterprise was Jerusalem. Its municipality chose 13 elementary schools that started the three years' transition process. Moreover, it ordered accompanying research in order to draw practical conclusions.

Besides describing the process from the point of view of the various participants, Friedman and Brama (1998) draw some conclusions regarding this transformation:

1. Local authority attempts to gain power may damage and slow the process
2. The participation of principals and financial functionaries in formal teamwork may help to reduce their fear and objection
3. Principals expected to gain more resources and plan them independently, but feared bureaucracy and an overload of work
4. Supervisors still expected to gain a higher degree of control over the chosen schools' resources and functioning.

Key issues that emerged at this stage (State of Israel, Department of Planning, 1997) concerned mainly the public inspection of budgeting, school profits and risks, and the benefits and risks for local authorities and the Ministry of Education.

Middle East: Dubai College

Dr Steve Lewis, Dubai College, United Arab Emirates.

Dubai College is a fee-paying, British curriculum, selective, mixed secondary school that serves the needs of children of expatriate families in Dubai. There are currently around 710 pupils, and the fees are between £6,000 and £6,800 per annum. It is a non-profit making school administered by a board of governors.

There is a bursar and an accountant. The budget is submitted annually to the board for approval, who delegate financial responsibility to the bursar for the running of the school. He allocates the budget into cost centres, which are subdivided, and decisions are taken in consultation with the headmaster, who shares the responsibility. The board do not intervene in the day-to-day financial running of the school unless targets are exceeded, and the bursar therefore not only has a great deal of control over the budget but also a high level of accountability in his position as bursar and clerk to the governors. The bursar has the authority to allocate funds and pay bills, although if the sum exceeds dirhams 500,000 (£8,500), the concurrence of the treasurer on the board is required. Therefore there are checks and balances within the system. For example, if there is an excess of 10% on a cost centre it must be reported to the board treasurer. The role of the accountant is to look after the accounts and not be involved in policy.

The role of the board of governors is to establish the overall strategy of Dubai College rather than the running of the school, and this is therefore a non-executive role since the running of the school is the responsibility of the head and the bursar. The board will therefore not disagree with decisions made, but will determine costs and timings. One function of the board is the appointment of the head and bursar, who report directly to them, but not the appointment of other staff. The board will only intervene in the running of the school if they feel policies are being adopted that conflict with their overall strategic vision.

The composition of the board is subject to the Ruler of Dubai's edict and consists of 11 members, with a chairman, deputy chairman and treasurer. Board members are invited to join and they are prominent people within professions, and it is hoped that at least some of the members within this category will be a parent (currently two). There is no staff member.

The main financial issues for a self-managing school of this type are as follows:

1. To set the right level of fees to provide sufficient resources. This must be realistic, particularly in view of the cost of recruiting staff from the UK – the school provides flights and free accommodation – which is a large expense that goes far beyond basic salary.
2. To ensure the local Ministry of Education approves the fee structure.
3. To take into account fluctuations in exchange control, although this is not a major issue for this school.
4. To make sure the school is run cost-effectively and that parents can see their fees are being properly deployed.

The financial situation of Dubai College is very healthy. The school always pays its bills on time and is highly respected within the community because of this, as well as its excellent academic reputation. Financial systems need upgrading to take into account school expansion over the years, but the appointment of a full-time school accountant who is a UK-qualified chartered accountant, the assistant bursar who takes care of local issues and the bursar in overall control ensures Dubai College is managed financially very effectively.

New Zealand

John O'Neill, Massey University, Palmerston North, New Zealand.

New Zealand was, perhaps, a surprising context for radical experimentation in self-management. Not only were the reforms introduced by a Labour government but, unlike in England and the USA, there had been no widespread concern about educational standards in the public system (Whitty *et al.*, 1998, p. 21). However, it seems that after a period of 'progressivist policies typical of earlier Labour administrations' (Snook *et al.*, 1999, p. 2) education policy was seen to be out of step with the New Right (Conservative) reforms of the Finance Minister, Roger Douglas. Pressure from Douglas and the Treasury (Codd, 1991) resulted in a taskforce being set up under the chairmanship of businessman, Brian Picot. The report that emerged from this group, the *Picot Report* (Picot, 1988), together with the government's response, *Tomorrow's Schools*, provided the basis for the reforms.

At one swoop, in 1989, responsibility for budget allocation, staff employment and educational outcomes shifted from central government and regional educational boards to individual schools. Boards of trustees were appointed that initially consisted of parents, although 'up to four others could be co-opted to provide additional expertise, or to provide gender, ethnic or class "balance" ' (Wylie, 1994, p. 65). This was followed in 1991 by the introduction of dezoning (open enrolment), which created a schooling market-place as well as the option for schools to be 'bulk funded' for teachers' salaries. The latter was based on average teacher costs initially and it was not until 1999 that the fully funded option was introduced whereby (most) schools in the scheme were funded at the top of the teachers' salary scale irrespective of actual costs of their teachers. However, at the time of writing, the serving Labour–Alliance coalition government's Education Amendment Bill 2000 had just been approved by Parliament and was about to reverse both these situations. Zoning control was to be reintroduced and bulk funding abolished. From the start of the school year 2001, all schools were to be centrally resourced for teachers' salaries once again.

Wylie (*ibid.*, p. xv) argues that the New Zealand reforms 'offer a model of school self management which is more balanced than the English experience' in that there is a 'great emphasis on equity . . . on community involvement . . . on parental involvement [and on] partnership: between parents and professionals'. This view is supported by Beckett (1991), who suggests the reforms in New Zealand gave 'parents a great deal more power than the British version, and arrived without the ideological baggage'. However, Caldwell and Spinks (1998, p. 8) point out that the reforms 'stopped short of what occurred in Britain and Victoria [Australia] in respect to budgeting for staff'. Only a small proportion of schools took up the 'bulk funding' option for teachers' salaries.

Pakistan

The nationalisation of private schools and colleges in Pakistan in 1972 under the Martial Law regulation 118 (Government of Punjab, 1982) brought with it a heavy financial burden on the exchequer as well as causing local initiative to come to a halt. This situation was summarised in the government's sixth Five Year Plan:

> The nearly comprehensive nationalisation of educational institutions and accompanying policy of free education ten years ago had at least two casualties. An already impoverished Government was landed with a large financial burden which restricted it from expanding education. And many of the schools of high quality, some of them run by education conscious communities, lost excellence under public control. This, in both quantity and quality, was counter-productive (Government of Pakistan, 1983, pp. 318–19).

It was clear the policy had to be reversed, and the ban on private schools and colleges was lifted and, through various measures, the private sector was given a boost.

Following on from this, the report of a World Bank delegation on the current circumstances and possible future developments in education in 1989 recommended financial and administrative autonomy for schools and colleges (see World Bank, 1989, paras. 132, 133, 134). In particular, it found favour with 'this neutral status in the case of Degree Colleges' (Khan, 1993) and recommended that 'Some colleges should be accredited with full operational autonomy . . . The Board of Trustees would establish the rules and standards and procedures under which the institutions would function, and those would of course vary across institutions' (World Bank, 1989, para. 158).

Consequently, in 1989, the Government of Punjab introduced a new scheme that granted autonomy initially to a few prestigious institutions and then extended it gradually to other colleges. The policy required each autonomous institution to be run by a board of governors comprising ex-officio members, local industrialists, public representatives and 'eminent educationalists' with the board chairman appointed by the Governor of Punjab Government. The board of governors have responsibility for formulating the budget of the institution for approval by the government, for the recruitment of staff and the determination of their terms and conditions of service, for the acquisition and disposal of property and other contracts, for the management of the college and for fund-raising. The government grant was fixed at the 1989/90 level, and colleges were free to set their own fee structure. Student admissions were to remain on a merit basis according to government instructions and a liberal scholarship programme provided for 'poor and talented' students. Decentralisation – or even 'privatisation in the guise of autonomy' (Khan, 1993) – and the involvement of the community in the management of education were seen to be the main objectives of the policy.

Iqbal and Davies (1994) report on their study of two autonomous colleges in Punjab, based on the reactions of principals and heads of departments (senior managers), teachers, students and parents. Their findings pointed up seven themes:

1. types of autonomy desired;
2. political interference;
3. social divisiveness;
4. teacher resistance;
5. consumers;
6. standards; and
7. competition between institutions.

From these results they suggest that 'autonomy' was not working and that the negative perceptions of staff outweighed the more optimistic interpretations from user groups. They conclude by concurring with Bolam (1993) in being pessimistic about the impact of self-management on schools and colleges and their users.

South Africa

Professor Mike Thurlow, University of Natal, Durban, South Africa.

The end of apartheid in 1994 marked the start of a period of change in South Africa in nearly every aspect of society. Education was no exception. The new Department of Education radically shifted the direction and vision of the education system with a series of policy initiatives and new legislation (Department of Education, South Africa, 1996). By 1996, education administration had been devolved from national to provincial level and the South African Schools Act 1996 introduced legislation that established school governing bodies on a country-wide basis. This placed substantial decision-making authority in the schools and is significant in that the required composition of governing bodies put parents in the majority. Additionally, from grade 8 upwards, learners (pupils) are also represented and have full rights as school governors.

At the same time, in February 1996, the Minister of Education appointed a Task Team on Education Management Development with a nine-month brief to address four education management development objectives. In their report (*ibid.*, p. 29) they set out a new approach to education management and management development, and state: 'At the heart of the policy and legislative initiatives is the process of decentralising decision making about the allocation of resources to school level.' They proposed an integrative and collaborative approach to education management that involves all staff and stakeholders and informs all management processes and outcomes in an organisational setting.

The task team's report was endorsed by the Minister of Education and, since 1997, all those involved with education, be it at the national, provincial, regional, district or individual school level, have been working to prepare and implement a whole host of initiatives that are aimed at addressing the inequalities among South African schools with a view to raising educational standards across the country. One way in which this is being tackled is through the allocation of recurrent funding of public schools on the basis of need, determined according to the conditions at the school and the poverty of the community served by it. These two factors are weighted equally and are used to produce five groups of schools. Resources are then allocated by group to favour the poorest schools with the overall effect that the 'better off' schools may receive just 5% of resources available.

Despite this approach, for many schools serving the deprived urban areas as well as the vast majority of the rural ones, the lack of resources is a key issue. It seems that even the allocation of teaching staff is being reduced as a result of the government's policy of 'right sizing'. The principle of this policy is to equalise staffing across schools that were formerly categorised for different groups of pupils, but research undertaken by the staff from the University of Leicester's Educational Management Development Unit suggests staff allocations at most schools are being reduced.

There is considerable variation as to the actual opportunity for educational managers in South African schools to manage finance and resources. There is little devolution to schools and no choice about the few resources that are provided. Many schools, particularly the former 'black' and 'coloured' ones, are just grateful for whatever resources come to them. However, there is an opportunity for schools to generate income through fees and other means. One of the governors' responsibilities is to hold an annual meeting for parents at which the fees for that year are set, and thereafter to implement the decision made. Inevitably, there is a wide range in the fee rates that are applied. These vary according to the school setting and background of the pupils.

In some former 'white' schools parents pay termly fees that generate significant income which, in turn, enables governors to employ additional staff – both teaching and support – over and above the number supported by the state so they are able to compensate for the reduction in staffing levels mentioned above. Furthermore, these schools are able to provide generous teaching resources and high-quality accommodation. In other schools, especially rural former 'black' and 'coloured' schools, the fees have to be set at a very low rate because of the local circumstances. These, of course, are the schools with extremely poor facilities and inadequate resources. Some schools attempt to generate additional income through tuck shops and/or growing produce to sell.

Similar developments are taking place in post-compulsory education. National restructuring has led to the development of a policy for further education and training as well as the establishment of a 'National Qualifications Framework' and a shift to outcomes-based education in all phases of education. As Lumby (2000b, p. 102) notes: 'there is recognition that further education has a particular role to play in reconstruction, in offering the second chance so desperately needed by large numbers of the population, and in training the craftspeople, technicians and entrepreneurs who will be critical to economic development'.

However, she goes on to note that, as with schools, the resources provided by the state and/or the provincial education department are extremely limited and, like schools, colleges also depend on student fees. These are paid by the individual or his or her employer. Additionally, colleges also receive donations from business and industry.

From her research, Lumby concludes that planning links between the macro-level – national, provincial and regional – and local needs are inadequate and require urgent attention (*ibid.*, p. 116) in order to ensure the ongoing development of further education in South Africa as a means of 'offering life enhancing opportunities to individuals and contributing to local and national economic prosperity' (*ibid.*, p. 117).

Sweden

Despite a strong tradition of centralism, Sweden, too, embarked on a process of restructuring and devolution during the last quarter of the twentieth century. Hirsch (1994) identifies a two-stage process of devolution that began in the mid-1970s with decentralisation of responsibility from central government to municipalities or local *kommuns*. In 1991 the central state ceased to regulate teaching appointments and headships and the municipalities eventually took over full responsibility for organising and implementing school activities (Swedish Institute, 1995). Since 1996, each municipality has received a government grant to fund obligatory services, including education. Thus, Swedish reforms appear to differ from those in other countries in terms of an enhanced, rather than reduced, role for local democratic influence (Whitty *et al.*, 1998, p. 28).

However, Englund (1993) has identified a gradual shift from collectivism to individualism within the Swedish school system during the 1980s, with education being regarded as a private rather than public good. This view is supported first by the Social Democratic government's approved proposal to distribute funds to private schools before it lost power in 1991 and, secondly, by the 'free choice revolution' that took place on the election of a centre–right coalition government at that time. This 'revolution' emphasised competition and choice by supporting the private provision and by encouraging state schools to develop specialisms within the national curriculum and, in some cases, between schools. Schemes were also put in place whereby funding follows the pupil – for example, in the municipality of Nacka, 85% of its budget is allocated directly to schools on the basis of pupil numbers (Chapman *et al.*, 1996, p. 7).

Although the move towards quasi-markets in Sweden was largely driven by economic pressure and the political and ideological motivation of the centre–right government, these markets were, in the main, not abandoned but modified when the Social Democrats were returned to power in 1994 (Whitty *et al.*, 1998, p. 29). Furthermore, alongside the trend to devolved management and financial responsibility, in line with other countries, the central government in Sweden has maintained a significant measure of control over curriculum content and evaluation of performance. As Lundgren (undated, p. 1) comments, the reforms can be 'characterised as a deregulation, but . . . also a sharpening of rules and demands'.

United States of America

Not surprisingly, as the federal system of the USA makes education primarily a state matter, the range of forms and purposes of initiatives concerned with school self-management – or school-based management as it is termed in North America – over the past 30 years make it difficult to generalise (Caldwell and Spinks, 1998, p. 9). Caldwell and Spinks (*ibid.*) describe developments in California and Florida in the 1970s, and more in Florida in Dade County in the 1980s, as 'significant'. However, the 1990s brought widespread reform in a bid to improve the quality of public education. Indeed, Ogawa and White's (1994) claim was that three quarters of America's school districts had introduced school self-management, while Newmann (1993) includes parental choice, greater school autonomy and shared decision-making as among the 11 most popular restructuring reforms. During the 1990s there were federal interventions as seen in the context of 'America 2000' (1991) and 'Goals 2000' (1994) which, according to Whitty *et al.* (1998, p. 26), 'exhibit something of the same tension between centralising and decentralising measures to be found in England and Wales and New Zealand . . . [therefore] the role of the federal Department of Education has had to be largely one of exhortation'. Indeed, Caldwell and Spinks' (1998, p. 9) comment that 'only rarely did these developments involve a central determined framework of the kind that emerged in Britain and Victoria' adds support to this view.

Among the most well known were the reforms in Chicago. Even though the Illinois legislature passed three major education bills, each promoting strategies to improve public education during the late 1980s and the 1990s, the reforms were very particular to the city (Whitty *et al.*, 1998, p. 26). They stress community empowerment in the form of school councils and state-directed accountability rather than the marketisation of education as elsewhere.

The localised nature of reforms is further demonstrated by the 'Charter School' initiative. Although the policy enjoys cross-party support and is underwritten financially by a programme of federal grants, charter school legislation has to be adopted on a state-by-state basis. Thus, there is variability in the way the policy is interpreted and implemented (*ibid.*, p. 27). Furthermore, Wells *et al.* (1996, p. 8) argue 'charter schools reflect the unique political struggle over the meaning of this reform in each state and local community'. None the less, according to Caldwell and Spinks (1998, p. 10), about half of the states have adopted the legislation.

The charter schools movement represents a 'bottom-up' approach in that it allows a group of teachers, parents or others who share similar educational views and interests to draw up an agreement – or charter – and to organise and operate a school. Charter schools are vested with decision-making authority in areas such as the budget, staffing and the curriculum, in exchange for which they are held accountable for agreed standards of performance (Wohlstetter and Anderson, 1994). Comparisons have been made between charter schools and the UK's grant-maintained schools (Wohlstetter and Anderson, 1994) although, as Caldwell and Spinks (1998, p. 10) point out, charter schools 'go further'.

References

Adler, M., Petch, A. and Tweedie, J. (1989) *Parental Choice and Educational Policy*, Edinburgh, Edinburgh University Press.

Advisory Committee on School-Based Management (2000) *Transforming Schools into Dynamic and Accountable Professional Learning Communities: School-Based Management Consultation Document*, Hong Kong, The Government Printer.

Ainley, P. and Bailey, B. (1997) *The Business of Learning: Staff and Student Experiences of Further Education in the 1999s*, London, Cassell.

Anderson, L. (2000a) Farewell to grant maintained status: the future of self-governing schools, *School Leadership and Management*, 20(3) 371–85.

Anderson, L. (2000b) The move towards entrepreneurialism, in Coleman, M. and Anderson, L. (eds.) *Managing Finance and Resources in Education*, London, Paul Chapman.

Angus, L. (1993) Democratic participation or efficient site management: the social and political location of the self-managing school, in Smyth, J. (ed.) *A Socially Critical View of the Self-Managing School*, London, Falmer Press.

Angus, L. (1995) Devolution of school governance in an Australian state school system: third time lucky?, in Carter, D.S.G. and O'Neill, M.H. (eds.) *Case Studies in Educational Change: An International Perspective*, London, Falmer Press.

Ardley, B. (1994) College marketing and the management of change, *Journal of Further and Higher Education*, 18(1) 3–13.

Arthur, J. (1993) Policy perceptions of headteachers and governors in Catholic schooling, *Educational Studies*, 19(3) 215–87.

Atkinson, D. (1997) *Towards Self-governing Schools*, London, The Institute of Economic Affairs Education and Training Unit.

Audit Commission (1993) *Unfinished Business: Full Time Educational Course for 16–19 Year Olds*, London, Ofsted.

Bacon, W. (1978) *Public Accountability and the School System: A Sociology of School Board Democracy*, London, Harper & Row.

Baginsky, M., Baker, L. and Cleave, S. (1991) *Towards Effective Partnerships in School Governance*, Slough, NFER.

Bagley, C., Woods, P. and Glatter, R. (1996) Scanning the market: school strategies for discovering parental preferences, in Preedy, M. *et al.* (eds.) *Educational Management: Strategy, Quality and Resources*, Buckingham, Open University Press.

Ball, S.J. (1990a) *Politics and Policymaking in Education*, London, Routledge.

Ball, S.J. (1990b) Management as a moral technology, in Ball, S.J. (ed.) *Foucault and Education*, London, Routledge.

Ball, S.J. (1994) *Education Reform: A Critical and Post-Structural Approach*, Buckingham, Open University Press.

Barker, R. (1994) Community service: review of David Selbourne's 'The principle of duty: an essay on the foundation of civic order', *The Times Higher Educational Supplement*, 14 October.

Beare, H. and Boyd, W.L. (eds.) (1993) *Restructuring Schools*, London, Falmer Press.

Beare, H., Caldwell, B. and Millikan, R. (1992) *Creating Excellent Schools: Some New Management Techniques*, London, Routledge.

Beckett, F. (1991) Power to whom?, *Education*, 8 March.

Beckett, F. (1999) Oratory belies the empty rhetoric, *The Times Educational Supplement*, 8 October, p. 20.

Bell, L. (1998) Back to the future: the development of site-based management in England with messages, challenges and a vision for Australia. Keynote address to the twenty-fifth Australian Council for Educational Administration international conference, Conrad Jupiters, Gold Coast, 27–30 September.

Bell, L. (1999) Primary schools and the educational market place, in Bush, T. *et al.* (eds.) *Educational Management: Redefining Theory, Policy and Practice*, London, Paul Chapman.

Bell, L. (2000) The management of staff: some issues of efficiency and cost-effectiveness, in Coleman, M. and Anderson, L. (eds.) *Managing Finance and Resources in Education*, London, Paul Chapman.

Bisschoff, T. (2000) Functions of school governing bodies in South Africa – first steps towards school-based management, *Management in Education*, 14(3) 12–13.

Bolam, R. (1993) School-based management, school improvement and social effectiveness: overview and implications, in Clive, D. (ed.) *School-Based Management and School Effectiveness*, London, Routledge.

Booth, C. and Hill, J. (1996) Power without responsibility, *The Times Educational Supplement*, 21 June, p. 20.

Bowe, R. and Ball, S.J. with Gold, A. (1992) *Reforming Education and Changing Schools*, London, Routledge.

Bray, M. (1990) The quality of education in multi-shift schools: how far does a financial saving imply an educational cost?, *Comparative Education*, 26(1) 73–81.

Brehony, K.J. (1992) 'Active citizens': the case of school governors, *International Studies in Sociology of Education*, 2(2) 199–216.

Briggs, A.R.J. (in press, due for publication 2001) Managing the learning environment, in Burton, N. and Middlewood, D. (eds.) *Managing the Curriculum in Schools and Colleges*, London, Paul Chapman.

Briggs, P. (1992) Finance, in Limb, A. *et al.* (eds.) *The Road to Incorporation*, Blagdon, The Staff College and the Association of Colleges for Further and Higher Education.

Brigley, S. (1990) The recomposition of school governing bodies: does parent power exist?, *Open University Education Reform Research Group. Occasional Paper Series 2*, Milton Keynes, Open University.

Brigley, S. (1994) Voice trumps choice: parents confront governors on opting out, in Thody, A. (ed.) *School Governors: Leaders or Followers?*, Harlow, Longman.

Brooks, C. (1993) Further education, in Morris, R. (ed.) *Education and the Law*, Harlow, Longman.

Brown, D. (1990) *Decentralization and School-Based Management*, London, Falmer Press.

Brown, M. and Rutherford, D. (1998) Changing roles and raising standards: new challenges for heads of department, *School Leadership and Management*, 18(1) 75–88.

Bullock, A. and Thomas, H. (1997) *Schools at the Centre?*, London, Routledge.

Burton, N. (1999) Efficient and effective staff deployment, in Brundrett, M. (ed.) *Principles of School Leadership*, Dereham, Peter Francis.

Burton, N. (2000) Lessons from the first Beacon schools, in Brundrett, M. and Burton, N. (eds.) *The Beacon Schools Experience: Case Studies in Excellence*, Dereham, Peter Francis.

Bush, T. (1986) *Theories of Educational Management*, London, Harper & Row.

Bush, T. (1994) Accountability in education, in Bush, T. and West-Burnham, J. (eds.) *The Principles of Educational Management*, Harlow, Longman.

Bush, T. (1995) *Theories of Educational Management*, London, Paul Chapman.

Bush, T. (1999a) The vanishing boundaries: the importance of effective external relations, in Lumby, J. and Foskett, N. (eds.) *Managing External Relations in Schools and Colleges*, London, Paul Chapman.

Bush, T. (ed.) (1999b) *Educational Management: Redefining Theory, Policy and Practice*, London, Paul Chapman.

Bush, T., Coleman, M. and Glover, D. (1993) *Managing Autonomous Schools: The Grant Maintained Experience*, London, Paul Chapman.

Bush, T., Coleman, M. and Si, X. (1998) Managing secondary schools in China, *Compare*, 28(2) 183–95.

Bush, T. and Middlewood, D. (1997) *Managing People in Education*, London, Paul Chapman.

Bush, T. and West-Burnham, J. (1994) *Principles of Educational Management*, London, Paul Chapman.

Cairns, J. (1998) Placing value on consensus: an elusive goal, *Curriculum Journal*, 9(1) 23–39.

Caldwell, B. (1993) Paradox and uncertainty in the governance of education, in Beare, H. and Boyd, W.L. (eds.) *Restructuring Schools*, London, Falmer Press.

Caldwell, B. (1994) Structural reform in a global context: an international perspective on self-managing and self-governing schools and their potential for improving the quality of schooling. Paper given at Loughborough University, March.

Caldwell, B. and Spinks, J. (1988) *The Self-Managing School*, London, Falmer Press.

Caldwell, B. and Spinks, J. (1992) *Leading the Self-Managing School*, London, Falmer Press.

Caldwell, B. and Spinks, J. (1998) *Beyond the Self-Managing School*, London, Falmer Press.

Campbell, R. (1985) *Developing the Primary School Curriculum*, London: Holt, Rinehart & Winston.

Cardno, C. (1998) Working together: managing strategy collaboratively, in Cheadle, A. (ed.) *Towards Developing a Customer Care Strategy for the Marketing of the Primary School*, London, Paul Chapman.

Cave, E. and Demick, D. (1990) Marketing the school, in Cave, E. and Wilkinson, C. (eds.) *Local Management of Schools: Some Practical Issues*, London, Routledge.

Chapman, D., Boyd, W.L., Lander, R. and Reynolds, D. (eds.) (1996) *The Reconstruction of Education*, London, Cassell.

Chitty, C. (1997) Comprehensive schooling and the 'neighbourhood' debate, *Forum*, 39(3) 73–76.

Clark, D. (1996) *Schools as Learning Communities*, London, Cassell.

Codd, J. (1991) Curriculum reform in New Zealand, *Journal of Curriculum Studies*, 23(2).

Coleman, M. (1994) Marketing and external relations, in Bush, T. and West-Burnham, J. (eds.) *The Principles of Educational Management*, Harlow, Longman.

Coleman, M. (1998) *Marketing in Education*, Leicester, University of Leicester.

Coleman, M. and Anderson, L. (eds.) (2000) *Managing Finance and Resources in Education*, London, Paul Chapman.

Coleman, M. and Briggs, A.R.J. (2000) Management of buildings and space, in Coleman, M. and Anderson, L. (eds.) *Managing Finance and Resources in Education*, London, Paul Chapman.

Connor, M. (1997) Community support in a local comprehensive school, *Emotional and Behavioral Difficulties*, 2(1) 41–48.

Cookson, P.W. (1995) Goals 2000: framework for the new educational federalism, *Teachers College Record*, 96(3) 405–17.

Coombs, P. and Hallak, J. (1987) *Cost Analysis in Education*, New York, Johns Hopkins University Press.

Cordingly, P. (1996) Who are the stakeholders?, *The Times Educational Supplement*, 7 June, p. 22.

Covrig, D. (1997) Fundamentalists, social capital and children's welfare, *Journal of Education Policy*, 12(1–2) 53–60.

Cowell, D. (1984) *The Marketing of Services*, Oxford, Butterworth/Heinemann.

Creese, M. and Earley, P. (1999) *Improving Schools and Governing Bodies: Making a Difference*, London, Routledge.

Crego, E. and Schiffrin, P. (1995) *Customer Centred Engineering*, New York, Harper & Row.

Crisp, P., Nightingale, A. and Street, H. (1991) *Cost Centres and College Budgets: post ERA*, Bristol, The Staff College.

Davies, B. (1994) Models of decision making in resource allocation, in Bush, T. and West-Burnham, J. (eds.) *The Principles of Educational Management*, London, Paul Chapman.

Davies, B. and Anderson, L. (1992) *Opting for Self-Management*, London, Routledge.

Davies, B. and Ellison, L. (1997) *Strategic Marketing for Schools*, London, Pitman.

Davies, B. and Ellison, L. (1999) *Strategic Direction and Development of the School*, London, Routledge.

Davies, P.N. (1999) Colleges and customers, in Lumby, J. and Foskett, N. (eds.) *Managing External Relations in Schools and Colleges*, London, Paul Chapman.

Deem, R. (1993) Educational reform and school governing bodies in England 1986–92: old dogs, new tricks or new dogs, new tricks, in Preedy, M. (ed.) *Managing the Effective School*, London, Paul Chapman.

Deem, R. (1994) Free marketeers or good citizens? Education policy and lay participation in the administration of schools, *British Journal of Educational Studies*, 42(1) 23–37.

Deem, R., Brehony, K.J. and Heath, S. (1995) *Active Citizenship and the Governing of Schools*, Buckingham, Open University Press.

DeHayes, D. and Lovrinic, J. (1994) ABC model for assessing economic performance, *New Directions for Institutional Research*, (82) 81–93.

Department of Education, South Africa (1996) *Changing Management to Manage Change in Education*. Report of the Task Team on Education Management Development, December.

Department for Education, Welsh Office (1992) *Choice and Diversity: A New Framework for Schools*, London, HMSO.

DES (1988) The Education Reform Act, London, HMSO.

DfE (1993) *Local Management of Schools*. Draft circular, London, Department for Education,

October.

DfE (1994) *Local Management of Schools*. Circular 2/94, London, DfE.

DfEE (undated) *Registration of Independent Schools Information Pack*, Darlington, DfEE.

DfEE (1996) *Guidance on Good Governance*, London, DfEE.

DfEE (1998) *Fair Funding: Improving Delegation to Schools*. Consultation paper, London, DfEE.

DfEE (1999a) *The Standards Fund 2000–2001*. Circular 16/99, London, DfEE.

DfEE (1999b) *A Fast Track for Teachers*. Green paper, London, DfEE.

DfEE (1999c) *The Standards Fund 2000–2001*. Supplement to Circular 16/99, London, DfEE.

DfEE (2000a) *Requirements of Nursery Education Grant 2000–2001*, London, DfEE.

DfEE (2000b) More spending power for schools and less red tape – Blunkett, *News 247/00*, London, DfEE.

Dimmock, C. (ed.) (1993) *School-Based Management and School Effectiveness*, London, Routledge.

Doe, B. (1998) Tory competition fails to raise standards, *The Times Educational Supplement*, 9 January, p. 1.

Earley, P. (1994) *School Governing Bodies, Making Progress?*, Slough, NFER.

Earley, P. and Creese, M. (1999) Working with governors: a bridge to the community?, in Lumby, J. and Foskett, N. (eds.) *Managing External Relations in Schools and Colleges*, London, Paul Chapman.

Education Department, Hong Kong (1991) *School Management Initiative*, Hong Kong, The Government Printer.

Education and Manpower Branch and Education Department, Hong Kong (1991) *The School Management Initiative: Setting the Framework for Quality in Hong Kong Schools*, Hong Kong, The Government Printer.

Englund, T. (1993) Education for public or private good, in Miron, G. (ed.) *Towards Free Choice and Market-Orientated Schools: Problems and Promises*, Stockholm, Institute of International Education, Stockholm University.

Esp, D. and Saran, R. (1995) *Effective Governors for Effective Schools*, London, Pitman.

FEDA (1998) Online at www.feda.ac.uk/funding/commentaries/1.asp

FEFC (1992) *Funding Learning*, Coventry, FEFC.

FEFC (1994) *Guide for College Governors*, Coventry, FEFC.

Feintuck, M. (1994) *Accountability and Choice in Schooling*, Buckingham, Open University Press.

FEU (1985) *Marketing Further Education: A Feasibility Study*, Blagdon, FEU.

FEU (1991) *Quality Matters*, Blagdon, FEU.

Field, L. (1993) School governing bodies: the lay–professional relationship, *School Organisation*, 13(2) 165–74.

Fitz, J., Halpin, D. and Power, S. (1993) *Grant Maintained Schools: Education in the Market Place*, London, Kogan Page.

Foor, D. (1985) Autonomy in education, in *Curriculum Planning – A vision for the future*. Ministry of Education, Department of Curriculum (in Hebrew)

Foreman, K. (1999) Schools and the state, in Lumby, J. and Foskett, N. (eds.) *Managing External Relations in Schools and Colleges*, London, Paul Chapman.

Foskett, N. (1996) Conceptualising 'marketing' in secondary schools – deconstructing an alien concept, *Conference Papers, Southampton University*, pp. 39–51.

Foskett, N. (1999) Strategy, external relations and marketing, in Lumby, J. and Foskett, N. (eds.) *Managing External Relations in Schools and Colleges*, London, Paul Chapman.

Foskett, N. and Helmsley-Brown, J. (1999) Communicating the organisation, in Lumby, J. and Foskett, N. (eds.) *Managing External Relations in Schools and Colleges*, London, Paul Chapman.

Fouts, J.T. and Chan, J.C.K. (1997) The development of work-study and school enterprises in China's schools, *Journal of Curriculum Studies*, 29(1) 31–46.

Friedman, Y. (1994) Parents' choice of schools – a beginning, *Megamot*, 36(2–3) 151–57 (in Hebrew).

Friedman, Y. and Brama, R. (1998) *The Transition of Jerusalem Schools to Self-Management*, Jerusalem, The Szold Institute.

Gamage, D. (1996) *School-Based Management: Theory, Research and Practice*, Colombo, Karunaratne & Sons.

Gilbert, C. (1990) Local management of schools: an introductory summary, in Gilbert, C. (ed.) *Local*

Management of Schools: A Guide for Governors and Teachers, London, Kogan Page.

Glatter, R. (ed.) (1989) *Educational Institutions and their Environments: Managing the Boundaries*, Buckingham, Open University Press.

Gleeson, D. and Shain, F. (1999) By Appointment: governance, markets and managerialism in further education, *British Educational Research Journal*, 25(4) 545–61.

Glover, D. (2000) Financial management and strategic planning, in Coleman, M. and Anderson, L. (eds.) *Managing Finance and Resources in Education*, London, Paul Chapman.

Glover, D., Gleeson, D., Gough, G. and Johnson, M. (1998) The meaning of management: the development needs of middle managers in secondary schools, *Educational Management and Administration*, 26(3) 279–92.

Golby, M. (1992) School governors: conceptual and practical problems, *Journal of Philosophy of Education*, 26(2) 165–72.

Golby, M. and Brigley, S. (1989) *Parents as School Governors*, Tiverton, Fairway Publications.

Gomez, C.A. (1991) Vocational education financing: an example of participation by employers in Brazil, *Prospects*, XXI(3) 457–65.

Gorringe, R. (1994) Devising a new funding methodology for further education – the funding learning approach, in Flint, C. and Austin, M. (eds.) *Going Further*, Blagdon, The Staff College in association with the Association for Colleges.

Government of Pakistan (1983) *The Sixth Five Year Plan 1983–1988*, Islamabad, Planning Commission.

Government of Punjab (1982) *A Compendium of Acts, Ordinances, Laws and Rules*, Lahore, Bureau of Education, Education Department.

Grant Maintained Schools Foundation (1992) *The Role of Governors and Heads in Grant Maintained Schools*, Harlow, Longman.

Gray, L. (1989) Marketing educational services, in Glatter, R. (ed.) *Educational Institutions and their Environments: Managing the Boundaries*, Milton Keynes, Open University Press.

Gray, L. (1991) *Marketing Education*, Buckingham, Open University Press.

Gray, L. and Warrender, A. (1993) Cost-effective technical education in developing countries, *Coombe Lodge Report*, 23(5) 359–424.

Graystone, J. (1991) The new governing bodies for the 21st century, in *Governing Colleges into the 21st Century*, Bristol, The Staff College, Coombe Lodge.

Greenfield, T. (1973) Organisations as social inventions: rethinking assumptions about change, *Journal of Applied Behavioural Science*, 9(5) 551–74.

Gregory, I. (1994) Some reflections on Golby and governors, *Journal of Philosophy of Education*, 28(2) 205–10.

Guanyu quanguo zhiye jishu jiaoyu gongzuo huiyi qigkuangde baogao (1986) [Report on the National Conference of Vocational and Technical Education] (Excerpt). Trans. in Cheng, K.M. (guest ed.) (1992) Theme edition: reform in the financing of education in Mainland China (II), *Chinese Education*, 25(2) 59.

Guimaraes, E. (1996) The school under siege: the relationship between the urban environment and the education system in Rio de Janeiro, *Prospects*, 26(2) 272–92.

Hall, G. (1999) Quantitative overview of the technical colleges of KwaZulu Natal, in Kraak, A. and Hall, G. (eds.) *Transforming Further Education and Training in South Africa*, Pretoria, HSRC Publishers.

Hall, V. (1997) Managing staff, in Fidler, B. *et al.* (eds.) *Choices for Self-Managing Schools*, London, Paul Chapman.

Hallinger, P. and Heck, R.H. (1998) Exploring the principal's contribution to school effectiveness: 1980–1995, *School Effectiveness and School Improvement*, 9(2) 157–91.

Halpin, D., Fitz, J. and Power, S. (1993) The early impact and long term implications of the grant-maintained schools policy, in *Warwick Papers on Education Policy No. 4*, Stoke-on-Trent, Trentham Books.

Halstead, M. (1994) Accountability and values, in Scott, D. (ed.) *Accountability and Control in Educational Settings*, London, Cassell.

Hanford, I. (1992) Liaising with parents, in Foskett, N. (ed.) *Managing External Relations in Schools: A Practical Guide*, London, Routledge.

Hans, J. (1996) *Cost Accounting in Higher Education – Simple Macro and Micro Costing Techniques*,

Washington, DC, NACUBO.

Hardcastle, L. (2000) Lift hearts of heads, *The Times Educational Supplement*, 12 May, p. 33.

Harris, K. (1996) The corporate invasion of schooling: some implications for pupils, teachers and education, in AARE SET: *Research Information for Teachers*, 2.

Helmsley-Brown, J. (1999) The state and colleges, in Lumby, J. and Foskett, N. (eds.) *Managing External Relations in Schools and Colleges*, London, Paul Chapman.

Hill, E. and O'Sullivan, T. (1999) *Marketing*, London, Longman (2nd edn).

Hinds, D. (2000) Leaders in battle for diversity, *The Times Educational Supplement*, 5 May, p. 28.

Hirsch, D. (1994) *School: A Matter of Choice*, Paris, OECD/CERI.

Horngren, C., Foster, G. and Datar, S. (1994) *Cost Accounting: A Managerial Emphasis*, London, Prentice-Hall.

Howson, J. and Mitchell, M. (1995) Course costing in devolved institutions: perspectives from an academic department, *Higher Education Review*, 25(3) 7–35.

Hoy, W.K. and Miskel, C.G. (1987) *Educational Administration: Theory, Research and Practice*, New York, Random House.

Hoy, W. and Miskel, C. (1989) Schools and their external environments, in Glatter, R. (ed.) *Educational Institutions and their Environments: Managing the Boundaries*, Buckingham, Open University Press.

Innes, J. and Mitchell, M. (1991) 'ABC': *A Review with Case Studies*, London, CIMA.

Iqbal, Z. and Davies, L. (1994) The early impact of the grant of autonomy to government educational institutions in Pakistan, *Journal of Educational Policy*, 9(3) 197–210.

Johnes, G. (1993) *The Economics of Education*, London, Macmillan.

Johnson, D. (1988) *The School's External Relations*, Milton Keynes, Open University Press.

Johnson, D. (1990) *Parental Choice in Education*, London, Unwin Hyman.

Johnson, V. and Davies, D. (1996) Crossing boundaries: family, community and school partnerships, *International Journal of Educational Research*, 25(1) 1–105.

Kahin, M. (1998) Somali children: the need to work in partnership with parents and the community, *Multicultural Teaching*, 17(1) 14–16.

Karstanje, P. (1999) Decentralisation and deregulation in Europe: towards a conceptual framework, in Bush, T. *et al.* (eds.) *Educational Management: Refining Theory, Policy and Practice*, London, Paul Chapman.

Kedney, R.J. (1993) Costing open and flexible learning, *OLS News*, Part 30, 1–14.

Kedney, R.J. and Davies, T. (1994) *Cost Reduction and Value for Money*, Bristol, Coombe Lodge Report 24, pp. 441–524.

Kelly, R. and Kedney, R.J. (1992) *Designing a College Accommodation Strategy*. Mendip Papers MP053, Bristol, The Staff College.

Kennedy, H. (1997) *Learning Works: Widening Participation in Further Education*, Coventry, FEFC.

Kenway, J. and Fitzclarence, L. (1998) Institutions with designs: consuming school children, *Journal of Educational Policy*, 13(6) 661–77.

Keys, W. and Fernandez, C. (1990) *A Survey of School Governing Bodies. Vol. 1*, Slough, NFER.

Khan, A.I. (1993) *Education: Concept and Process*, Lahore, Izhar Sons.

Knight, B. (1983) *Managing School Finance*, Oxford, Heinemann.

Knight, B. (1993) *Financial Management for Schools: The Thinking Manager's Guide*, Oxford, Heinemann.

Knight, P. and Hesketh, A. (1998) Secondary school prospectuses and educational markets, *Cambridge Journal of Education*, 28(1) 21–35.

Kogan, M. (1984) *School Governing Bodies*, Oxford, Heinemann.

Kogan, M. (1986) *Education Accountability*, London, Hutchinson.

Kogan, M. (1988) Normative models of accountability, in Glatter, R. *et al.* (eds.) *Understanding School Management*, Buckingham, Open University Press.

Kogan, M., Johnson, D., Packwood, T. and Whitaker, T. (1984) *School Governing Bodies*, London, Heinemann.

Kotler, P. and Armstrong, G. (1994) *Principles of Marketing*, Englewood Cliffs, NJ, Prentice-Hall.

Kotler, P. and Fox, F.A. (1995) *Strategic Marketing for Educational Institutions*, London, Prentice-Hall (2nd edn).

Kruchov, C. and Hoyrup, S. (1994) Development of the school system in Gladsaxe Municipality. Paper presented to the Seventh International Congress for School Effectiveness and Improvement, Melbourne, Australia, January.

Kucukcan, T. (1998) Community, identity and the institutionalisation of Islamic education, *British Journal of Religious Education*, 21(1) 32–43.

Leithwood, K., Jantzi, D. and Steinbach, R. (1999) *Changing Leadership for Changing Times*, Buckingham, Open University Press.

Levačić, R. (1989) *Financial Management in Education*, Buckingham, Open University Press.

Levačić, R. (1990) *Financial and Resource Management in Schools*, Buckingham, Open University Press.

Levačić, R. (1992) Local management of schools: aims, scope and impact, *Educational Management and Administration*, 20(1) 16–29.

Levačić, R. (1993) Managing resources effectively, in *E326 Managing Schools: Challenge and Response*, Milton Keynes, Open University Press.

Levačić, R. (1995) *Local Management of Schools*, Buckingham, Open University Press.

Levačić, R. (2000) Linking resources to learning outcomes, in Coleman, M. and Anderson, L. (eds.) *Managing Finance and Resources in Education*, London, Paul Chapman.

Levačić, R., Hardman, J. and Woods, P. (1998) Competition as a spur to improvement? Differential improvement in GCSE examination results. Paper presented to the International Congress for School Effectiveness and Improvement, Manchester.

Levin, H. (1983) *Cost Effectiveness: A Primer*, London, Sage.

Lingard, B., Knight, J. and Porter, P. (eds.) (1993) *Schooling Reform in Hard Times*, London, Falmer Press.

Lockheed, M. (1998) Decentralisation of education: eight lessons for school effectiveness and improvement. Keynote address presented at the International Congress on School Effectiveness and Improvement, Manchester, 5 January.

Lucey, T. (1996) *Costing*, London, DP Publications (5th edn).

Lumby, J. (1998) Restraining the further education market: closing Pandora's box, *Education and Training*, 40(2) 57–62.

Lumby, J. (2000a) Restructuring vocational education in Hong Kong, *The International Journal of Educational Management*, 14(1) 16–22.

Lumby, J. (2000b) Technical colleges in South Africa: planning for the future, *Journal of Vocational Education and Training*, 52(1) 101–18.

Lumby, J. (2000c) Funding learning in further education, in Coleman, M. and Anderson, L. (eds.) *Managing Finance and Resources in Education*, London, Paul Chapman.

Lumby, J. and Foskett, N. (eds.) (1999) *Managing External Relations in Schools and Colleges*, London, Paul Chapman.

Lumby, J. and Li, Y.P. (1998) Managing vocational education in China, *Compare*, 28(2) 197–206.

Lundgren, U.P. (undated) The knowledge base for national education policy-making: the case of Sweden. Mimeo, National Agency for Education, Sweden.

Lundgren, U.P. and Mattsson, K. (1996) Decentralization by or for school improvement, in Chapman, J.D. *et al.* (eds.) *The Reconstruction of Education*, London, Cassell.

Lynn, P. and Davis Smith, J. (1991) *The 1991 National Survey of Voluntary Activity in the UK*. Second Series Paper no. 1, Berkhamstead, Volunteer Centre UK.

MacBeath, J., Boyd, B., Rand, J. and Bell, S. (1996) *Schools Speak for Themselves*, London, NUT.

Macbeth, A. (1993) Parent–teacher partnership: a minimum programme and a signed understanding, in Preedy, M. (ed.) *Managing the Effective School*, London, Paul Chapman.

Macbeth, A. (1995) Partnership between parents and teachers in education, in Macbeth, A. *et al.* (eds.) *Collaborate or Compete? Educational Partnerships in a Market Economy*, London, Falmer Press.

Maha, A.C. (1997) Governance of education in Papua New Guinea: the role of boards of governors, *International Review of Education*, 43(2–3) 179–92.

Mahoney, T. (1994) A little learning is a dangerous thing: governor training, in Thody, A. (ed.) *School Governors: Leaders or Followers*, Harlow, Longman.

Marriott, D. (2000) Wanted: public spirit and expertise, *The Times Educational Supplement*, 26 May, p. 29.

Maslen, G. (1999) GM look-alikes to be scrapped, *The Times Educational Supplement*, 19 November, p. 5.

McAleese, K. (2000) Budgeting in schools, in Coleman, M. and Anderson, L. (eds.) *Managing Finance and Resources in Education*, London, Paul Chapman.

McAlister, D. and Connolly, M. (1990) Local financial management, in Cave, E. and Wilkinson, C. (eds.) *Local Management of Schools: Some Practical Issues*, London, Routledge.

McCreath, D. and Maclachlan, K. (1995) Realizing the virtual: new alliances in the market model education game, in Macbeth, A. *et al.* (eds.) *Collaborate or Compete? Educational Partnerships in a Market Economy*, London, Falmer Press.

Middlewood, D. and Lumby, J. (1998a) *Human Resource Management in Schools and Colleges*, London, Paul Chapman.

Middlewood, D. and Lumby, J. (1998b) *Strategic Management in Schools and Colleges*, London, Paul Chapman.

Morris, A. (1998) By the fruits you will know them: distinctive features of Catholic education, *Research Papers in Education*, 13(1) 87–112.

Mortimore, P. and Mortimore, J. with Thomas, H. (1994) *Managing Associate Staff: Innovation in Primary and Secondary Schools*, London, Paul Chapman.

Munn, P. (1991) School boards, accountability and control, *British Journal of Educational Studies*, 40(1) 173–89.

Murgatroyd, S. and Morgan, C. (1993) *Total Quality Management and the School*, Buckingham, Open University Press.

Murphy, M. (1994) Managing the use of space, in Warner, D. and Kelly, G. (eds.) *Managing Educational Property: A Handbook for Schools, Colleges and Universities*, Buckingham, Society for Research into Higher Education and Open University Press.

Nadirbekyzy, B. and DeYoung, A. (1997) Redefining schooling and community in post-Soviet Kazakstan, *Journal of Education Policy*, 12(1–2) 71–78.

National Consumer Council (1996) *Sponsorship in Schools*, London, National Consumer Council.

Naybour, S. (1989) Parents: partners or customers?, in Sayer, J. and Williams, V. (eds.) *Schools and External Relations: Managing the New Partnership*, London, Cassell.

Newmann, F. (1993) Beyond common sense in educational restructuring: the issues of content and leadership, *Educational Researcher*, 22(2) 4–13.

Nkata, J. and Thody, A. (1996) Who is allowed to speak? Ugandan and English school governance. Part 1, *International Studies in Educational Administration*, 24(1) 67–77.

Odden, A. (1995) Decentralised school management in Victoria, Australia. Paper prepared for the World Bank, Consortium for Policy Research in Education, Madison, WI.

Ofsted (1998) *Secondary Education 1993–97: A Review of Secondary Schools in England*, London, HMSO.

Ofsted (2000) *Handbook for Inspecting Schools*, London, HMSO.

Ogawa, R.T. and White, P.A. (1994) School-based management: an overview, in Mohrman, S.A. *et al.* (eds.) *School-Based Management: Organizing for High Performance*, San Francisco, Jossey-Bass.

O'Neill, J. (1994) Organisational structure and culture, in Bush, T. and West-Burnham, J. (eds.) *The Principles of Educational Management*, London, Financial Times/Prentice-Hall.

O'Neill, J. (1998) Beyond partnerships – a corporate strategy?, *Journal of Sport Pedagogy*, 4(2) 29–42.

Open University (1988) *Course E325, Block 6, Part 3: Turbulence*, Milton Keynes, Open University Press.

Packwood, T. (1989) Models of governing bodies, in Glatter, R. *et al.* (eds.) *Understanding School Management*, Buckingham, Open University Press.

Palfreyman, D. (1991) The art of costing and the politics of pricing, *Promoting Education*, Part 2, 26–27.

Pascal, C. (1989) Democratising primary school government: conflicts and dichotomies, in Glatter, R. (ed.) *Educational Institutions and their Environments: Managing the Boundaries*, Buckingham, Open University Press.

Patel, C. (2000) Missing the big picture?, *The Times Educational Supplement*, 14 April, p. 27.

Pettifor, J. (1974) The economics of the polytechnic sector of higher education: a study of the determinants of unit cost variations in polytechnics. Thesis, Nottingham Trent Polytechnic.

Picot, B. and members of the Taskforce to Review Educational Administration (1988) *Administering for*

Excellence (Picot Report), Wellington, NZ, Government Printer.

Pierson, C. (1998) The new governance of education: the Conservatives and education 1988–1997, *Oxford Review of Education*, 24(1) 131–42.

Plank, D. (1997) Dreams of community, *Journal of Education Policy*, 12(1–2) 13–20.

Power, S. and Whitty, G. (1999) Market forces and school cultures, in Prosser, J. (ed.) *School Culture*, London, Paul Chapman.

Pyke, C. (1998) Costing and pricing in the public sector, in Wilson, J. (ed.) *Financial Management for the Public Services*, Buckingham, Open University Press.

Radelescu, E. (1993) The decentralisation of educational management, in Bolam, R. and van Weiringen, F. (eds.) *Educational Management across Europe*, De Lier, Academic Book Center.

Ranson, S. (1996) Markets or democracy for education, in Ahier, J. *et al.* (eds.) *Diversity and Change: Education, Policy and Selection*, London, Routledge with The Open University.

Resef, Sh. (1985) School autonomy – a new era, in Friedman, Y. (ed) (1987) *Autonomy in Education and Processes of Performance*, The Sold Research Centre, Jerusalem (Hebrew)

Robinson, V.M.J. and Timperley, H. (1996) Learning to be responsive: the impact of school choice and decentralization, *Educational Management and Administration*, 24(1) 65–78.

Rumble, G. (1987) Why distance learning can be cheaper than conventional education, *Distance Learning*, 8(1) 2–94.

Ryan, B. (1993) And your corporate manager will set you free . . . Devolution in South Australian education, in Smyth, J. (ed.) *A Socially Critical View of the Self-Managing School*, London, Falmer Press.

Ryan, P., Chen, X.D. and Merry, R. (1998) In search of understanding: a qualitative comparison of primary school management in the Shaanxi region of China and England, *Compare*, 28(2) 171–82.

Sallis, J. (1988) *Schools, Parents and Governors: A New Approach to Accountability*, London, Routledge.

Sallis, J. (1991) *School Governors: Your Questions Answered*, London, Hodder & Stoughton.

Sallis, J. (1995) *School Governors: A Question and Answer Guide*, London, Times Educational Supplement.

Saqeb, G. (1998) Spiritual and moral development in school and the British Muslim, *Muslim Education Quarterly*, 16(1) 4–17.

Sayer, J. (1989) The public context of change, in Sayer, J. and Williams, V. (eds.) *Schools and External Relations: Managing the New Partnership*, London, Cassell.

Scott, B. (1989) *Schools Renewal: A Strategy to Revitalise Schools within the New South Wales Education System. Management Review*, Milsons Point, NSW Educational Portfolio.

Scott, D. (1999) Accountability in education systems: centralising and decentralising pressures, in Lumby, J. and Foskett, N. (eds.) *Managing External Relations in Schools and Colleges*, London, Paul Chapman.

Scott, P. (1989) Accountability, responsiveness and responsibility, in Glatter, R. (ed.) *Educational Institutions and their Environments: Managing the Boundaries*, Buckingham, Open University Press.

Sergiovanni, T.J. (1987) The theoretical basis for cultural leadership, in Sheive, L.T. and Schoenheit, M.B. (eds.) *1987 Yearbook of the Association for Supervision and Curriculum Development*, Alexandria, VA, ASCA.

Sergiovanni, T.J. (1998) Moral authority, community and diversity: leadership challenges for the twenty-first century. Paper presented at the inaugural meeting of the Centre of Educational Leadership, Hong Kong, University of Hong Kong.

Shain, F. and Gleeson, D. (1999) Under new management: changing conceptions of teacher professionalism and policy in the further education sector, *Journal of Education Policy*, 14(4) 445–62.

Shapira, R. and Cookson, P. (1997) *Autonomy and Choice in Context: An International Perspective*, Oxford, Pergamon.

Shattock, M. (1994) *Derby College: Wilmorton. Report of an Enquiry into the Governance and Management of the College*, Coventry, FEFC.

Shattock, M. (2000) Governance and management, in Smithers, A. and Robinson, P. (eds.) *Further Education Re-formed*, London, Falmer Press.

Shearn, D., Broadbent, J., Laughlin, R. and Willig-Atherton, H. (1995) The changing face of school governor responsibilities: a mismatch between governor intention and actuality?, *School Organisation*, 15(2) 175–88.

Sherratt, B. (1994) *Grant Maintained Status: Considering the Options*, Harlow, Longman.

Simkins, T. (1986) Patronage, markets and collegiality: reflections on the allocation of finance in secondary schools, *Educational Management and Administration*, 14(1) 17–30.

Simkins, T. (1989) Budgeting as a political and organisational process in educational institutions, in Levačić, R. (ed.) *Financial Management in Education*, Milton Keynes, Open University Press.

Smith, I. (2000) Learning to be better, *The Times Educational Supplement*, 14(1) July, p. 28.

Smyth, J. (ed.) (1993) *A Socially Critical View of the Self-Managing School*, London, Falmer Press.

Smyth, J. (1996) The socially just alternative to the self-managing school, in Leithwood, J. *et al.* (eds.) *International Handbook of Educational Leadership and Administration*, Boston, MA, Klumer.

Snook, I., Adams, P., Adams, R., Clark, J., Codd, J., Collins, G., Harker, R., O'Neill, J. and Pearce, D. (1999) Educational reform in New Zealand 1989–1999: is there any evidence of success? An unofficial briefing paper for journalists and others attending the APEC Summit, September, Massey University.

State of Israel, Ministry of Education (1993) *Recommendations of the Steering-Committee for Self-Managed Schools*. Second draft (in Hebrew).

State of Israel, Ministry of Education, Department of Planning (1997) *The Contents of the Course/ School Principals*. From www.education.gov.il/planning/shemesh.htm (downloaded on 5 October 2000).

Stoll, L. and Fink, D. (1996) *Changing our Schools*, Buckingham, Open University Press.

Stone, M. (1992) Cost analysis in an educational setting, *Studies in Educational Administration*, 7(1) 1–11.

Swedish Institute (1995) *Factsheets* (www.si.se/english/factsheets/school.html), Swedish Institute.

Thody, A. (1992) *Moving to Management: School Governors in the 1990s*, London, David Fulton.

Thomas, A. and Dennison, B. (1991) Parental or pupil choice – who really decides in urban schools?, *Educational Management and Administration*, 19(4) 25–34.

Thomas, H. (1990) *Education Costs and Performance: A Cost-Effective Analysis*, London, Cassell.

Thomas, H. (1993) The education-reform movement in England and Wales, in Beare, H. and Boyd, W.L. (eds.) *Restructuring Schools*, London, Falmer Press.

Thomas, H. and Bullock, A. (1992) Local management funding formulae and LEA discretion, in Simkins, T. *et al.* (eds.) *Implementing Educational Reform: The Early Lessons*, Harlow, Longman.

Thomas, H. and Martin, J. (1996) *Managing Resources for School Improvement*, London, Routledge.

Thornton, K. (2000) With friends like these . . ., *The Times Educational Supplement*, 7 July, p. 27.

Travers, T. (1993) Postgraduate arithmetic, *The Times Educational Supplement*, 15 January, p. 14.

Tshireletso, L. (1997) They are the government's children, *International Journal of Educational Development*, 17(2) 173–88.

Turner, B. (1997) Local learning partnerships: the Birmingham experience, *Forum*, 39(1) 24–26.

Turner, C.K. (1996) The role and tasks of a subject head of department in secondary schools in England and Wales: a neglected area of research, *School Organisation*, 16 203–17.

Turney, P. (1996) *ABC – The Performance Breakthrough*, London, Kogan Page.

Walford, G. (ed.) (1991) *Private Schooling: Tradition, Change and Diversity*, London, Paul Chapman.

Wallace, M. (1988) Towards a collegiate approach to curriculum management in primary and middle schools, *School Organisation*, 8(1) 25–34.

Waring, S. (1999) Finding your way: sensing the external environment, in Lumby, J. and Foskett, N. (eds.) *Managing External Relations in Schools and Colleges*, London, Paul Chapman.

Warwick, D. (1989) Interpretation and aims, in Warwick, D. (ed.) *Linking Schools and Industry*, Oxford, Blackwell.

Wells, A.S., Grutzik, C. and Carnochan, S. (1996) The multiple meanings of US charter school reform: exploring the politics of deregulation. Paper presented at the British Educational Research Association annual conference, University of Lancaster, 12–15 September.

West, A., Pennell, H., West, R. and Travers, T. (2000) Financing school-based education in England: principles and problems, in Coleman, M. and Anderson, L. (eds.) *Managing Finance and Resources in Education*, London, Paul Chapman.

West, A., Scott, G and Varlaam, A. (1991) Choice of high school: pupils' perceptions, *Educational Research*, 37(3) 205–15.

West-Burnham, J. (1992a) Total quality management in education, in Bennett, N. *et al.* (eds.) *Managing Change in Education: Individual and Organisational Perspectives*, London, Paul Chapman.

West-Burnham, J. (1992b) *Managing Quality in Schools*, Harlow, Longman.

West-Burnham, J. (1994) Strategy, policy and planning, in Bush, T. and West-Burnham, J. (eds.) *The Principles of Educational Management*, London, Financial Times/Prentice-Hall.

Westcott, E. (2000) Mark out your territory with red tape, *The Times Educational Supplement*, 21 April, p. 26.

Whitear, B., Guthrie, D. and Gordon, I. (1997) Stopping them starting: evaluation of a community-based project to discourage teenage smoking in Cardiff, *Health Education Journal*, 56(1) 42–50.

Whitty, G. (1990) The New Right and the National Curriculum: state control or market forces?, in Flude, M. and Hammer, M. (eds.) *The Education Reform Act*, 1988, London, Falmer Press.

Whitty, G., Power, S. and Halpin, D. (1998) *Devolution and Choice in Education: The School, the State and the Market*, Buckingham, Open University Press.

Wirt, F. (1981) Professionalism and political conflict: a development model, *Journal of Public Policy*, 1(1) 61–93.

Wohlstetter, P. and Anderson, L. (1994) What can US charter schools learn from England's grant-maintained schools?, *Phi Delta Kappan*, 75 486–91.

Wong, E.K.P., Sharpe, F.G. and McCormick, J. (1998) Factors affecting the perceived effectiveness of planning in Hong Kong self-managing schools, *Educational Management and Administration*, 26(1) 67–81.

Woodhall, M. (1987) Cost analysis in education, in Psacharopoulos, G. (ed.) *Economics of Education: Research and Studies*, Oxford, Pergamon Press.

Woods, P., Bagley, C. and Glatter, R. (1998) *School Choice and Competition: Markets in the Public Interest?*, London, Routledge.

World Bank (1989) *Higher Education and Scientific Research for Development: A Discussion Paper*, Washington, DC, World Bank.

Worrall, C. (1994) Keeping the customer satisfied. Unpublished assignment for the MBA, University of Leicester.

Wylie, C. (1994) The shift to school-based management in New Zealand – the school view, in Carter, D.S.G. and O'Neill, M.H. (eds.) *Case Studies in Educational Change: An International Perspective*, London, Falmer Press.

Yarnit, M. (1992) Formula funding in Sheffield: towards planning and collaboration, in Simkins, T. *et al.* (eds.) *Implementing Educational Reform: The Early Lessons*, Harlow, Longman.

Yonai, J. (1984) *Pedagogical Independence – Guidelines for Implementation*, Ministry of Education, The Pedagogical Secretaryship (in Hebrew).

Author Index

Subject Index

accommodation
management of, 50–1
accountability, 3, 28, 29, 62–5,114

Beacon School Initiative, 89
budgeting, 27–30,43
approaches to, 29–30
as a resource management tool,
28–9
delegated budget
management of, 45–7
reasons for, 27

Charter Schools, 7–8, 124
city technology colleges, 18
competition and collaboration,
86–9
customer relationships, 81–6
and funding, 81
and parents and students, 82–6
definition, 81–2
partnerships in, 84–6
repercussions of parental choice,
84

Education Reform Act, 13, 14, 86,
98
external relationships
management of, 55–73

fair funding, 14–16
and accountability, 15
increased delegation in, 16
principles of, 14–15
working of, 15– 16
finance and resources
(see also: budgeting)
and economic realities, 42–3
management of, 2
accommodation, 50–2
activity-based costing (ABC),
35–6
and cost centres, 35–6
and costing in, 30–9
key factors in, 38–9
types of cost, 31–4
and models of, 39–41
costing and pricing in, 37
learning resources, 52–4
staffing, 47–50
the delegated budget, 44–7
theoretical perspectives of, 21–43
effectiveness and efficiency,
24–7,43

financial and real resources, 23
resource management cycle,
22–3
other sources of, 17
formula funding, 1, 13
funding in Scotland, 17–18
further education colleges
incorporation of, 19, 21, 111–2
(see also: governing bodies)

governing bodies, 95–113
and management issues, 113
definition of, 96
in FE, 111–2
lay participation in, 107–8
membership of, 99–101
models of, 96–9
nature of, 95–6
participation in, 106–7
pressures on, 97–9
roles and responsibilities of,
101–3, 109–10
structure of, 103–6
tensions within, 109
training of, 112
Grant Maintained schools, 14, 15,
18, 98, 109

independent schools, 18–19,81
and funding of, 37
Individual Schools Budget, 15
institutions
and collaboration among,
86–7,88–9
and relationships among, 87–8

Learning and Skills Council, 19,20
learning resources
management of, 52–4
local communities
managing relations with, 89–93
local management of schools
(LMS), 13–14
in action, 13–14
principles of, 13
Local Schools Budget (LSB), 15

management of external
relationships, 2–3
and business links, 91–3
and the local community, 89–93
and the state, 93–4
theoretical perspectives of, 55–73
marketing, 65–73

and mix, 68–9
and promotion, 69–73
and strategic planning, 65–6
strategies for, 66–8

open enrolment, 1
open organisation, 57–62
implications for the management
of, 62
resources perspective, 59–61

PASCI report, 84
Public Finance Initiative (PFI), 61

resource management cycle, 22–3
resources
components of, 5

Schools of the Future, 8, 115
self-management, 4–10
and degrees of autonomy, 7–10
and LMS, 13–14
definition of, 5, 21
in Australia, 115–6
in England and Wales, 12–16
in Hong Kong, 116–7
in Israel, 117–8
in New Zealand, 119–20
in Pakistan, 120–1
in South Africa, 121–3
in Sweden, 123
in the United Arab Emirates,
118–9
in the United States of America,
123–4
international trend in, 5–10
terminology of, 6
U.K. perspective of, 12–20
Specialist Schools, 17
staffing
management of, 47–50
stakeholders
(see also: customer relationships)
different groups of, 74–6
increasing influence of, 55–7
management of, 2–3
and accountability, 3
boundaries, 75
communication, 75–7
image, 79–80
relationships with, 74–94
reputation, 77–9
Standards Fund, 17